DISASTER
Betting the Farm on God in Life's Storms

Dr. Michael Sprague

Copyright © 2011 by Dr. Michael Sprague

Disaster
Betting the Farm on God in Life's Storms
by Dr. Michael Sprague

Printed in the United States of America

ISBN 9781613798423

All rights reserved solely by the author. The author guarantees all contents are original and do not infringe upon the legal rights of any other person or work. No part of this book may be reproduced in any form without the permission of the author. The views expressed in this book are not necessarily those of the publisher.

Unless otherwise indicated, Bible quotations are taken from The New American Standard Bible®. Copyright © 1960, 1962, 1963, 1968, 1971, 1972, 1973, 1975, 1977, 1995 by The Lockman Foundation. Used by permission. (www.Lockman.org); The King James Version (KJV); The Message (MSG) by Eugene H. Peterson. Copyright © 1993, 1994, 1995, 1996 by NavPress Publishing Group (www.navpress.com). Used by permission; The Holy Bible, New International Version (NIV). Copyright © 1973, 1978, 1984 by International Bible Society. Used by permission of Zondervan Bible Publishers; and The New Living Translation (NLT). Copyright © 1996, 2004, 2007 by Tyndale House Publishers. Used by permission.

www.xulonpress.com

Table of Contents

Acknowledgments... xi
Preface: A Tempest Called Katrina xiii
Introduction xix

Part One: Spiritual Formation

1. Your Faith...29
2. Surrender – God's Plan Is Better 39
3. Your Brokenness 53
4. Fearless Moral Inventory 64
5. Your Calling 71

Part Two: Theological Underpinnings

6. Our Culture 83
7. Where Is God When Things Go Wrong 96
8. God of the Resupply 103
9. Our Jesus 114

Part Three: Overcoming Knockout Punches

10. Surviving Bouts with Doubts 127
11. Sustainability—Surviving for the Long Haul 139
12. When Sheep Act Like Wolves: Revealing the Dirty Little Secret in the Church 156
13. Spiritual Warfare 170

Part Four: Kingdom Building

14. Be Dangerous 183
15. Do Good Deeds 196
16. Ripples 208
17. Volunteer Revolution 219
18. Divine Appointments 227

Epilogue: God Doesn't Play Dice 239
Appendix: Externally Focused Churches 243
Notes 263

I know of no one else more qualified to write about leading the Church to be the Church of Jesus Christ in the midst of crisis. I have been in his church. I have talked with God's people. I have seen the transforming results. I have heard the testimonies. Your heart will be expanded — your horizons lengthened — and your vision focused as you read this book by Michael Sprague. But be careful, it will change you!

—Mark L. Bailey
President, Dallas Theological Seminary

This is a story of trials and triumphs as Sprague shows us by word and personal testimony how big God is. Through God's provision and grace, any obstacle can be used for good. Sprague exemplifies faith in a big God.

—Dr. David A. Anderson, Senior Pastor
Bridgeway Community Church, Columbia, Maryland
author of *Multicultural Ministry*

Michael Sprague gets it. TouchGlobal Ministry has done phenomenal work post-Katrina in New Orleans and beyond to come to the aid of those affected by disaster, answering God's call to help the poor and needy. You will be uplifted by his walk of faith and encouraged by his obedience.

—Danny Wuerffel
Heisman Trophy winner
Executive Director of Desire Street Ministries

The odds are you will find Betting the Farm, personally challenging, but also extremely encouraging to know that serving others can change the world. I've known Pastor Sprague since I was a Louisiana legislator working with pastors to strengthen marriage, the foundation for strong families and the key to rebuilding our culture. In Betting the Farm, you'll see how the covenant of faith serves as the foundation for people from all walks of life to work together to serve and rebuild a hurting community. Take the challenge - Bet the Farm!

—Tony Perkins
President of the Family Research Council

Through his eyes and experiences surviving Hurricane Katrina, Michael Sprague demonstrates how God can faithfully get us through our own personal Katrina's. Weaving scriptural examples alongside the miraculous provisions God made as Michael and his family, community, and church, waded through the trials Katrina wrought, we are reminded afresh of our Faithful Provider. This book is not only a celebration of how God brought an entire state through a monster storm, but it is a huge encouragement to anyone going through difficulties.

—Russ Olmon
Pastor, Lakepointe Church Town East, Mesquite, Texas
President, Ministry Advantage Coaching

Disaster: Betting the Farm on God in Life's Storms will challenge your spiritual complacency with practical biblical teaching. Your faith in the Father, who walks with us through crisis, will grow as you read the many amazing stories of how God provided specific needs at just the right moment. This book will prepare you and your church for the "Katrina's" you will face in your journey with the Savior and inspire you to extend the compassion of Jesus to those around you.

—William J. Hamel
President
Evangelical Free Churches of America

Few people can speak to the issue of pressing into faith and God in the midst of life storms as Michael Sprague. Not only did he experience a personal trauma that irrevocably changed him but in the vortex of "Katrina" he experienced the trauma of a whole city undone, desperate and needy. Faced with this disaster, Michael bet the farm on God and called the entire congregation to a ministry of hope and the rebuilding of homes, lives and hearts. It changed him forever and it changed his congregation forever. Everyone experiences the storms of life. Michael's book, written in candor and from real life experience can give you a path of faith to follow. It is a reliable and helpful guide.

—T. J. Addington
Senior Vice President
Evangelical Free Churches of America, ReachGlobal

Seeking godly counsel on matters of real life? To be challenged and encouraged to grow as a Christ-follower? Having walked beside Michael as a ministry partner and friend in the aftermath of Hurricane Katrina, my eyes teared on certain pages, while other chapters challenged and inspired my heart. In "Betting the Farm on God", Michael speaks truth and offers guidance into living a fulfilled Christian life...leaving nothing on the table. It's a must read for compassionate Christians.

—Mark Lewis
Director
Evangelical Free Churches of America, TouchGlobal

Acknowledgments

There are so many I want to thank who have impacted my life and ministry. First and foremost to the Lord Jesus Christ. I will forever be amazed by grace as seen in a blood stained cross and an empty tomb. Knowing You is the most significant truth of my life.

Donna, you more than any one, live your faith before me. No one depicts and dispenses grace like you do. I love betting the farm with you. My love always!

Jonathan, my son, from the start you were a wonder to me, your future brings excitement to me and I always want the best for you. God has a cherished plan for you and your bride Patricia. Great choice!

Mom and Dad, many thanks for giving your all, and Lois for raising an incredible daughter. Tommy and Jaimie for the memories.

Gerald Small, Phil Powers and the whole gang at Forcey Memorial Church, thanks for helping me cut my teeth in ministry. You will never be forgotten.

Trinity Church in Covington, LA – I loved being your pastor and forever will love you all.

Thanks for the almost 20,000 volunteers who have marked my life and given to the dear people of New Orleans and the Gulf Region who have endured so much. Thanks to Mark Lewis and the TouchGlobal team, and John Gerhardt and the Urban Impact Team.

Thanks multiplied to Bill Hamel, President of the Evangelical Free Churches of America and the entire association; to Dallas

Theological Seminary, Capital Bible Seminary and Ministry Advantage.

Thanks to my friends for life ... Fred, Earl, Brad, Scott, James, Jim, Chuck, Shannon, Jerry, Hank, Barry, Pete, John, Joey, Stephen, Craig, Joe, Greg, Jay, Tom, Gary, Chris, Forrester, Zeke, Kevin, Brian, Van & Laura, Larry, David, Sam, Dave (in heaven), Jeff, Glenn, Gary, Larry and Pam Reed. Thanks to Pastor Waylon Bailey, Sam and the ABF and Aaron and the gang.

So many others ... you know who you are. You believe in me. We are partners in "Grace Adventures." May we give it all we've got and when we are 100 years old, and sitting in the rocker at the nursing home, while gumming Jello and drooling, say, "Wasn't it a great ride!"

Finally, to you the reader, I thank you for reading this book and pray you will learn to Bet the Farm on God!

Preface

A Tempest Called Katrina

My life was so normal, so extremely normal, until August 29, 2005. Instantly everything changed. I was about to enter the adventure of a lifetime, a roller coaster ride that keeps on blowing. A Category 5 hurricane named Katrina barreled across my life and the entire Gulf Coast, breaking levees and drowning the nation's beloved city of New Orleans. That week, 1,836 Americans lost their lives, 480,000 homes were damaged or destroyed, and 80 percent of a major American city was underwater. This book is set against the backdrop of the worst natural disaster in United States history.

The week leading up to August 29, 2005, reveals just how normal my life really was. Our nice, safe, comfortable, God-fearing church was buzzing with activity as the summer came to a close. The new church year was launching with gusto, and my newly approved long-range church plan was being implemented. A new 15,000-square-foot family discipleship center was being built. The slab was poured and some of the steel and studs were in. Trinity Church was loving and messy all at the same time. Church life was good, and it was all so normal.

Six days before Katrina hit we returned from taking our son, our precious only child, off to Baylor University in Texas. It was a proud day to turn him over to God in this next season of his life. We gave him roots; now we were giving him wings. Donna, Fluffy (our dog), and I were poised to enter the empty-nest days with anticipation and joy. Family was good, and it was all so normal.

The weekend Katrina arrived we spent Friday night with five couples in a long-awaited, carefree respite from the demands of life – a three-hour social time that included dinner, swimming, and a competitive game of survival sloshing through a swamp to conquer an orienteering challenge. Our minds were fixed on friendships and plain old-fashioned fun. Amazing, all this frolicking fifty hours before Katrina hit. The storm wasn't even on our radar screen. The day gave way to a beautiful evening of stars filling the sky. Indeed, it was the bliss of ignorance in New Orleans. In fact, my next morning included a special six-hour leader's meeting. Then Donna and I had an afternoon date. Months before, we had received tickets to a live taping of *Wheel of Fortune*. We were going to spend the afternoon with Vanna White and Pat Sajak. Oh, the bliss of ignorance. Our social life was good and so normal.

For outsiders, you need to know that New Orleans folks become somewhat numb to hurricane reports. Meteorologists can only "cry wolf" so many times before their reports are ignored. A dozen possible hurricane hits come in a season. For instance, the summer before Katrina hit thousands of us fled out of state for Hurricane Ivan. Packing up our valuables and dog Fluffy, we caravanned to Jackson, Mississippi, in unbelievable traffic. It took some people twelve hours to get to Baton Rouge (normally a one-hour trip). Ivan ended up being a total miss. In fact, didn't even rain at our house. Time loss, money, and chaos lead people to be skeptical about the next supposed threat. After all, can major metropolitan areas evacuate ten times every season? We think, "What is the chance of this being the Big One?" Oh, the bliss of ignorance.

Then everything changed. Some have their world rocked by a call in the middle of the night, a pink slip, a letter, or a diagnosis. For us, it was the mother of all storms, a Category 5 hurricane that ravaged everything in its path. The hurricane picked up steam across the warm waters of the Gulf of Mexico and came ashore leaving a 300-mile-wide swath of destruction, winds up to 175 mph, and a storm surge that swelled as high as 28 feet. New Orleans and its outlying areas were built below sea level. Manmade engineering failures caused the levees to breach, and the city pumping station personnel were evacuated. This was coupled with dwindling wetlands, rising seas, and a series of government miscues and fiascos. Junior Rodriguez, former president of decimated St. Bernard Parish, told of how he saw the Canadian Mounties before he saw his own nation's government. This was the perfect storm that had been feared for years, and turned out to be worse than expected.

New Orleans was torn apart, with $60 billion of damage. As Mitch Landrieu, the current mayor of the city, said, "…for four horrific days, there was anarchy on the streets of America."

These days should never be rejected or forgotten. Hunger, thirst, and unbearable conditions prevailed at the convention center. The Superdome floor was filled with cots, crying babies, and families holding garbage bags filled with all of their remaining earthly belongings. A giant hole tore through the roof of this well-known sports complex. Many lost everything. We were battered, beaten down, and displaced. Everyone had a story. Every conversation was about the storm. The loss. The pain.

The early days after the disaster are forever etched into our memories and often flood back in seconds with a torrent of sights, sounds, and smells. Screams from rooftops. Corpses lying facedown in the water. Daring rescues. Oppressive heat. Pitch-black nights. Houses mud-caked with 2 feet of standing water. The stench of rotten refrigerators left on the curbs to be hauled away, spray-painted with graffiti that read: "Only a fool would open this… and I was that fool," "Katrina Leftovers," "Levee Board Victim," "Maggot Motel," "Smells like FEMA," and others. Mold growing in the walls like ivy. Blue tarps everywhere. Giant X's spray-painted on houses denoting the number of those who survived and perished. Tens of thousands of trees fallen or beheaded by Katrina. Debris and overturned cars. Homes decimated. Boats in trees. Mountains of red tape. The region turned gray as everything lost its color. Dead quiet. No birds in the air. The stench of dead fish. A ghost town. Today, eighty-five bodies still lay unclaimed at the Katrina Memorial.

Huge military planes refueled helicopters over our heads. Red Cross vehicles. Military convoys. National Guard. FEMA trailers.

Disaster

Power company and tree-removal trucks from all over the United States. No water. No gas. No sewage. No telephone. No electricity.

Our personal wakeup call came Sunday afternoon when the mayors enacted mandatory evacuations, for indeed this was the "big one." We boarded up, stocked up, gassed up, and decided to get out of town. Mass evacuation brought traffic nightmares. Some reported going ten miles in five hours. Over one million people fled to all fifty states. Evacuees registered in almost half of the zip codes in the United States. Donna, Fluffy, and I became refugees in a Super 8 motel in Birmingham, Alabama. In our "miniature world" of the Super 8, we had the complete micro-chasm of the Gulf Coast. Everyone's world had changed instantly. The mad scramble for information—any information—back home was on. Cell phones didn't work, rumors abounded. People walked around in a zombie-like daze. It was the combination of grief, exhaustion, shell shock, fear, loss, and uncertainty. Everyone was missing a spouse, sibling, parent, or child. Despite the heavy hearts, everyone tried to watch out for everyone else. We were in this together.

I had to get back home as soon as possible. The drive home left me speechless. So much had disappeared and trees looked like toothpicks. We wondered if we could get across our state line since reports were that our parish was closed.

Sprague home immediately after Hurricane Katrina

We finally reached our home. The backyard looked like a nuclear explosion had taken place. Eight gigantic pines had come down on top of each other. Fortunately they fell away from the house; however, one additional pine in the front yard came down on the house and rested in the attic. The hole in the roof produced the biggest skylight you have ever seen. Inside the house, we found structural and water damage to five rooms and a hallway. Floors and counters were warped and carpets were wet.

We went from the empty nest to the refugee nest to no nest to eventually the messy nest of a house needing rebuilding. The town had curfews at night. Much of the city looked like a ghost town, but those who remained or returned were committed to protecting and rebuilding their homes. Because of reports of looting at night, five or six men with guns would keep watch at the front of communities to safeguard their homes and families. People worked together and watched out for each other. It was community at its best in many ways. Heroic acts by everyday people abounded.

It is chilling to look back and see all our favorite places on FOX or CNN replayed over and over during Katrina specials with the captions of death, looting, devastation, and body counts. All of this was surreal. Was it really happening to us? I can relate to Dorothy: "I don't think we're in Kansas anymore, Toto." I don't think we are in my nice, safe, comfortable, normal world anymore. August 29, 2005, changed everything.

Yet, with all the pain and darkness, I can say that God's grace has abounded. Beauty has come out of the ashes. Good has come from bad. Triumph has come from tragedy. Walls have come tumbling down between groups. Divisions have been set aside and differences forgotten or become insignificant. Turf is shared with affection.

Trinity Church was transformed from a nice, safe, comfortable, God-fearing suburban church to a dangerous, unsafe, uncomfortable, Holy Spirit-dependent mobilization center. Trinity was dubbed "The church of the stained carpet." To date, almost twenty thousand volunteers from forty-two states and seven countries have slept on our floors, eaten in our worship center, and been deployed to rebuild homes and lives and share Jesus Christ. I have witnessed modern-day miracles week after week all done in "Jesus' name." Amazing things have unfolded before our very eyes, and it has definitely been a "God thing."

America, know this: the people of New Orleans live, stand, and will overcome. What doesn't kill us makes us stronger. In so many ways the community has come back stronger and better. Even with the 2010 BP oil spill, New Orleans chooses to survive. We are poised to serve America and the world with our oil, coastal fisheries, port system, tourism, culture, food, and people.

Though I won't wish what happened to us upon anyone, I wouldn't trade what I've learned for anything. I choose to adjust to the new realities by *Betting the Farm on God*. With life so crazy, abnormal, and overwhelming, what else can you do? Who else could I possibly have bet upon? Jesus Christ has changed my life, and this book recounts the deed!

The following pages lay out the lessons learned in disaster and address the sticky issues of how such catastrophe can be reconciled with a God who is able, aware, and caring. The book tackles issues of doubt, depression, betrayal, and grief while challenging you to slow down, reflect, sort out, and think through some of life's quandaries. You won't walk away with neat, tidy, packaged, easy-nickel answers to million-dollar questions, but you will receive dialogue, thoughtfulness, new insights, and most importantly hope.

Introduction

We live in a dangerous world. All too often crisis and disasters hit without warning. In a moment, the unthinkable happens. Need proof? Read through the following list. What images and feelings do you associate with these recent disasters?

- Hurricane Katrina
- 9/11
- Columbine
- Oklahoma City bombing
- Chernobyl nuclear disaster
- Unabomber
- Virginia Tech massacre
- Japan tsunami
- Haiti earthquake
- D.C. sniper
- Fort Hood shooting
- Anthrax scare
- Mumbai horror
- West Nile virus
- California fires
- Indian Ocean tsunami
- Mount St. Helens
- Hudson River miracle
- Minneapolis bridge collapse
- F-5 Alabama and Missouri tornadoes

It takes but a moment to recall the feelings and emotions disasters produce in our lives. Amanda Ripley, author of *The Unthinkable*, writes,

> It is, however, quite likely that you will be effected [sic] by a disaster. In an August 2006 *Time* magazine poll of one thousand Americans, about half of those surveyed said they had personally experienced a disaster or public emergency. In fact, about 91 percent of Americans live in places at a moderate-to-high risk of earthquakes, volcanoes, tornadoes, wildfires, hurricanes, flooding, high-wind damage, or terrorism, according to an estimate calculated in 2006 for *Time* by the Hazards and Vulnerability Institute at the University of South Carolina.[1]

We live in risky times. New threats rise above the horizon almost daily. In our times, prophets aren't needed to foresee likely disastrous scenarios. Consider the following:

1. **Bio-threats:** Global pandemics are real threats today. Dr. Stuart Levy, M.D., says, "Certain bacterial infections now defy all antibiotics."
2. **Food supply threats:** Tommy Thompson, former Health and Human Services Secretary, said on CNN's *Paula Zahn Now* (December 6, 2004), "For the life of me, I cannot understand why terrorists have not attacked our food supply because it is so easy to do."
3. **Technological threats:** Tom Clancy and Hollywood's action films, though exaggerated, reveal the real possibility of cyber-terrorism from criminals, terrorists, hackers, or state-sponsored activity. The enormous cyber-security industry attempts to protect our world which is profoundly dependent upon technology.
4. **Eco-threats:** Eco-systems weaken, super-storms increase, and water shortages challenge vast communities in the United States and around the world. The now famous FEMA emergency training session in August 2001 concluded that the three major disasters most likely to strike the United

States were: a New York terrorist attack, a massive New Orleans hurricane, and a major California earthquake. Two out of three ain't bad. The third is quite likely. In 2002, a U.S. Geological Survey Group report estimated a 62 percent probability of a 6.7 or greater earthquake on the Richter scale in the San Francisco Bay area by 2032. A 6.9 earthquake in the Bay area could leave 360,000 people homeless, according to the Association of Bay Area Governments. William Lettis of the U.S. Geological Survey Group said, "Certain communities in the East Bay have the potential to become ghost towns."

5. **Nuclear/Chemical threats:** Graham Allison, founding dean of Harvard's John F. Kennedy School of Government, and author of *Nuclear Terrorism,* says a nuclear attack on U.S. soil within the next ten years is probable. Other experts, according to a survey by Senator Richard Lugar, estimate the likelihood over the next ten years at 30 percent.
6. **Terrorist threats:** About the only thing our presidential candidates agree on these days is the serious threat of terrorism to American national security.
7. **Energy threats:** Prices at the gas pump remind us of our looming energy challenges worldwide.
8. **War threats:** Here to stay are the days of wars and rumors of wars. 9/11 woke Americans up to war on our soil. Wars fought on foreign soil are all too commonplace to much of the world.

Personal Disasters

Are you living right this moment in the midst of a raging hurricane, the aftermath of a wildfire, or in a war-torn community? Probably not, but just because you're not in a capital "D" disaster does not mean you are not in the midst of a small "d" disaster. Maybe your own personal whirlwind brings challenges that you would easily label "The Unthinkable." This disaster scales to serious and sizable proportions. For you it's real, it's dangerous, and it's inescapable!

Disaster

Personal disasters hit all too often. Without warning the unthinkable happens. Need proof? Read through the following list. What images and feelings do you associate with these personal disasters?

- Divorce/Separation
- Medical Challenge/Injury
- Financial Struggle/Debt/Foreclosure
- Depression/Anxiety/Fear
- Significant Conflict/Betrayal
- Job Loss/Uncertainty
- Death
- Aging Challenges/Aging Parents
- Retirement Issues
- Children's Needs/Issues
- Addictions/Habits/Hang-ups
- Moving
- Trouble with In-laws
- Friendship/Neighbor/Co-worker Tension
- A Legal Case
- Death of a Dream
- Pregnancy, Miscarriage, Infertility

One moment your life is sunny, calm, predictable, and happy. You enjoy healthy relationships, job security, amazing kids, and great mental and physical fitness. Then suddenly…life crashes all around you. Unexpectedly, cataclysmically, disaster hits. The whirling, violent, turbulent life storm strikes with vengeance. Rough winds howl, thunder roars, lightning strikes, and precious cargo evaporates. Life implodes, exasperates, and challenges; yet perplexingly, the heavens manifest silence, and your dreams wash out to sea. Your soul shakes. You waver, mourn, protest and cry. You wonder, "Will I survive?

Personal Disaster Quotient

Before you jump into the meat of this book, determine your Personal Disaster Quotient (PDQ). Pause a few minutes to reflect on this simple inventory to identify your PDQ. Be honest, vulnerable, and as open as possible. The inventory reveals nothing God does not already know, but it may reveal something to you. After reading each statement, circle the appropriate number on the ten-point scale. Choose the first response that comes to mind. Your instinct is usually the best. The scale is:

10	9	8	7	6	5	4	3	2	1
Strongly Agree	/Agree		/Neither Agree or Disagree			/Disagree			/Strongly Disagree

1. Life circumstances and burdens weigh me down.
   10 9 8 7 6 5 4 3 2 1
   Strongly Agree /Agree /Neither Agree or Disagree /Disagree /Strongly Disagree

2. I want to experience more in life.
   10 9 8 7 6 5 4 3 2 1
   Strongly Agree /Agree /Neither Agree or Disagree /Disagree /Strongly Disagree

3. I feel ashamed and unworthy before God and others.
   10 9 8 7 6 5 4 3 2 1
   Strongly Agree /Agree /Neither Agree or Disagree /Disagree /Strongly Disagree

4. I am too often most interested in creature comfort.
   10 9 8 7 6 5 4 3 2 1
   Strongly Agree /Agree /Neither Agree or Disagree /Disagree /Strongly Disagree

5. No good thing comes from evil and suffering.
   10 9 8 7 6 5 4 3 2 1
   Strongly Agree /Agree /Neither Agree or Disagree /Disagree /Strongly Disagree

6. I am reluctant to be honest about my doubts, grief, hurts, and hang-ups.
   10 9 8 7 6 5 4 3 2 1
   Strongly Agree /Agree /Neither Agree or Disagree /Disagree /Strongly Disagree

7. I do not have a healthy plan to sustain my emotional, spiritual, physical, and social life.
   10 9 8 7 6 5 4 3 2 1
   Strongly Agree /Agree /Neither Agree or Disagree /Disagree /Strongly Disagree

8. I do not understand the purpose of "disasters" in my life.
   10 9 8 7 6 5 4 3 2 1
   Strongly Agree /Agree /Neither Agree or Disagree /Disagree /Strongly Disagree

9. I pretend rather than reveal my losses and disappointments.
   10 9 8 7 6 5 4 3 2 1
   Strongly Agree /Agree /Neither Agree or Disagree /Disagree /Strongly Disagree

10. I need more understanding on what God says about suffering.
    10   9   8   7   6   5   4   3   2   1
    Strongly Agree /Agree /Neither Agree or Disagree /Disagree /Strongly Disagree

11. I need more understanding on what the Bible says about the sovereignty of God.
    10   9   8   7   6   5   4   3   2   1
    Strongly Agree /Agree /Neither Agree or Disagree /Disagree /Strongly Disagree

12. I rarely think of the world as a spiritual battleground.
    10   9   8   7   6   5   4   3   2   1
    Strongly Agree /Agree /Neither Agree or Disagree /Disagree /Strongly Disagree

13. I need a fresh vision of Jesus' calling on my life.
    10   9   8   7   6   5   4   3   2   1
    Strongly Agree /Agree /Neither Agree or Disagree /Disagree /Strongly Disagree

14. I need to integrate my faith in the world and marketplace more consistently.
    10   9   8   7   6   5   4   3   2   1
    Strongly Agree /Agree /Neither Agree or Disagree /Disagree /Strongly Disagree

15. I need to devote time to understand the unique ways God has gifted me and can use me.
    10   9   8   7   6   5   4   3   2   1
    Strongly Agree /Agree /Neither Agree or Disagree /Disagree /Strongly Disagree

16. I am hesitant to evaluate unknown or weak parts of myself to allow for transformation.
    10   9   8   7   6   5   4   3   2   1
    Strongly Agree /Agree /Neither Agree or Disagree /Disagree /Strongly Disagree

17. I have stopped going to church, or I am simply going through the motions because I was used or mistreated.
    10   9   8   7   6   5   4   3   2   1
    Strongly Agree /Agree /Neither Agree or Disagree /Disagree /Strongly Disagree

18. I have been verbally, financially, sexually, emotionally manipulated or abused by someone in a position of spiritual authority.
    10   9   8   7   6   5   4   3   2   1
    Strongly Agree /Agree /Neither Agree or Disagree /Disagree /Strongly Disagree

19. I need to live more in the confident expectation of biblical hope as opposed to the up and down approach of manmade hope.
    10   9   8   7   6   5   4   3   2   1
    Strongly Agree /Agree /Neither Agree or Disagree /Disagree /Strongly Disagree

20. I tend to isolate, judge, or conform to the world rather than be bold to reach out.
    10   9   8   7   6   5   4   3   2   1
    Strongly Agree /Agree /Neither Agree or Disagree /Disagree /Strongly Disagree

Disaster

Inventory Results:
Add your scores from the 20 statements to get your total PDQ. Write the total in the box below.

TOTAL PDQ = ☐

The Key:
Locate your score below to find out your assessment.
- If you scored 7 or higher on any one statement this book will help you in that area.
- If you scored above 150 total this book may be very significant for you.
- If you scored between 100 and 150 you will find this book extremely helpful.
- If you scored between 50 and 99 you will find this book beneficial.
- If you scored less than 50...congratulations! You are either in denial, in a sweet time of life, or in a position to help others in significant ways. May this book sharpen your call to aid others.

Time to Start

If you are currently hitting rock bottom, it is time to start fresh. If you are ready to take on the world, it is time to soar. Whether you're facing an idyllic moment of calm or in the midst of disaster, today is the day to press on toward new opportunity. The opportunity awaits to:

1. discover what you value
2. discover the strengths and weaknesses of your current spiritual conditioning
3. allow God to renew your mind and heart
4. recreate a meaningful life
5. honor God
6. start fresh and envision new possibilities
7. break down old barriers
8. impact others

LET'S GO! It's time to bet the farm on God!

Part One
Spiritual Formation

Chapter 1

Your Faith

It was a day shortly after Hurricane Katrina slammed into the Gulf Coast, bringing unspeakable devastation and misery, that I decided to "bet the farm on God." It was a day that will be forever marked in my own personal history—a day of no turning back.

As a senior pastor in New Orleans, I stood at my Ground Zero, perplexed and not knowing a twenty-four-hour divine appointment awaited me. This would be holy ground.

Actually, my day was spent at two Ground Zeroes. Half my day was spent at Ground Zero in New Orleans with eighteen helicopters hovering overhead, scores of mobilized military units patrolling the city armed to the hilt, and much of the city underwater. Treasured, well-known sections of New Orleans were now ghost towns, untold cars were flipped over, fires burned along the horizon, and buildings were turned into rubbish. The beloved Superdome was ruined and the convention center had a stench that made it unbearable to come near, even though that was the only place food and water resided for pickup. It was a hellish sight.

My other Ground Zero was the command center at Trinity Church to the devastated community on the Northshore of New Orleans. Katrina ripped through this community with such ferocity that trees fell everywhere, and much was destroyed by flooding. Most of the community was scattered as refugees across the entire Southeast. Life as we knew it did not exist anymore, and everyone struggled to figure out how to survive day-to-day. The needs were overwhelming and the resources horribly inadequate.

The situation was so impossible that we who could so easily trust our own strength, wit, and resourcefulness were forced to trust God totally. What a novel idea, to trust God—the God who provides manna from heaven and raises the dead. Being a desperate man, I decided to "bet the farm on God." Six memorial stones will forever mark that day.

Memorial Stone #1

My day started with an early morning call that we had been given use of an 8,000-square-foot warehouse for free. This was amazing because people told us that if we were going to make a difference in the community we would need warehouse space to accommodate truckloads of disaster supplies that would eventually come our way. Yet we had also been told that it was impossible to find warehouse space since FEMA and businesses had gobbled it all up.

A few of us were foolish enough to knock on the door of heaven and ask for 5,000 to 10,000 square feet of warehouse space. When the call came, we were giving high-fives and praising God. In the midst of our nothingness the Father provided. This was cool.

Memorial Stone #2

Moments later, a twelve-person SWAT team from Indiana called me. They had been asked to work security of the Mississippi Coast, but when they tried to get in FEMA rebuffed them. They tried again, and FEMA told them no one was getting in. When they called me they said, "Nobody down South wants us. Do you want us?"

I was desperate and told them to come on over. A short time later they arrived with a big eighteen-wheeler filled with supplies, another supply truck, and a third truck pulling their gear. Now you have to realize that in the early days after Katrina there was tremendous fear in the community and rumors of looting and other atrocities. The remnant of people left in the community took things into their own hands, providing their own security. It seemed that everyone had a gun except Donna and me. It was like the Wild West. Communities would have big signs at their entrance that read "You loot, we shoot." And the signs in the rural areas read "Please loot. We love to shoot."

The head of the SWAT team took me to the last truck and wanted to show me something. There in the truck were more machine guns and artillery than I'd ever seen. This was my lucky day. If I could stay on the good side of the SWAT team, we'd have the whole Northshore outgunned. However, my bubble of euphoria quickly popped when I was told their 18-wheeler had to have the supplies unloaded immediately so it could be returned home.

I was stumped. We couldn't leave the equipment and supplies outside, and I didn't have a spot for it. All I knew to do was send up a quick 911 to God. I called my associate into my office and asked him to go into town, spot the first eighteen-wheeler truck driver he could find, and say, "God needs your truck."

Looking back, I can't even believe I said those words. Steve looked at me like I was crazy yet went into town, saw a trucker, and said in his own words, "My pastor said to tell you that God needs your truck."

The trucker thought Steve was crazy, but he put his head down then looked up and said, "Okay," and the truck trailer was on the back of our lot in two hours and stayed there for two and a half months. All the supplies from the one truck were moved into the other. This was now the coolest thing I had ever seen. What a novel way to live – ask the Father!

Memorial Stone #3

Moments later I realized that a number of missionaries had landed at Trinity. Some of them had lost homes in New Orleans. As a pastor, I personally felt responsible for putting a roof over their heads since they were God's missionaries. Instantly, I remembered I had just been a refugee myself. My home was unlivable; Donna, our dog, and I were bunking in one room with another family. What was I to do? My cell phone rang and a friend said, "I'm going to Austin, Texas, for four days. Do you want my house?"

Bingo! I knew this was the Father's provision.

Memorial Stone #4

A few minutes later Donna found out I had taken responsibility for the missionaries. She called and asked me what we were going to feed these people. Good question! Indeed, for the first time in my life I didn't know where my next meal was coming from. We would work eighteen-hour days. Someone would bring you something or you could get an MRE (field ration) from the soldiers.

I said, "Donna, you're going to have to ask the Holy Spirit to provide supernaturally. I'm so busy. I've got so much to do. I've got to go. Goodbye."

Now it was Donna's turn to think I was crazy. A couple of hours later, she went to the home of a friend. The woman had just driven in from another town and brought food to feed the twelve emergency workers sleeping on the floor of her house. While Donna was in the kitchen watching the woman unpack the groceries, one of the workers walked in. He told her the entire group had been called out on security detail and would not be eating with them. The woman was perplexed. She had bought all this food! Donna looked at her and said, "Michael said to pray and ask the Holy Spirit to provide food for our missionaries tonight." Our wonderful friend smiled and provided us the manna God had sent from heaven.

All this happened in the morning of one day. It was like God was burning into me the truth that the Father always provides. He might not give us all we want, but He will give us all we need moment by moment. I needed to learn this truth and walk by faith.

It was like God was speaking loud and clear: "Trusting the Father is not just the way to live in disaster times, but for the rest of your life." It makes sense, doesn't it? A Father-dependent approach to life. Wow!

Memorial Stone #5

Around noon, a few of us decided to check on our mission church, Urban Impact, in the city of New Orleans. The only problem was that no one was getting into the city without proper authorization. However, we prayed and were prompted to proceed. At the 24-mile causeway bridge that takes people across Lake Pontchartrain into New Orleans, we found a barricade and a heavily guarded checkpoint. A hardnosed military gatekeeper pointed his gun right at us. Our driver worked for Food for the Hungry. Knowing we had no official authorization, he pulled out his Food for the Hungry American Express credit card, held it up, and told him we'd like to check on our mission church.

As I sat in the backseat, I thought, "We're going to get shot. Second, what's up with the credit card approach, and third, if this soldier lets us through, he can't be doing his job."

Sure enough, the soldier was sharp. He went into a rant about our having no authorization and asked if we knew the city was underwater. Curiously, halfway through the ranting and raving, his tone and demeanor suddenly changed. I'm convinced Proverbs 21:1 kicked in where it says, "God can move the heart of a king." I believe God moved the heart of that soldier as he said, "Well, go ahead, but do not come back tomorrow without proper authorization."

Off we went to the next checkpoint four miles ahead on the bridge. The same deal—barricade, gun, American Express credit card, a soldier ranting, "How did you get through the first checkpoint? Where's your authorization?" Midway through the rant, Proverbs 21:1 kicked in again and we were waved through. At all six checkpoints, hardnosed gatekeepers with machine guns mysteriously waved us through.

As we got into the city it was indeed 80 percent underwater. Military helicopters buzzed overhead, doing search-and-rescue and delivering supplies. The city was burning in two places. We picked our way around the city. This was not the beloved city of jazz, streetcars, and beignets I once knew. The good news – we descended into Central City and found our mission church, Castle Rock Church, on dry ground. One block over was underwater. We spent the afternoon with people who rode out the storm. Military patrols came through every twenty minutes urging a mandatory evacuation. These people weren't going anywhere unless they were dragged out. They were worried that their minimal earthly belongings would be stolen if left unattended. They had little or no money, and some were staying with their pets.

We listened to stories of those who rode out Katrina, gave them water in Jesus' name, and prayed with many. It was a time I will never forget.

As we traveled across the bridge on our way home later that afternoon, it was like the Father was speaking a second time saying, "Michael, if I want to get you into a city, I can get you into a city, and the power of the United States military can't stop me. I am ABLE!" This was something I needed to hear—something God wanted me to know and live.

Memorial Stone #6

Like most days, I worked till midnight that evening. Even though I had seen God's fingerprints all throughout the day, I was still concerned about how I would pay my staff and how Trinity Church would survive financially. There were no offerings, people were scattered, many jobs were gone, and a lot of people did not plan to return.

At midnight that night, I read an email on the computer Donna had hooked up to a generator. As I read it, I cried. A seven-year-old girl in Maryland overheard her mom and dad discussing the plight of New Orleans at the dinner table. She went to her room, brought her entire piggybank to her parents, and said that if she could get some money for a loose tooth, there would be enough money to buy one Barbie doll for a little refugee girl in New Orleans.

It was like the Father was speaking for a third time that day saying, "Michael, if I can move the heart of a seven-year-old girl on the East Coast, don't you think I can move the heart of big boys and big girls to take care of you and Trinity Church?"

Right after midnight I bowed my head and prayed, "God, I'm going to bet the farm on You. No matter what happens from now on, I'm going to bet the Farm on God." I can tell you I have, and He has been absolutely faithful.

All of this really happened in one day! I was learning a new approach to living by faith. Without touching any money or seeing one newspaper, and with very little news – still I had all I needed. Yea, God! In the middle of devastation, inadequacy, and the impossible, we were forced to not trust in our own wit, strength, and resourcefulness, but forced to trust God totally. Late that night someone asked me about some provision for the next day. My first thought was *what do I know about that?* Yet what came out of my mouth was, "I think we should ask the Father to supernaturally show up tomorrow." I'm learning that whatever your need is today, you might try asking the Father. What a novel idea!

Betting the Farm on God

In the month prior to Katrina, I happened to be meditating upon an old C.S. Lewis statement: "The man who has God and everything has no more than the man who has God and nothing." It certainly made sense in my head, but pre-Katrina it was simply a theoretical statement that seemed plausible.

After Katrina, I continued to meditate upon the C.S. Lewis statement, and the truth moved from my head to my heart. You never know Jesus is all you need until Jesus is all you have, and then you discover Jesus is all you need. You can literally bet the farm on God. He will not let you down.

Here's a story that means a lot to me:

> Bishop Ken Ulmer, the pastor of a mostly African-American congregation in Los Angeles that meets in The Forum where the L.A. Lakers used to play basketball, told about two men who were in an art museum and came upon a painting of a chess game. One character looked like a man; the other character looked a lot like the Devil. The man is down to his last piece on the chessboard. The title of the painting is "Checkmate."
>
> Ken says that one of the two men looking at this painting was an international chess champion, and something about the painting intrigued him. He began to study it. He became so engrossed that the man with him grew impatient and asked him what he was doing.
>
> He said, "There's something about this painting that bothers me, and I want to study it for a little while. You go ahead and wander around."
>
> He studied it. His head started nodding, and his hands started moving. When his friend came back, he said, "We have to locate the man who painted this picture and tell him that either he has to change the picture, or he has to change the title. I have deter-

mined that there is something wrong with this painting, and I am an international chess champion."

His friend asked, "What's wrong with the painting?"

The man said, "Well, it's titled 'Checkmate,' but the title is wrong. The painter's either got to change the painting or change the title, because the King still has one more move."

When Ken tells this story and reaches the line "the King has one more move," the people get very excited. I trust that you can do the same.

The King Still Has One More Move

A little boy named David is up against the giant named Goliath. David is in trouble. He tries to put on King Saul's armor, but Saul's a 52-Long and David's a 36-Short. He can't even handle a grown-up's sword. It looks like checkmate, but...*the King still has one more move.*

A man named Daniel gets thrown into a den of lions because he refuses to stop praying to his God. The lions are hungry. He's in there all night. At the first light of dawn, King Darius calls down. Daniel tells him the lions have been put on a "low protein diet" and he's fine, because...*the King still has one more move.*

A man named Moses convinces a nation of oppressed slaves to run away from the most powerful man on earth. Pharaoh sets out after them. They're standing on the shore of the Red Sea with the greatest army in the world behind them, and the people say to Moses, "What were you thinking?" And Moses says to God, "God, what were You thinking?" But...*the King still has one more move.*

I don't know what challenge you face. Maybe there is stress at work. Maybe you're in a marriage that is falling apart, or has already fallen apart. Maybe a son or daughter, somebody that you love, is struggling or estranged from you. Maybe you have financial pressures. Maybe you have done the wrong thing or said the wrong thing or made a mistake that feels so big it could never be redeemed.

Or maybe things are going pretty well, and there is no crisis at all. But there will be one day. The mortality rate is still hovering at right around 100 percent. Whatever you face, whether it's today or tomorrow, the promise of Jesus to everyone who puts their trust in Him in this: there is hope, even when it feels like checkmate, because...*the King still has one more move.*[1]

Do You Need a Miracle?

In the middle of the hurricane response, a fellow Christ-follower stopped by my house and said, "Michael, I have a birthday gift for you." She reached into her purse and presented me with a carnation and said, "Remember?"

I responded with a "Well...kinda...sorta...maybe...remind me."

My friend continued. "Four years ago you preached on God being a miracle-working God." I vaguely remembered that at the end of a Sunday service I invited the congregation to come up front to pick up one of the carnations that had been placed on a set of tables. The carnation was to be put in a prominent location as a reminder to pray for a miracle by a miracle-working God. I had said, "When you get your miracle, return your carnation to me." At this point, I was now very curious.

"Michael," she said, "I put the carnation on a mirror and have prayed daily for four years because I needed a miracle. My daughter was not where she needed to be. I especially didn't like her friends. I've prayed for four years. Recently, my daughter started walking close with the Lord and wants to join a Bible church. She still has those old friends, but she is talking to them about the Lord. I got my miracle and here is your carnation. I don't need it anymore. Happy birthday!"

Wow! For a pastor, it doesn't get any better than that.

Then she added, "I have another birthday gift for you." She presented a second carnation to me. "Even though you said to take one carnation, I took two. That means I stole one and need to ask your forgiveness, but I needed two miracles. My son needed a work of God also. I prayed for four years for my son. He called this week and said he will be baptized on Sunday. He wants us to come and watch. Happy birthday!"

Let me ask you, where do you need to bet the farm on God? Where do you need a miracle, a breakthrough? What seems so impossible? Where is your hurricane? Your storm? Is it a terrifying diagnosis? A disillusioning church experience? Are you destined for a corner office but stuck in a cubicle? Do you face infertility mountains? Addiction struggles? Friendship fiascos? A financial reversal? Divorce papers? A prodigal? A dream fizzled? A dead-end job? A mediocre marriage? A child in prison? Fired at fifty-two? Depressed at thirty-five? Single at forty?

Everyone has a personal Katrina. Everyone has brokenness, disappointment, and shattered dreams. Everyone needs a miracle. If you need to put a carnation on your dashboard or mirror to remind you to pray, do it! Our God is still in the miracle-working business. The King still has one more move.

Chapter 2

Surrender — God's Plan Is Better

May all your expectations be frustrated. May all your plans be thwarted. May all your desires be withered into nothingness....That you may experience the powerlessness and poverty of a child.... And then sing and dance in the compassion of God, Who is Father, Son and Holy Spirit.
—Brennan Manning

"Abraham!...Take now your son, your only son, whom you love, Isaac, and go to the land of Moriah; and offer him there as a burnt offering on one of the mountains" (Genesis 22:1b-2a). For years as a seminary student and then as a pastor, I never taught or preached on Genesis 22. To be honest, it was the one chapter in the Bible I could least identify with and emotionally understand. Oh, I knew the facts of the account, believed them to be true, and knew it had something to do with faith, but it perplexed me. It didn't all make sense. I didn't know what to say regarding application for today.

As a couple, Donna and I had infertility issues for years and then had one son. If anyone told me to kill my son, I'd say they were crazy. If anyone tried to hurt my son, they would have a fight on their hands. If God were to tell me to sacrifice my son, I would wonder, "Do You really mean this?"

The Road to Mt. Moriah

Truthfully, I grappled with this chapter for years. When you are in your twenties everyone you know is healthy and getting into careers or homes or starting families. As a young pastor, nobody tells you their problems. You are too young. When you hit thirty people start to let you in on their real-life dramas, and you agonize with people who ache over life.

As the years go by you get to the point where you daily enter into the deep heartaches of people, often multiple times in a day. When people go through disaster, catastrophe, crisis, death, loss, shock, grief, or surprise, you discover we all are so very human.

At these times it is often hard to comprehend the depth of darkness. It is hard to get our minds around certain things, things that are simply not in the original DNA of planet earth. We attempt to process the world's horrors or our own, but it is impossible. We stare, we stand dumbfounded, saddened as we ask why—and still find no answers.

One day it dawned on me that my perplexity over Genesis 22, and the very heart of this mysterious chapter, had to do with the wild-at-heart God who could not be put into a box. Sure, it's a crazy story, and the road to Mt. Moriah was dark, but the truth is **every Christ-follower eventually ends up on a road to Mt. Moriah.**

Some of you are on that road right now; the rest of you will be there eventually. The road to Mt. Moriah is a place of loneliness, pain, and disappointment. It's where you end up when you lose a job, a dream, a relationship, your health, or are simply depressed. It's the road upon which you wonder:

- Is God a good God?
- Why does God seem so distant or silent?
- Why does God seem to contradict Himself?
- How will things turn out?

There are so many questions and so few answers. On the road to Mt. Moriah you pray, "God, get me out of here!" But God does not because He wants to reveal Himself further and do something in you.

Remember, the background to the Mt. Moriah episode is that Abraham and Sarah waited seemingly forever to have the son God promised. Abraham was one hundred and Sarah was ninety. They named the boy Isaac, which means laughter. As John Ortberg notes, the aged couple laughed because the boy was born in the geriatrics ward and Medicare picked up the tab. They laughed because parents and baby had to eat strained vegetables for there wasn't a single tooth in the family. They laughed because when all their friends were buying Depends, they were buying Pampers.[1]

The baby made them laugh. The toddler made them laugh. The boy made them laugh. But then God said, "Take your son, your only son, whom you love, Isaac, and sacrifice him on Mt. Moriah." In fact, Isaac was to be sacrificed as a "burnt offering," meaning completely, nothing saved or held back. Surely Abraham was not laughing anymore.

God's Voice

If I had looked close enough at the first sentence in this Mt. Moriah account, I would have discovered that Isaac was never in any danger. This was a "test" (Genesis 22:1) for God's servant Abraham. Just like our school tests as kids, you don't like them, but you learn a whole lot because of them.

God called Abraham, and Abraham knew God's voice. It was unmistakable. It was the voice he first heard at age seventy-five that told him to give up everything and leave his homeland for the sake of a promise (Genesis 12). Abraham didn't have a clue where he would end up, but he put one foot in front of the other and launched out. It was the same voice that came to him at age eighty-seven (Genesis 15:1) and reminded him that his descendants would outnumber the stars. It was the voice that came to him at age ninety-nine and told him that he and Sarah would have a son in their old age (Genesis 17:1, 16-17). In Genesis 22, God comes to Abraham one more time and asks him to give up the promise, his dream.

You want to scream out to Abraham, "It will all work out! I know the end of the story. God is good!" But you can't.

Indeed, Abraham leaves early the next morning (Genesis 22:3) to walk the three-day journey. He has to walk it one day at a time, one step at a time by faith. When he arrives at the outskirts of Mt. Moriah, he says to his two servants, "stay here with the donkey, and I and the lad will go yonder, and we will worship and return to you" (Genesis 22:5).

What does he mean "we will return"? What is going through his mind? Is he keeping Isaac and the servants in the dark? Does he question his ability to execute the plan? Does he really believe God will work it all out? Does he think God will raise Isaac from the dead?

We don't know the range of thoughts and emotions flowing through Abraham's mind, but we do see his obedience. Can you relate to times when your mind is frazzled and frustrated by the seemingly impossible situation you are in?

The Sacrifice...and Provision

At Mt. Moriah, they had the wood, the knife, and the fire, but something was missing. A very perceptive son asks, "Where is the lamb for the burnt offering?" (Genesis 22:7) and Abraham's answer is classic: "God will provide the lamb, my son" (Genesis 22:8).

Abraham had no idea how prophetic those words would be in their immediate context as well as in God's redemptive plan for the ages to come. Yes, God will provide the lamb! As the father and son walked on together, you can imagine the agony, the inner struggle, and the feeling of aloneness Abraham experienced. Yet when they reached their final destination, he did not hesitate. He built the altar and bound Isaac (Genesis 22:9). This was the son Abraham had prayed for, rocked at night as a baby, built model chariots with, and giggled with. This was his dream. This was the promise. This was his son, his only son, whom he loved.

I wonder, what's your dream? What's your agenda...your way... your wish...your expectation? What fight do you need to lay down?

Abraham raises the knife in the air (v. 10), the knife that will remove laughter and joy. How will he ever explain this to Sarah? Can you imagine?

Pause here. It's easy to rush past this gut-wrenching moment to the "they lived happily ever after" part, but this really happened. Maybe this is where you find yourself. Perplexed. Life doesn't make

Disaster

sense. Impossible circumstances. Maybe you are on the road to Mt. Moriah and it's dark right now. Maybe it has been three days, maybe thirty days, maybe three years. This is Abraham's story, but it's also your story and mine.

Abraham starts to bring the knife down. He chooses to honor the voice of God despite his fears and doubts. He simply takes God at His word. That's faith.

And suddenly the angel of the Lord interrupts and says, "Do not stretch out your hand against the lad and do nothing to him; for now I know you fear God, since you have not withheld your son, your only son from Me" (Genesis 22:12).

Whew…that was close! Abraham passed the test, a test that to my knowledge has not been and I believe never will be asked of anyone else in human history.

You may have thought, as I did years ago, that this story is barbaric. Yet in a barbaric, broken world in which human sacrifice was an all too common way to satisfy the heart of the gods, the God of the Bible models and teaches another way. God does not believe in child sacrifice. He has a different heart. God provides a ram in the thicket (Genesis 22:13). Isaac will live! Abraham names that place *"The Lord will provide."*

Faith, Not Perfect Faith

What faith! Faith that moves past doubts and despair. Faith that obeys. Faith that is not a feeling but an action. Faith that knows God will make a way.

Now realize that Abraham didn't have perfect faith. The patriarch's faith wasn't perfect when Sarah suggested Abraham sleep with her servant girl Hagar to start a family and fulfill the promise. This is a curious suggestion made by a desperate wife for sure, but it's even odder for Abraham to reply, "Okay, honey, if that's what you really want." Abraham didn't win Husband of the Year honors that year.

Abraham didn't have perfect faith when he told Pharaoh that his sixty-five-year-old "knockout" wife was his sister. In fact, Scripture says that in his fear Abraham repeated this wherever he went. He didn't have perfect faith when he was first told that Sarah was expecting at age eighty-nine. Abraham laughed in God's face. It was a belly laugh.

At times Abraham's faith wavered. Isn't it encouraging the Bible doesn't just hit the high spots of the patriarch's career? He didn't have perfect faith, but he sure had real faith.

So often we are like the guy who fell off a cliff and grabbed a branch on the way down. Hanging high above the ground, he looks down, realizing his predicament, and yells, "Someone help me!"

God answers, "What do you want Me to do?"

"Help me!" screams the man.

God replies, "Then let go."

The man looks down and then up and says, "Is there anyone else up there?"

Yes, at times we may be confused, unsettled, perplexed, and full of questions, but we too can choose to have faith and act upon God's Word.

The Surrender of the Soul

The sacrifice of the soul is at the heart of biblical faith. In the dead of night before Abraham launched out to Mt. Moriah, he made a decision. His decision was to put his mind, will, and body on the altar of God. I don't know how much he doubted or wrestled with that decision, but he chose well. This was the most important sacrifice of Genesis 22.

The sacrifice of surrender was my most valuable lesson during and after Katrina—and I'm still learning it. When Katrina hit and all the props, crutches, and security blankets were kicked out from my life, for a time everything was uncertain. Friends were dispersed, communities shattered, and I wondered if the church would survive.

I found out that Jesus was, is, and always will be absolutely faithful. My job is to stay on the altar as a sacrifice of surrender.

What are you and I called to put on the altar?

- My hopes
- My comforts
- My dreams
- My traditions

- My rights
- My agendas
- My ambitions
- My control
- My politics
- My pride
- My image
- My self-sufficiency
- My self-interest
- My greed

The challenge is to put these things on the altar and keep them there. The trouble with living sacrifices is that we are always tempted to crawl off the altar. During the trials of life, we need to *actively* choose to surrender. At these times we may shake upon the rock, but the rock does not shake under us. We may struggle, limp, or take baby steps, but we can always choose to step in the direction of obedience. We look for our ram in the thicket, and when it comes, we stand on sacred ground we can label *"God will provide."*

Not long ago, after preaching this "surrender" topic, I got a heart-wrenching email from a friend who had met the woman of his dreams. This sincere Christ-follower went from months of bliss, even talking of marriage, to the pain of a breakup. He was blindsided and undone. He questioned and wrestled with his Mt. Moriah moment. His dream was shattered and he had no idea where to go except to let go and wait for, as he put it, his ram in the thicket.

I don't know what your Mt. Moriah moment is. It may be a disability, a chronic disease, a dark secret, a dissolving marriage, a distant son or daughter, or a difficult career. Your Moriah may seem like all hell has broken loose…suddenly, unexpectedly, catastrophically. One day it's sunny. The next it's dark, turbulent, and out of control. Your heart is singed, your faith is scorched, and smoldering ashes permeate the landscape of your life.

No one is exempt. We all yearn for the ram in the thicket, don't we?

Dreams Can Become Dangerous Lovers

Many books, even so called Christian books, teach us to chase our dreams and pursue bigger, better, more audacious goals. The truth is that dreams, if not stewarded well, can become dangerous lovers.

Why would God ever want us to let go of "our" dream? Because anything I am unwilling to let go of is an idol, and idols come in all shapes and sizes. The truth is that idols can be anything: our job, our family, our title, our religion, our money, our addiction, our need for control, our picture of a preferable future, or our Isaac. It's easy for our dream to become our security and what we cling to for identity. It's what we use as a measuring stick with others; it's what holds us back from intimacy with God.

I don't know what your idol is, but everyone is tempted to have someone or something replace God. These "Isaacs" need to be taken to the mountain and sacrificed. Is this easy? No. Is it wise? Yes. Quit clutching. Give up. Surrender. You will get a whole lot lighter. Die to whatever you need to.

In C.S. Lewis' *The Voyage of the Dawn Treader*, Aslan (the Christ figure) deals with the boy, Eustace:

> ... so selfish, prideful, and greedy that he wakes up one day to find he has literally turned into a dragon. Life as a dragon proves so lonely and the dragon skin so uncomfortable that he soon longs to return to his friends, longs to be human again. In this scene, Aslan the lion leads Eustace the dragon to a pool. Eustace enters the pool and tries unsuccessfully to scratch off the aching dragon skin. Then Aslan says, "Lie down. This is going to hurt." And with a long, terrible claw, Aslan digs deep into Eustace's skin, ripping it wide open. It is the most painful thing Eustace has ever experienced, but when it is over, he stands up, a boy again. Reborn.[2]

God could keep our dreams alive, but misplaced dreams sometimes need to be killed—even ripped off like dragon skin. You are left with God alone, and He is enough, really enough.

Hitting a Wall

God will allow you to hit a wall if an idol needs to be stripped away. As we've already discussed, He knows how to get our attention. A well-timed wall in our way will make us admit, "I can't handle this on my own. I need God's strength. I need to surrender to His plans."

Here's what I am slowly learning: **Sometimes when God seems to be killing me, He is actually making me, and sometimes even killing an idol.** In Genesis 22, though it looked from the outside that God was cruel, God was actually turning Abraham into Abraham, or at least revealing him.

Look at Abraham. Isaac was his dream, his promise, his everything. You can imagine God saying, "Abe, who do you love more, Me or your dream?"

Abraham says, "That's easy. You, God."

God says, "Prove it. Offer up Isaac on the altar. Sacrifice him."

Abraham says, "But...but...but God, he is my son, my only son, my dream, my promise, my future."

What we learn from Abraham is that in the end he was willing to let go of everything before he would let go of God. The truth is, in many cases, **just because my will won't be done doesn't mean God's will won't be done.** If I need occasionally to abandon my dream, it does not mean I have to abandon my God.

When a Dream Dies

A few years ago I was at a meeting where Phil Vischer, the creator of VeggieTales, told how he wanted his company, Big Idea Inc., to be the Christian version of Disney, complete with media and theme parks. He was on his way with sales of more than fifty million videos and annual revenues hitting over $44 million, but then came a lawsuit, followed by bankruptcy, and the dream died.

Vischer said, "Fourteen years worth of work flashed before my eyes – the characters, the songs, the impact, the letters from kids all over the world. It all flashed before my eyes, then it all vanished."[3]

Big Idea wasn't a dream; it was the work Vischer was doing for Christ. "Big Idea was so much more important than me – more important to the world, more important to God," Phil admitted.[4]

Perplexed, fatigued, and desperate, he listened to a tape in which the pastor stated, "What does it mean when God gives you a dream, then He shows up in it and the dream comes to life and then without warning the dream dies? What does that mean?"[5]

At the end of the tape, the pastor said, "If God gives you a dream, and the dream comes to life and God shows up in it, and then the dream dies, it may be that God wants to see what is more important to you, the dream or Him. And once He's seen that, you may get your dream back. Or you may not, and you live the rest of your life without it. But that will be okay, because you'll have God."[6]

Vischer was undone. God was enough. God is infinite and you can't add anything to Him. God can meet our needs. God alone. No matter the circumstances. Just God without all the crazy work effort and need to perform. Everything minus God equals nothing. God plus nothing equals everything.

We must abandon ourselves to God. The adventure takes off when we abandon our purposes for His...when we flow not in our own strength but in His...when we build His kingdom, not ours. It is about Him, not us. The best thing we can do is resign from trying to control our universe and let God be God.

Phil Vischer's eyes were opened to the fact that his dream of Big Idea and the desire to impact the world had become an idol that defined his identity rather than his finding his identity in God. The more he dove into Scripture, the more he realized he was "drinking a dangerous cocktail – a mix of the gospel, the protestant work ethic, and the American dream. My eternal value was rooted in what I could accomplish....The Savior I was following seemed, in hindsight, equal parts Jesus, Ben Franklin, and Henry Ford."[7]

We are not to be people of vision but people of revelation. Proverbs 29:18 says, "For lack of wisdom, the people perish." Interestingly, as Vischer pointed out, in the language of the sixteenth-century KJV, "vision" is not synonymous with creative brainstorming, visionary thinking, big goals, and rah-rah meetings. Proverbs 29:18 literally should be interpreted, "Where there is no revelation, the people cast off restraint." The verse is all about what happens when God's people ignore what God has revealed to them in His Word. Our job is not to dream up our own good works but to enter into the good works that God has "prepared in advance for us to do" (Ephesians 2:10).

These truths may rock your world. We aren't called to make up a vision but to stop and listen. To wait upon the Lord, to walk with God, and to listen—as opposed to running around like a maniac. It's about listening and obedience. It's not about impact but about God. It's not about ambition but about dying to me.

And Phil Vischer? He found himself living life with ever increasing love, peace, patience, kindness, goodness, faithfulness, gentleness, and self-control. As he waited upon God, in time new creative ideas came his way that seemed to come from above. He wasn't concerned about five-year plans and big goals, but about trusting God for daily guidance. God even led him to publicly tell his story of broken dreams. He said to let them go. Quit clutching. Give up. Fall into God's arms – relying solely on His power and His will for life. That's where the fun starts. It's worth it. Vischer stated, "The impact God has planned for us doesn't occur when we're pursuing impact. It occurs when we're pursuing God."[8]

As you can imagine, people were moved, undone, encouraged, and energized by his message. I was fortunate to be among those in that initial crowd who never forgot it, and in some ways I needed to learn the same truths. **God works best when you are not wholly abandoned to impacting your world, but wholly abandoned to God.** Jesus said, "If you save your life, you'll lose it, but if you lose your life for my sake and the gospels, you'll find it."

His Plan Is Better

Thinking back over my life, I wonder how many times I have blamed God for the collapse of a dream, but when the dream was dusted for fingerprints, mine were all over it.

Henry Blackaby said, "If you start something and it does not seem to go well, consider carefully that God, on purpose, may not be authenticating what you told the people because it did not come from Him, but from your own head. You may have wanted to do something outstanding for God and forgot that God does not want that. He wants you to be available to him and more important, to be obedient to him."[9]

What is interesting to me is that for most of the year before Hurricane Katrina I had worked on a major strategic planning initiative for Trinity Church. I worked with elders, pastors, and key ministry leaders, but I was the point person. Finally, three weeks prior to the hurricane, I presented my plan to the leadership of the church. It was over seventy pages long, complete with graphs, charts, and projections, and included how Trinity could launch out into new ministry in September (remember, the hurricane hit August 29). It detailed what we would do through the fall and into the next year. There were even three- to five-year plans.

To be honest, the plan I put together was so well done that even I was impressed. In fact, the leaders adopted and unanimously approved the entire plan in one evening. This was surprising because normally in church circles proposals need to be discussed, prayed over, tweaked, sent to a committee, or sent back for more research. Not my plan—it was thoroughly approved in one evening. Everyone liked "my plan." We all went home and went to bed.

I'm convinced, however, that the Trinity (Father, Son, and Holy Spirit) did not sleep. The old saying is that when we make our plans God laughs. I imagine the Father might have said to the Son, "Jesus, have you seen Michael's plan?"

I think they started laughing, and the Son said to the Holy Spirit, "Michael thinks he's going to accomplish something through HIS plan!"

Then they all broke out in belly laughs. Late in the evening, I envision the Holy Spirit saying to the Father, "I think we can do better. In fact, I think he can do better. If he is willing to go along with our plans, something bigger and longer lasting will take place."

Even though I wouldn't wish Katrina on anyone or any community, I wouldn't trade it for anything. God's plan has been far better than my plan. His plan accomplished what my plan could never accomplish. The truth is **His plans are always better than our plans, even when they are hard.**

G.K. Chesterton said it this way: "How much happier you would be, how much more of you there would be, if the hammer of a higher God could smash your small cosmos."[10]

Adventure

It was Oswald Chambers who said, "To be certain of God is to be uncertain in all our ways, you never know what a day may bring. This is generally said with a sign of sadness; it should rather be an expression of breathless expectation."[11]

When we release our grip and surrender on the altar, the fun stuff begins and the adventure is amazing. We can then pedal like the old poem "The Road of Life" explains:

The Road of Life

At first, I saw God as my observer, my judge, keeping track of the things I did wrong,
so as to know whether I merited heaven or hell when I die.
He was out there sort of like a president.
I recognized His picture when I saw it, but I really didn't know Him.
But later on when I met Christ, it seemed as though life were rather like a bike ride,
but it was a tandem bike, and I noticed that Christ was in the back
helping me pedal.
I don't know just when it was that He suggested
we change places, but life has not been the same since.
When I had control, I knew the way.
It was rather boring, but predictable …
It was the shortest distance between two points.
But when He took the lead, He knew delightful long cuts,
up mountains, and through rocky places at breakneck speeds,
it was all I could do to hang on!
Even though it looked like madness, He said, "Pedal!"
I worried and was anxious and asked
"Where are you taking me?"
He laughed and didn't answer, and I started to learn to trust.
I forgot my boring life and entered into the adventure.
And when I'd say, "I'm scared,"
He'd lean back and touch my hand.

He took me to people with gifts that I needed,
gifts of healing, acceptance, and joy.
They gave me gifts to take on my journey, my Lord's and mine.
And we were off again.
He said, "Give the gifts away; they're extra baggage,
too much weight."
So I did, to the people we met,
and I found that in giving, I received,
and still our burden was light.
I did not trust Him, at first, in control of my life.
I thought He'd wreck it;
but He knows bike secrets,
knows how to make it bend to take sharp corners,
knows how to jump to clear high rocks,
knows how to fly to shorten scary passages.
And I am learning to shut up and pedal
in the strangest places,
and I'm beginning to enjoy the view
and the cool breeze on my face
with my delightful constant companion, Jesus Christ.
And when I'm sure I just can't do anymore,
He just smiles and says…
"Pedal."[12]

Chapter 3

Your Brokenness

God will always do something to thwart our self-life for a better life. God will use brokenness. That is His plan. He will sometimes take our "bat" away.

In the movie *The Natural*, Robert Redford stars as an aging Roy Hobbs. This onetime high school wonder boy finally gets his shot in the big leagues. Almost singlehandedly, Hobbs leads the worst team to the playoff game that will determine the pennant. The climax of the film comes down to Roy's last at bat in the bottom of the ninth with two outs. A homerun will win the game, but an out will dash all hopes. Ballplayers young and old dream of the adventure of this kind of moment.

The drama gets even more intense when Roy hits a long foul ball that at first appears to be a homerun. When he returns to the plate, his lucky bat is lying in pieces. This is the bat he has used since high school, a bat he carved himself from a tree felled by lightning. Burned into the bat were a lightning bolt and the words "Wonder Boy." The bat symbolizes his giftedness, his resources, his greatness, and his identity. He has never trusted anything else. The bat is shattered.

Such is life. Sooner or later life comes crashing down and the lucky bat explodes. The foreclosure comes. The spouse leaves. The pink slip appears. The investment disintegrates. The dream collapses. The friend dies. Health deteriorates. Men and women get tested when they can no longer rely on what seemed so sure for so long. When the golden goose dies, when the crutch disappears, when the security blanket burns, when the idol proves worthless, when the old identity fails, when giftedness fades, when the favorite bat breaks ... what then? Will we quit? Will we try to paste together the old pieces? Will we stay in the game? Will we cling to the old or surrender to a new beginning?

Brokenness always puts a person at a crossroads. Roy Hobbs found himself holding his lucky bat that was broken beyond repair. Finally, with a spirit of humble surrender, he says to the batboy, "Go pick me out a winner, Bobby." He steps up to the plate and belts a homerun to win the game.

God is always looking for a few good men

God made men to be men, to be warriors, and to stand in the gap. Gideon is one such example. When God called Gideon to defend Israel against the Midianites, he put out the call for warriors (Judges 6:34-35) and a massive group showed up. Gideon stepped out, and that aroused courage and zeal in others. In all, 32,000 inexperienced recruits volunteered, and most had no weapon.

On the other hand, Midian had an army of 135,000 troops (Judges 8:10). Their transportation and supply system was formidable. Their herd of camels was like counting the sand on a seashore. Gideon's army was outnumbered 4 to 1. God said, "Gideon, you have a numbers problem."

Gideon replied, "You can say that again. We don't stand a chance."

God said, "You've got too many troops. Have a troop reduction. Get rid of anyone who is afraid." Why did God say this? "And the Lord said to Gideon, 'The people who are with you are too many for Me to give Midian into their hands, lest Israel become boastful saying, "My own power has delivered me"'" (Judges 7:2).

Gideon went to the troops with a divine waiver, a get-out-of-harm's-way-free card. They were at Mt. Gilead, the last point where the soldiers could exit. Once you crossed the next hill, you ran headlong into war with the Midianites. Gideon gave the men a choice:

"Men, talk is cheap. We've come to the point of no return. God said if anyone is afraid, you can go home."

No doubt Gideon was hopeful the men were thinking, "We're good. They're bad. We'll stay." But 22,000 bailed out! The troop level dropped to 10,000, changing the odds to 13 to 1. No matter how you look at this, it's not good odds!

Again God said, "You have a numbers problem. Let's whittle the numbers down again." By this time, Gideon probably didn't want any more help from God with the numbers, but God said there needed to be one more round of cuts.

"You shall separate everyone who laps the water with his tongue, as a dog laps, as well as everyone who kneels to drink" (Judges 7:5). The vast majority of the men fell to their faces and drank deeply from the stream, but a small number knelt and scooped up some water, lapping it like a dog: 300 men. God said, "Go with the 300."

The numbers had been reduced from 32,000 troops to 300 on Gideon's side. They were outnumbered 135,000 to 300, making the odds 450 to 1. If you want to get a modern-day picture of who the 300 were like, think of the deputy sheriff Barney Fife on the old *Andy Griffith* show. Some scholars maintain the dog-lapper types were not the Navy SEALs but rather the geeky guys in the army. Comparison to dogs in the Bible is not a complimentary thing or a sentimental thing, but a derogatory thing.

God was setting up a scenario such that when victory came, all would know who won it! Over and over when God wants to do something big, He stacks the odds against His own so the credit will go to Him alone. Think about:

- David vs. Goliath
- Moses vs. the most powerful man in the world
- Disciples vs. the Pharisees and scribes
- Shadrach, Meshach, and Abednego vs. the fiery furnace
- Daniel vs. the lions
- 100-year-old Abraham and 90-year-old Sarah vs. the aging process
- Early church vs. the Roman Empire

Disaster

God strips Gideon of everything so he will trust in God. The Lord said to Gideon, "I will deliver you with the 300 men who lapped and will give the Midianites into your hands; arise, go down against the camp for I have given it into your hands" (Judges 7:7a, 7b).

It was no longer 300 vs. 135,000; it was the Lord God Almighty vs. Midian. The 300 were simply God's instruments. A God-confidence oozed. Farmers and cave dwellers were turning into mighty warriors.

Before going into battle, God gave Gideon one more sign to enhance his resolve. God told Gideon and his servant to sneak into the enemy camp and hear what they were saying. Gideon overheard an enemy soldier recounting a dream and talking about Gideon himself and the great victory he would have. The victory is referred to as the "sword of Gideon" (Judges 7:9-14). This is fascinating because as far as we know, Gideon didn't even have a sword.

As his reputation began to grow larger than life, fear ran rampant in the enemy's camp. A scaredy-cat wheat thresher turned into an intimidating warrior, and even crazier is that his "top cheerleader" was a Midianite soldier. Only God!

Only God can move in a way that results in your enemy speaking courage into your life. All Gideon could do was worship God, and he told all his troops, "Arise, for the Lord has given the camp of Midian into your hands" (Judges 7:15).

Battle Strategy

The battle strategy for victory: Gideon "divided the 300 men into three companies, and he put trumpets and empty pitchers into the hands of all of them, with torches inside the pitchers" (Judges 7:16). Their weapons were not bombs, bazookas, or AK-47s, but a jar, a torch, and a trumpet. Puzzling.

At first this made no sense from a human reasoning or military strategy standpoint. Their combat size was grossly inadequate. They had no experience, non-conventional weaponry, and their opponents were professional killing machines. Yet God had called, and where God calls He provides.

At about ten o'clock that night, Gideon's 300 warriors circled the Midian camp. At that moment the following happened simultaneously:

- 300 clay pots were smashed
- 300 torches pierced the darkness
- 300 ram's horns blared
- 300 voices shouted, "The sword of the Lord and of Gideon!"

Imagine each man, stealth-like, moving into position. Hearts pounded. God was their rock. Though they shook upon the rock, the rock would not shake under them. They would not run away. It was time for battle. God alone would make the difference between victory and defeat. Finally, Gideon's horn pierced the night, followed by an ear-splitting blast of 300 ram's horns, which shook the camp. The battle cry "The sword of the Lord and of Gideon!" roared, pots were smashed, and a circle of blinding, blazing luminaries created one of the most startling experiences in military history.

Imagine being suddenly awakened, stumbling out of bed, and finding yourself encircled with glaring spotlights and the commotion of crashing noises and trumpet blasts. It was sheer terror and confusion. In the mayhem, the Midianites picked up their swords and sliced and diced each other. There is always failure and defeat when armies, friends, or families turn on each other. Self-slaughter and fear lead to irrationality and killing. Midianite soldiers killed their own, and all the surviving warriors could do was flee.

Imagine the 300 wide-eyed Hebrew warriors' awe at the power of God. This ragtag band chased the once-legendary Midian soldiers right out of the country. Even the 31,700 who went home were filled with a wave of courage and helped with mop-up duties. Escape routes were cut off and Oreb and Zeeb (Judges 7:24-25), the enemy princes, were captured. These were the sons of a king, the best-educated commanders in the region. Oreb had a rock named after him, and Zeeb, a winepress. This was the ancient version of a general today having a school or highway named after him for some great victory. Oreb and Zeeb were killed, respectively, at the places named for them. A place of status for the Midianites became known as a place of defeat.

An in-your-face message spread throughout the region: "Don't mess with us...or our God."

Here is the huge lesson from Gideon: **Power is not in the clay pot but in the one who resides in the jar.** "But we have this treasure in earthen vessels, that the surpassing greatness of the power may be of God and not from ourselves" (2 Corinthians 4:7). The same God who brought creation out of nothing, parted the Red Sea, broke down the walls of Jericho, ripped the veil in the Holy of Holies, and raised Jesus from the dead is the same God of Gideon and the same God who dwells in us. This God seldom uses fine china; instead He uses weak, cracked clay pots. The pots usually have to be broken for the power to be revealed.

This truth is known as brokenness.

Brokenness vs. the Kingdom of Me

Brokenness was not a term I ever remember encountering in seminary, and it wasn't brought out in my early discipleship training. In our world today that values self-reliance, image, youthfulness, and got-it-togetherness, brokenness certainly isn't a popular subject. Yet these days I can't seem to miss its call in Scripture. From Jacob wrestling with God to Gideon's charge to serve God with 300 rather than 32,000 to Paul learning that strength often comes in the midst of weakness, we find the call to brokenness.

Brokenness is the work of the Spirit of God in which He strips us of self-sufficiency, self-preserving agendas, self-will, self-wisdom, and self-trust and replaces it with a God-trust, God-reliance, God-wisdom, and God-strength so that the beauty of the life of Christ will shine in, through, and out of us!

Self-sufficiency	→	Sufficiency of God
Self-reliance	→	God-reliance
Self-wisdom	→	Wisdom of God and the Word of God
Self-will	→	Surrender to timing and plan of God
Self-resourcefulness	→	God's adequacy plus nothing
Self-life	→	Christ-centered life
Self-power	→	Freer flow of God's power

Brokenness crucifies self so that Christ might reign in our lives. Brokenness dislodges our self-life and substitutes utter dependence on God and God alone. Sometimes we are bucking broncos and sometimes we are stubborn mules, but God wants to tame our unbridled spirit. Whereas the world craves success, the broken yearn for blessing—the blessing of God. Dietrich Bonhoeffer said, "The cross is laid on every Christian. It begins with the call to abandon the attachments of this world. It is that dying of the old man which is the result of his encounter with Christ....When Christ calls a man, He bids him to come and die."

Jesus spoke of brokenness when He said, "I tell you the truth, unless a kernel of wheat falls to the ground and dies, it remains only a single seed. But if it dies, it produces many seeds" (John 12:24). A kernel of wheat in its hard outer shell cannot sprout or grow. However, when the hard shell is broken and cracked open, then the life of the wheat can blossom and bear much fruit. Christ-followers are like kernels of wheat with new life inside. We all have a hard outer shell of our self-life that restricts the life and power of God from fully flowing through us. Brokenness breaks the shell so the life of Christ can spill out through us. We move from flesh-driven to Spirit-driven. Our personalities, strengths, and temperaments are not changed, but they are purified.

The psalmist says, "The sacrifices of God are a broken spirit, a broken and contrite heart, O God, You will not despise" (Psalm 51:17). "For though the Lord is exalted, yet He regards the lowly, but the haughty he knows from afar" (Psalm 138:6). "God is opposed to the proud but gives grace to the humble" (James 4:6). I'm convinced the key question in discipleship is not "Are you living the Christian life" but "Have you died?"

We must die to our agendas and our ways. His path may include sacrifice, discomfort, being hidden, and fewer toys. However, dying to my plan, my program, my purpose, and my agenda is the path to transformation. It always costs, yet we receive the benefit of the soul. As Jesus put it, if you want to save your life, you'll lose it, but if you lose your life for My sake, you'll find it. To live before you die, you have to die before you live.

Paul ended up boasting in his brokenness. "Most gladly, therefore, I will boast about my weaknesses, so that the power of Christ may dwell in me" (2 Corinthians 12:9).

The Tools of Brokenness
God can use all sorts of things to bring us to brokenness:

- Catastrophe (Judges 7-8)
- Satan (Job 42:5-6)
- Thorns (2 Corinthians 12:9)
- Sin (Genesis 32:22-32; Matthew 26:33)
- Circumstances (Acts 13:13)

God can use anything to teach us greater dependence upon Him, but the key thing is how we respond. When we go through the "dark night of the soul," will we respond with humility, deeper grace, and character growth—or with cynicism or bitterness?

We often say, "God won't let you endure more than you can handle." Is that true? Yes, when it comes to temptation. It is an ironclad promise that we will not be tempted beyond what we are able (1 Corinthians 10:13). But "God will not give us more than we can bear" when it comes to trials? Where do we get such whacked theology? Hallucinations 21:12? This line may sound great on a needlepoint wall hanging or a Hallmark card, but you won't find it in the Bible.

When God is trying to work brokenness into our lives, He will break us using fire that burns off the old self-life, and He will reshape us into something new. We will be in situations completely over our heads. Paul knew about this all too much when he wrote, "…Our affliction, which came to us in Asia, that we were burdened excessively beyond our strength, so that we despaired even of life; indeed, we had the sentence of death within ourselves in order that we should not trust in ourselves but in God…" (2 Corinthians 1:8-9).

The Bible is packed with stories of situations beyond someone's ability to handle, situations in which people were forced to embrace or abandon God's plan. A.W. Tozer wrote, "It is doubtful whether God can bless a man greatly until He has hurt him deeply." Deep stuff, but true. Dr. Alan Redpath, in *The Making of a Man of God*, said, "When God wants to do an impossible task, He takes an impossible individual and crushes him."

God will root out escapism, sarcasm, arrogance, turf protection, or self-pity. To accomplish it, He strikes fatal blows to the heart of me. On a daily basis He makes a clarion call to funerals. Paul said, "I die daily," with the result being the matchless adventure of life in Jesus. God is simply not in the business of calling perfect, self-actualized, got-it-all-together people.

My Journey

Have you ever seen or ridden one of the world's tallest, fastest, scariest roller coasters? You know, the Cyclone, the Rebel Yell, the Tower of Terror II, or something else?

To be honest, my life has felt that way. I was on a slow, steady climb just like on a roller coaster...click, click, click, up we go. Ministry opportunity, success, compensation, some bumps along the way, but fruitfulness and not hype, the real stuff. This could have lasted forever; it was the good stuff.

But one day I realized there is a downside to the roller coaster that I wasn't expecting – unemployment, ministry crumbling, betrayal, and vulnerability. It's terrifying and shattering. All kinds of "niceness" boxes get exploded. Assumptions about the future get reshuffled. Friendships get tested. Idealism gets tempered. You have no earthly way of knowing where this will end up. My illusion of control exploded even though theologically I knew I was never in control in the first place.

Brokenness isn't easy or pain free, but it is liberating. God knocks the props and crutches out from under us. He snatches away our security blankets. He reduces us to Jesus plus nothing.

I am learning to respond to God's call to daily "die to self" with a greater glimpse of the matchless adventure of life in Jesus. Amazing how I can preach on Colossians or Galatians and expose their reliance on circumcision or other such things, while not being aware of my own propensity to rely on props and security blankets rather than on God alone.

Yes, brokenness is liberating. I'm fresher. I can see new understandings of grace. I can allow for greater mystery in the Godhead. I don't have to have the answers to everything. I'm learning there is a lot of "I don't know" and "wait" in my life and that discipleship involves learning to struggle well. I don't have to pretend all is well. The question is not "Are you struggling?" but "What are you doing with your struggles?" and "Where is God in the midst of these struggles?"

I love Jesus, who simply says, "Do you want to be well?" I love the truth that grace is available. In fact, less than 10 percent of the references to grace in the Bible refer to our justification; most refer to God's merciful restoring power for living. I must simply trust His hand and believe His heart. I'm learning to see people through a new lens, with greater delight and with greater discernment. I'm choosing to grow in being wise as a serpent even as I try to be harmless as a dove. I'm learning to look up and look ahead, for that's where my future lies.

Topics of forgiveness, reconciliation, justice, courage, and wisdom are not just topics to preach, but they are the stuff to be grappled with and lived out. These times give a greater reality of our own Achilles' heels. We want the barbed hooks out of our lives because they keep us from Him and from living life to the fullest, but it hurts to pull those hooks out!

I'm learning to listen to the voice of One and not to the loudest, most domineering voice. I'm resting in my gifts: shepherding, encouraging, preaching, and teaching. I'm willing to be true to my calling to be Christ-centered, substantive, Bible-focused, and grace-centered. I'm learning leadership is not always being the strong one, but instead sometimes being the weak one who is made strong by Jesus alone. In fact, I'm learning that in brokenness, weakness, and vulnerability before God and others, His grace is sufficient. Yes! That's liberating. That is where my life is right now.

Many times we portray "surrender" with negative connotations: failure, capitulation, waving the white flag, defeat, giving up, or giving in. I'm learning that to surrender to God is the boldest and smartest move I can ever make. It is always in my self-interest to surrender to Him. Saying "yes" to God-reliance and God-sufficiency changes everything.

Like a mother eagle that pushes her eaglets out of the nest before they think they're ready to fly, God often has to nudge us—even outright push us—out of our comfort zones to accomplish His purposes for our life.

Chapter 4

Fearless Moral Inventory

Savvy marketplace leaders audit their books and inventory regularly. Why? To make sure everything is on the up and up. It's a fiscal inventory. Smart seniors show up for the annual physical exam. It's no fun getting the prostate exam, but it's a health inventory. The NASCAR driver loses time entering the pits to check the tires and fuel, but it's worth it because it's a mechanical inventory. The soccer team watches game film and learns where things went wrong. Why? It's post-game analysis athletic inventory. A world traveler stops occasionally to look at a map. It's too costly to be going in the wrong direction. It's a geographic inventory.

If businesspeople examine books, racers read gauges, travelers read maps, sports teams look at film, and human beings get blood work, shouldn't Christ-followers slow down now and then to take a personal moral inventory? If people and organizations are smart to take inventory, shouldn't we audit our life, inventory our souls, take stock of our integrity, and reflect on our emotional state? As one man asked, "Why do we have CPAs to keep us liquid, lawyers to keep us legal, and medical doctors to keep us healthy, but no one to regularly assess our spiritual condition?" Where is the regular spiritual audit?

Spiritual inventories are particularly important in the middle of crisis, disaster, conflict, and turmoil. Yet it often is the road less traveled. That is a shame because catastrophes will come. The ICU stay. The pink slip. The early retirement. The lawsuit. The creditors. The

IRS. The foreclosure. The divorce papers. The cancer. The tornado. The flood.

No matter who you are, you will end up between a rock and a hard place, with no light at the end of the tunnel. At these times we almost always want to blame the other guy and defend ourselves.

Job was a man in the middle of a cosmic showdown at the OK Corral. Excruciating physical pain, attacks by trusted friends, perplexing circumstances, and grief beyond description—Job faced all this and still had the character, insight, and fortitude to pause and conduct a fearless moral inventory of his life, a careful reflection of his heart. Job's inventory encompassed five full chapters of his book (Job 27-31).

Let's look at the transferable principles:

➢ Conduct a Fearless Moral Inventory (Job 27:1-12)

Job starts with an ancient oath, "as God lives," vowing his reflection will be honest and serious, not phony. Job asserts his integrity and concludes the attacks of his so-called friends have not been on target.

Psychologists have coined the phrase "self-serving bias" to describe our human capacity for self-deception. We evaluate information in ways that are almost always beneficial to our own interests. These biases make us think we are better than the average person, and that gives us an illusory superiority.

Conducting a fearless moral inventory is the road less traveled. Examining yourself in the middle of a disaster separates the men from the boys and the women from the girls. Let down your guard. Take an honest look at yourself.

➢ Seek Divine Wisdom, Not Conventional Wisdom (Job 28:1-28)

As the spotlight gets shone inward, we need God's eyes (not natural eyes), divine wisdom (not conventional wisdom), and a word from God (not the voice of the streets). Wisdom is skill in living. Wisdom is saying or doing the right thing, at the right time, in the right way, for the right reason.

Wisdom is not about IQ or gathering lots of information. It's about right decisions; it's about being godly, not just smart. It involves very practical areas like money management, choosing words carefully, governing impulses, navigating relationships, and managing anger. Wisdom allows for the proper application of truth. Real wisdom comes from above and not from within. This contrasts with conventional wisdom, even if it comes from the so-called best and brightest.

Job discovered that the great treasure of wisdom can't be purchased; it has to be mined like silver and gold. Wisdom comes from God and is the result of pursuing the knowledge of God and fearing God with a spirit of reverence, honor, awe, and respect.

In taking a spiritual audit, especially in tough times, it's essential we see as God sees with supernatural insight. Otherwise, our issues and faults will be invisible blind spots and our relationships will suffer.

➢ Audit Your Past Blessings and Personal Strengths (Job 29:1-16)

Job remembers that he has been favored with God's presence (Job 29:1-6), that he has had the esteem of the community (Job 29:7-11), that he has been the joy of compassion to many (Job 29:12-17), and that he has hope for the future (Job 29:18-25). Job isn't bragging, he is being honest and recalling what God has done.

There is much to praise and thank God for as you audit your assets.

➢ Take Stock of Your Losses (Job 30:1-31)

Imagine Job scratching his boils. His tongue is parched and his lips are swollen. His skin is blistered and his body aches. He thinks through not only his gains, but also his losses. He doesn't live in denial. The man who was once revered is now disrespected and afflicted. Young men mock him (Job 30:1) and others spit in his face (Job 30:10). He is taunted and humiliated. The pain takes no rest. It seems as if even God is silent. Job feels like he has no help, no health, no future, and no ministry.

What a list! Job itemizes his losses.

> **Conduct an Internal Spiritual Audit (Job 31:1-40)**

Job allows the spotlight to go into the secret, often overlooked places. No stone is left unturned. His spiritual audit includes:

- His thought world (31:1-4)
- His ethical world (31:5-8)
- His family world (31:9-12)
- His business world (31:13-15)
- His community world (31:16-23)
- His financial world (31:24-25)
- His spiritual world (31:26-28)
- His social world (31:29-34)
- His stewardship world (31:35-40)

Moral inventories are often frightful, painful, time-consuming, and tedious. Taking stock demands slowing down, shining a spotlight, asking good questions with fearless honesty, and sometimes using the help of reflective tools, a counselor, or a good friend. Internal audits are not easy, but a life not worth examining is not worth living, as the saying goes.

Without inventories, we keep reaping certain consequences of our actions and face the possibility of a more serious downward spiral. It's easy to make excuses and bail out.

Just as Alcoholics Anonymous participants choose to reflect on their lives with a fearless moral inventory, so we must take out a spiritual notebook and pen and honestly engage in a moral inventory. In Brennan Manning's words, "we must lose our halo's and get honest."

There is an old saying in Texas: "If one person tells you that you're a horse's rear, forget it. If two people tell you that you are a horse's rear, look in the mirror. If three people tell you you're a horse's rear, go buy a saddle."

Do you need to buy a saddle in some area of your life?

> **To Stop Killing Yourself, You Have to Stop Kidding Yourself**

It's easy to get accustomed to our misery. Our peer group won't criticize us. In fact, they commiserate with us.

The reality is that people can know they are sick, know things could be better, and know there is a problem...but don't want to get well.

The key question is, "Do you want to get well?"

Denial is saying, "Who me? I don't have a problem. I can stop anytime. No big deal. I'm fine."

Recently, I went through a pretty thorough and intense self-evaluation. It was a time to take stock, to walk through the nooks and crannies of my life, and to check out my heart. I had to turn on the searchlight and:

- Evaluate my strengths
- Consider my weaknesses
- Audit my giftedness
- Tally my limitations, itemize friendships, examine woundedness
- Write off areas of failure under the banner of grace
- Rearrange priorities

This was no easy process. It was time-consuming. It wasn't convenient in the least. And it certainly wasn't comfortable, especially since a number of people were evaluating my life with feedback for greater accuracy and understanding. I felt vulnerable and humbled. I had a friend who knew how to take me apart and put me back together...to wound and heal...to be hard yet protect my spirit with encouragement. As the rewards started to come in, I knew I was preparing for the next five thousand miles of the journey.

One of the areas I've learned I need to grow in is overcoming "people pleasing" tendencies. On the one hand I desire to please God, but sometimes I waste time on the impossible task of trying to please everyone. Some modern-day writers refer to this as "approval addiction." Truth be told, in some ways I know what this drug tastes like. I know what it's like when it's withheld. I know what it's like to hear that inner voice, "What will they think of me?"

Disaster

Over the last few years, God has been rooting out of me the need to please others. I don't know the exact date that I started giving up the need to impress. This motivation came from a combination of personal experiences and the Word of God.

Personal experience is a great teacher, isn't it? You know when you run into a wall that your nose is soft and the wall is hard, and the wall wins every time. Over time you learn not to run into stuff that doesn't move. I'm learning that people pleasing doesn't work because people want more and more and more, and people want opposite things, and people don't really want what they ask for. You simply get weary from people pleasing.

I also learned from God's Word that Jesus always played to the audience of One—always! He was about God's will and not about His own. I learned:

> For am I now seeking the favor of men, or of God? Or am I striving to please men? If I were still trying to please men, I would not be a bond-servant of Christ.
>
> Galatians 1:10
>
> But just as we have been approved by God to be entrusted with the gospel, so we speak, not as pleasing men, but God who examines our hearts.
>
> 1 Thessalonians 2:4

I have been called by Scripture to a life of not measuring myself by someone else's measuring stick. I don't have to be someone else; I simply need to be who Christ made me to be. My worth comes not by performance but from the One who alone can satisfy: God.

Here are the Top 10 things I'm in the process of learning:

1. Live for an audience of One. If everyone applauds me but God, I'm a failure. If no one applauds me but God, I'm a success. The question is whose applause am I living for? I must not play to the audience who pays me but to the audience that made me.
2. Listen to criticism when it's appropriate and dismiss invalid criticism. No matter how hard I may try, I can't please everyone.

3. My life is not based on the unstable foundation of human opinion but on Christ.
4. Endure. Maturity is moving from a thin skin and a hard heart to a thick skin and a soft heart.
5. Learn to say no. Busyness does not equal fulfillment.
6. Refuse to ask permission from those who have no authority over my life.
7. Do not kowtow to someone with an opinion just because they are loud about it.
8. Controllers cannot control me unless I let them.
9. Love people without needing their approval.
10. Live in the loving care of the Father.

There is a freedom, security, and safety that comes from living to please One. Do you remember when you were in elementary school and your teacher needed something taken to the office? You were given a hall pass. You'd walk confident and secure past other classrooms. You smiled at your buddies stuck in their classes and flashed them your hall pass. If some teacher stopped you in the hall and said, "Young man, aren't you supposed to be in class?" you'd hold up your hall pass. You had a hall pass!

God gives us all a hall pass, an assignment. We are to do what He calls us to do! When people question you or doubt you, pull out your hall pass.

How About You?

I want to ask you to do a difficult thing. It's especially challenging to do in the middle of disaster, crisis, woundedness, or tragedy. It is easy to blame, rationalize, not take the time, or think you wouldn't know how. It takes courage and a brand of humility that defies embarrassment. Go ahead and take a stab at it:

- Audit your past blessings and personal strengths
- Take stock of your losses
- Conduct an internal spiritual audit
- Restock and move forward

Chapter 5

Your Calling

When speaking to churches or volunteers, one of my favorite illustrations involves a big, puffy, comfortable chair sitting on the platform. I ask for a volunteer to help me demonstrate why comfort can be dangerous.

I get the volunteer's name (let's say it's Sam) and say, "Sam, I want you to immerse yourself in comfort. I want you to go all out. Take your shoes off. Have a seat."

Guys always play this part with flair. I don't even have to tell them to pull the lever and lounge back; it's innate to the species. I bring the lights down a little and hand Sam some comfort food: chips and a Coke. Of course, every true American male has to have something in his right hand while residing in a chair like this – a remote control. I put on a little music. Sam shuts his eyes.

I ask the crowd, "Tell me, does Sam look like a man ready to spring into action and live an adventure? Is he ready to seize the day? Is life really maximized in a La-Z-Boy chair? Does the chair cause your heart to beat fast and your soul to be filled?"

We end up waking Sam up and everyone gives him a big ovation. One time I actually had a guy who stayed in the chair the whole service. He was too comfortable to move. But, paraphrasing John Ortberg on this chair illustration, I say, "What is so dangerous about the chair is not the stuff you do in the chair, but the stuff you don't do. Relationships that are never deepened, people never served, prayers never prayed, races never run, fights never fought, tears never wept, and adventure never gone on."

You were made for more than life in a La-Z-Boy chair. You were made for partnership with God. You were made for adventure, risk-taking, and maybe even something a little dangerous at times for the sake of the call.

The pattern of Scripture is that God calls us on adventure. He called Moses, "Go to Pharaoh and say 'Let my people go.'" He called Sarah, "You are going to have a baby at age 90." God called Noah to build a 20,000-ton box 450 feet long, 75 feet wide, and 45 feet high and tell people a flood would come out in the desert where it had never rained. God called Mary to conceive a son without a husband and have people forever question her on the real story.

God Calls

The fact that God calls is undeniable. We have already looked at Gideon and his triumphant battle with the Midianites, but when we look at his life from another perspective, we see a calling on his life that relates to the calling on our lives as well.

Judges 6:1-2 states, "Again the Israelites did evil in the eyes of the Lord, and for seven years he gave them into the hands of the Midianites. Because the power of the Midianites was so oppressive, the Israelites prepared shelters for themselves in the mountain clefts, caves and strongholds."

Notice the word "again." Here's a people who, after finally conquering and living in the Promised Land, get stuck in cycles of failure. They go from milk-and-honey to living in fear and hiding in holes on the side of mountains.

In Judges, the five-step failure cycle appears seven times:

- SIN leads to...
- SERVITUDE
- The people cry to God in SUPPLICATION
- God sends SALVATION through a deliverer
- In time prosperity leads to SLIPPAGE

The Midianites were the warring regional bullies who brought pain and harassment for six years and pushed the Israelites to the brink of starvation. Remember, Israel was an agricultural people: crops and livestock. You can't hide that stuff very well. The Midianite bad boys would wait until the livestock had given birth and the harvest was ready, and then they would descend upon Israel "like swarms of locusts" (Judges 6:5).

Imagine, year after year they came swarming, pillaging all that you needed to survive. Things were going from bad to worse. If you tried to fight, the savages would kill you for sure. Do nothing and you might starve. This once proud people now ran to holes in the ground. The people were resigned to misery and had almost nothing to show for themselves. You know how maddening it can be when someone cuts you off on the highway. This was a whole different league of injustice. What frustration, disillusionment, and hopelessness!

When people hit rock bottom and a certain threshold of pain, they say "That's it!" and cry out to God. It is at this point of pain, frustration, calamity, and disaster that God often does His best work.

What's your disaster? What's causing your greatest pain? What is overwhelming you? What failure do you need to face? What cycle are you trapped in? What is your treadmill? What has been going on six years for you? God always raises up a man, a woman, a couple, or a core team. Be ready. It may be you!

The Call

God is in the business of calling people. It happens over and over. He needs a few good men and women. God taps people on the shoulder and says, "I have something for you to do of eternal significance. It's a call, an assignment, a purpose."

God called the unlikely Gideon. "The Lord is with you, O valiant warrior" (Judges 6:11-12). Valiant warrior? Who is this guy? He is down in a winepress, not making grape juice but trying to thresh wheat! What a ridiculous sight. Threshing was done outside where the wind could separate the chaff from the wheat. It's a very visible operation. A winepress was cramped, small, and had no wind. It must have looked ridiculous as Gideon, covered head to toe with husks, threw grain into the air. It was like making coffee in a thimble. Gideon was trying to eek out a living for his family as he peeked out the window to see if the big bad Midianites were coming. Industrious? Yes. But also sad.

Yet God called Gideon as a mighty warrior to an assignment. The call comes to every Christ-follower. It came to me. One day God tapped me on the shoulder and said, "Will you respond?" He will come to you.

By the way, when God calls, how often does He give an easy assignment? Think about it. Never! He does not put a high premium upon comfort. All pay a price for their callings. Let me be frank. Some have obeyed the call and been martyred. Others have had unspeakable challenges and barely survived. Some have lived in obscurity and seen little measurable results. Sometimes it's draining and the hours are long.

However, the call is always unique, always customized, always special, and always a partnership with God. Calls are not the classified ads to volunteer for but a summons to be obeyed. In His own way, God taps you on the shoulder.

Response to the Call – Fear

When God calls, the response is almost never "Cool! Yes! What an opportunity…can you supersize it?" Instead, the response is usually one of fear. Many will resist because the call would take them outside of their comfort zone.

Fears, Insecurities

Mighty warrior? Save Israel out of the Midianites' hands? Can you imagine Gideon's initial thoughts when he heard his calling? It seemed preposterous, crazy. Gideon was neither nobility nor royalty.

A terrified Gideon reminded God that he was from the least impressive tribe and the runt of the worst family (6:15). God had the wrong guy. What self-regard! He was fearful and rationalizing away his passivity. He was declining the greatest invitation of his life. He couldn't picture a better tomorrow. There were no dreams for the future beyond subsistence; he was just dust in the wind, a little chaff in the air. Inadequate, fearful, cowardly.

Questions, Doubts

Gideon has real questions that spring out of his doubts and the injustices he observed. "If the Lord is with us, why has all this happened to us? And where are all the miracles our ancestors told us about? Didn't they say, 'The Lord brought us up out of Egypt?' But now the Lord has abandoned us and handed us over to the Midianites" (Judges 6:13 NLT).

Gideon feels abandoned and wonders where the power, miracles, and interventions of the past have gone. Questions…lots of questions about God and how He is running the universe. It's a mix of anger, frustration, and confusion, just like people have today:

- Why, God?
- Why is this bad stuff happening?
- Why do bad things happen to good people?
- Why didn't You do more?
- Why didn't You keep this from happening?
- Are You really all-powerful, all-caring, all-knowing?

C.S. Lewis, one of the greatest writers and thinkers about God, wrote this after losing his wife to cancer:

> When you are happy, so happy that you have no sense of needing Him, so happy that you are tempted to feel His claims upon you as an interruption, if you remember yourself and turn to Him with gratitude and praise, you will be – or so it feels – welcomed with open arms. But go to Him when your need is desperate when all other help is vain, and what do you find? A door slammed in your face, and a sound of bolting and double bolting on the inside. After that, silence. You may as well turn away. The longer you wait, the more emphatic the silence will become… What does this mean? Why is He so present a commander in our time of prosperity and so very absent a help in time of trouble?[1]

Richard Dawkins, author of *The God Delusion,* describes God in even stronger terms:

> The God of the Old Testament is arguably the most unpleasant character in all fiction: jealous and proud of it; a petty, unjust, unforgiving control-freak; a vindictive, bloodthirsty ethnic cleanser; a misogynistic, homophobic, racist, infanticidal, genocidal, filicidal, pestilential, megalomaniacal, sadomasochistic, capriciously malevolent bully.[2]

Wow, Richard. What are you really thinking? It is easy to get a call from God and initially say no. Fear, excuses, and discomfort can always try to hold us back.

God came repeatedly to me in my growing up years and through my youth leaders and asked me to preach. I said each year, "No, that will be the last thing I ever do." When I first told Donna about a ministry opportunity in Louisiana, she said, "Louisiana? Who would ever want to live in Louisiana?"

The call comes. Most respond with fear or excuses.

Assurance

Interestingly, God does not correct Gideon, criticize him, or chew him out. God responds with assurances and promises. To Gideon came these words:

- "The Lord is with you" (Judges 6:12).
- "Surely I will be with you, and you shall defeat the Midianites as one man" (Judges 6:16).

This is where the hinge point usually is in divine calls, not just for Gideon but also for everyone else. What is impossible for ordinary folks becomes possible when it's God plus one other person. The size of your God will determine the size of your faith.

You plus God equals a majority. A shrunken god will lead to fear, no dreams, anxiety, and a stomach tied up in knots. Those who worship shrunken gods will worship without awe, pray without expectation, suffer without hope, and live without courage. However, a

Disaster

BIG God changes everything. Life just works that way when you are with someone BIG.

What if God comes to Gideon, or you or me, and says, "Don't be afraid. Don't hide in a hole. You have a God you can count on. Get with it. Accept the call."

Over and over in the Bible God says "Fear not" and often with the words, "For I am with you." We do not have to live under the tyranny of fear.

Are you a teenager? You and God are a team that can't be beat. Are you in your eighties? You and God are a powerful team. Are you feeling beat-up? You and God can't lose. God has come to Gideon with assurance. "You are not Super Chicken...you are a mighty warrior!"

Isn't that what God does? Childless Abram's name meant "Father," and God says, "No, you are going to be Abraham, meaning 'the Father of many nations.'" God comes to "Simon, the little pebble" and renames him Peter "the Rock."

When God calls you, He sees you as special to Him. Too many of us walk around with labels someone else has pinned upon us. What labels do you need to cut off? Ugly, stupid, failure, DWI, unwanted, wrong family, wrong side of the tracks, wrong skin color...?

Too many of us say, "Not me. I'm too shy. I'm too old. I'm too young. I'm not smart enough." You will always act in accordance with how you think about yourself. If you think you are a loser, you will act as a loser. If you want to experience God's best, you need to stop thinking you are a failure. Right thinking leads to right actions. We don't think we are worth much. Too many of us have an inferiority complex.

Which of these excuses do you need to let go?

- So-and-so is walking all over me.
- I'm going to change jobs.
- I'd like to tell so-and-so...
- My dream is...

Who do you need to confront? What do you need to face? Where do you need to step?

Where do you need to change? Where do you need to stop playing the victim? If we hear His voice and know His presence, it will change us.

Decision Component

With every call there always comes choice. A decision has to be made. Yes or no. Fear or faith. Or faith in the midst of fear. Will you step out of the comfort zone? This isn't just having a good intention, it's launching out in obedience. Faith is the decision to trust God. It's not a feeling but an action. It's walking through experiences that are hard to comprehend. It's advancing when everything is going wrong, when expectations aren't met, when life is not fair. Faith is choosing God no matter what. It's not waiting until the circumstances change. It is trusting God now. It's overcoming peer pressure and family intimidation. It's overcoming "What would so-and-so think?" and asking "What does God want?" It's going in God's direction even when an abrasive personality doesn't agree, even when a "false voice" doesn't understand and gets angry. You choose in favor of God.

These words were for Gideon, "Go in the strength you have and save Israel out of Midian's hands. Am I not sending you?" (Judges 6:14). Gideon steps in the direction of obedience, and God's power comes along the way.

What false idol do you need to dethrone? What fear is trying to derail you? What words of mother/father/sister/brother/boss/bully do you need to disagree with?

Now, before God delivers Israel, they must get rid of their idols. The land was full of them, namely Baal, the fertility god. It worked like this: if you bow to Baal, he'll provide you with kids, crops, and cash. If you deny him, you are in big trouble. Baal was the sex god. Baal was worshipped through eroticism. Many worshipped at this altar of immorality, infant sacrifice, and pole dancing (yes, even back then they had an Asherah pole). It was a dark place, but here's the kicker: Gideon's family is the poster family for idolatry in the land. Gideon's backyard is Ground Zero for Baal's headquarters, the epicenter of the movement. It's like his dad is the priest of the cult.

How often do you think Gideon has ever taken on his dad? So Gideon takes ten friends in the middle of the night and gets the job done. He's scared to death, but he's obedient. Gideon's obedience is even contagious, and his dad stands up for him.

This is the decision component. It matters not if we feel adequate, only whether we say yes to God. What ledge has God asked you to jump off? In what area do you need to cross the line of faith?

Empowerment

When God calls and you step in the direction of obedience, God's power comes along the way. Judges 6:34 says, "Then the Spirit of the Lord came upon Gideon." Obedience brings power. Obedience causes strength to flow in your direction. Power comes when the tests are passed.

Gideon ignites a firestorm across the nation, and all the enemy armies come. Gideon still wrestles with fear and wants a sign that this call is real. He wants to make sure this isn't a bad dream or a product of bad pizza the night before. Gideon says, "Uh, God, show me again that You are really who You say You are" (see Judges 6:33). You may have heard the expression "There's no need for signs or fleeces." But Gideon has just met God in the winepress, his life has been turned upside down, and now the greatest army in the world is bearing down on him. Let's cut him some slack. Gideon wants to believe, but he wants confirmation that God is with him and that he is to lead an army against the Midianites. He puts out a fleece.

Now sometimes people use fleeces as superstitious things or as a way to manipulate God or to stall or as a loophole not to act. One time I was in a crowd listening to comedian Ken Davis, and Ken told about a guy who drives near a bakery and prays, "Lord, if there's a parking space in front of the bakery when I drive by, then I'll know it's Your will I go inside and get a doughnut." And sure enough, his fifth time around the block there is an open parking space in front of the bakery.

This wasn't Gideon's heart. The fleece was about encouragement and growth. Gideon lays out a sheepskin fleece and asks God to soak the fleece with dew the next morning but keep the ground dry. God didn't condemn this request. Sure enough, the next morning water pours out when he squeezes the fleece, yet the ground is dry. To be doubly sure, Gideon asks the next night for the fleece to be dry and the ground wet. God honors his request, and Gideon's faith goes off the charts. Isn't God tender? He wants to grow our faith. Even though we need to be cautious with signs, God gives holy experiences. All Christ-followers have them in time.

Everybody who says yes to God is empowered and ends up with a story to tell. Every time you say yes to God you grow a bit. Your courage gets enhanced, your faith is stretched, your joy level increases, you find more pleasure in God, and your endurance muscles are strengthened. The truth is if you save your life you lose it, but if you lose your life for Christ and the gospel, you find it.

Not long ago one of our teams needed a Bobcat to finish clearing a big stump from a yard. Where could they get a Bobcat? On the way to the person's home, they got stuck in traffic. A drawbridge went up and traffic came to a standstill. Someone joked that there was a Bobcat three vehicles up. One of the team members jumped out of the vehicle, ran up, and tapped on the window of the truck hauling the Bobcat. "We work with a church and have no money, but we will give you a sandwich for lunch if you will come to New Orleans and help us," he said. Unbelievably, the man said he would. Indeed, he arrived later in the day, but when he saw the stump he said it was too big. The team said, "You pull, we'll pray." The stump came right out! The Bobcat guy felt so good about it that he called his wife and told her, "I did some free work today. If you don't believe me, I will put some people on the phone who will tell you."

Watch for divine appointments. Listen for God's callings. They often come in the most unusual of places.

Sometimes we are asked, "Isn't the work hard?" I like TouchGlobal Crisis Response director Mark Lewis' answer. He says it's like being in the Super Bowl of God's work and having seats on the 50-yard line. Who wouldn't want to be there?

Part Two
Theological Underpinnings

Chapter 6

Our Culture

During the height of the Cold War, Billy Graham traveled to the Soviet Union and spoke to hundreds of leaders in the Brezhnev regime. Critics in other parts of the world couldn't understand why he treated the enemies of America and detractors of the Western church with such courtesy and respect. Shouldn't he condemn Soviet human rights abuses and their restraints on religious liberty? One person scoffed that Graham set the church back fifty years.

Graham responded, "I am deeply ashamed. I have been trying very hard to set the church back two thousand years."

Oh, to recover the radical, dangerous, scandalous way of Jesus!

First-century Israel faced many of the same challenges we face today. High taxes, terrorism, poverty, military challenges, religious extremism, governmental ineptitude, and a shrinking middle class, to name a few. Solutions were championed through elaborate theological, political, and social systems in an effort to improve the culture and bring forth a new kingdom of God. Talk of revolution and hope, particularly from the top four philosophies, pervaded the land.

Zealots

The Zealots were deeply patriotic, activistic, and fervent for the Law of God. The Zealots proposed solutions through revolt. These solutions would usher in the kingdom of God through might, force,

Disaster

and revolution. Zealots believed a zealous anger would lead people to rise up and arm themselves, thus bringing new world order through military coup. Their motto resounded through the call to take action, come out swinging, slit a few throats, and take the country back.

	APPROACH	STYLE	CULTURE	METHOD	RESULT	EXAMPLES
Zealots	Revolt Might Force Revolution Hostility	Combative	Fight	Lunacy	Suicidal	Far extreme religious right and left

The Zealots thought passivity and cowardliness identified the reasons for the oppression. They viewed themselves as freedom fighters, but many looked upon them as terrorists. Today, the name al-Qaeda elicits the same emotion that many in the first century felt when they heard the word "Zealot."

Some of the Zealots even embraced assassination as a means to an end. These men concealed daggers in their robes and waited at crowded events to strike their targets. This group's popularity was on the ascendancy in Jesus' day, yet Zealot philosophy led the people to ruin. During Nero's reign, the Zealots moved from guerrilla resistance to major initiatives. The Romans brought in General Titus, whose armies destroyed Jerusalem in A.D.70, including burning the temple to the ground. Some of the Zealots, 960 of them, survived this holocaust and holed up on top of the mountainous fortress called Masada until A.D.73. It is said that 15,000 Roman troops came in to crush the resistance. In the end, the Zealots committed suicide rather than surrender.

Today, there are cultural warriors of every stripe. Rally the troops. Take a stand. Protest. Shout louder. Every new issue is a defining moment. Isn't it tempting, on the far religious right and left, to value elections over Easter and political petitions over prayer? Isn't it easy to think of Jesus simply as the honorary chaplain of the Democratic Party or the Republican Party, or whatever your persuasion, believing for political utopia?

But, as Chuck Colson stated, "The kingdom of God will not be ushered in on Air Force One."

Sadducees

The Sadducees thought the Zealots' militant approach against Rome was stupid or even suicidal. Resistance was futile. They believed making the best out of a bad situation through compromise, collaboration, and pragmatism would ensure greater progress. Their motto resounded with the common phrase, "If you can't beat 'em, join 'em."

	APPROACH	STYLE	CULTURE	METHOD	RESULT	EXAMPLES
Sadducees	Compromise Collaboration Pragmatism Expedience	Conforming	Imitate	Liberalism	Shaped by others	Liberal religion

In part, this thinking flowed out of their theology. Sadducees did not believe in spirits, angels, or resurrection (Acts 23:8). They centered their thinking upon the here and now. Caesar rewarded them handsomely for paying allegiance to Roman rule. The Sadducees maintained the high priest and chief priest positions in the temple. They profited immensely by managing its affairs, which was by far the economic engine of the region. People from all over traveled to Jerusalem for religious festivals and paid dearly for sacrifices and relics. The Law required all males to come three times a year to pay the temple tax.

The Sadducees' approach was problematic because when you don't shape culture, culture shapes you. Conforming leads to constant compromise, which results in little influence. Metaphorically speaking, there is no problem launching a boat into the water. The problem comes when the water enters into the boat. Likewise, there is no problem having a believer in the world; the problem comes when the world gets in the believer.

Even today, faith blenders fit right in. They are cultural Christians. Faith is a private matter. They go along for the ride, do good, and fill many church pews. They don't obsess over their faith. Their lifestyles are not that different from anyone else's. In the book *UnChristian*, young non-Christians were asked if they perceived the lifestyle of a Christian to be much different from their own. Of the 84 percent who knew a Christian personally, only 15 percent thought the lifestyle of the Christian was different.[1]

Essenes

The Essenes thought the Zealots' military coup was impossible, and the Sadducees' compromise turned their stomachs. Withdrawal, isolation, and retreat defined the strategy of the Essenes. They withdrew from society to devote themselves to a life of exclusivity and purity. Ritual cleansing and purification often became an obsession. Legalism was pervasive, and many pursued mystical encounters with God.

The Essene wilderness commune in Qumran provided the locale for the discovery of the Dead Sea Scrolls in 1947. The Essenes preserved the oldest surviving copies of biblical documents we have today.

	APPROACH	STYLE	CULTURE	METHOD	RESULT	EXAMPLES
Essenes	Withdrawal Retreat Isolation	Cocooning	Ignore	Legalism	Irrelevance	Amish

The Essenes believed they had a deal with God. They considered themselves sons of light and that everyone else was a son of darkness. Graphic wording permeated their writings. They believed God's wrath would soon come upon the sons of darkness like a blowtorch, but as sons of light they would return to Jerusalem and take over temple worship.

Though they didn't see it, their withdrawal made them irrelevant. Those who ignore the culture are ignored by the culture. The Essenes simply chose to curse the darkness rather than light a candle. For the most part they were left alone, but society thought they were crazy.

Today it's easy to gravitate to this religious subculture of choice where we avoid the world at all costs. Create church basketball, church summer camps, Christian radio, schools, T-shirts, and toys. On and on it goes. Retreat to the fortress.

Pharisees

Of our four groups, the Pharisees are the most famous and infamous. They ushered in their brand of hard-line religion with passion and conservatism. Separation, moralism, and an active spirit of condemnation toward all outsiders defined their approach.

	APPROACH	STYLE	CULTURE	METHOD	RESULT	EXAMPLES
Pharisees	Separation Moralism Draw Lines	Corrective	Condemn	Legislation	Condemnation returned	Religious subculture

The Pharisees believed their goodness far exceeded the goodness of anyone else. They looked down their noses at everyone, while conveniently overlooking their own shortcomings. The lists of sins kept getting longer and longer. These religious elitists dressed differently, walked on the opposite side of the street than ordinary people, and set up moral boundary marker after moral boundary marker. In their viewpoint, the sin of Israel prevented God from ushering in the kingdom. It was their job to whip everyone else into shape.

Sadly, the sinners of the first century saw arrogance, self-righteousness, and judgmentalism in the Pharisees. How can people be won to Christ when all they do is dodge the stones you throw at them?

The Pharisees' amazing efforts to separate themselves from worldly infection brought little effect to those they yelled at across the fence. Condemning the culture leads to condemnation from the culture. Aren't there better alternatives than just pointing a finger?

Are There No Good Options?

These four groups constantly vied for power and ascendancy. They were always arguing, counteracting, and forming and dissolving alliances. When the Zealots killed someone, the Sadducees would decry the terrorism and pledge greater allegiance to the Roman government, the Essenes would write words of disdain, and the Pharisees would wonder why everyone wasn't following their great Pharisaic example.

The people of the land wondered, "Which path is the right path? How do we live in this world and honor God?"

	APPROACH	STYLE	CULTURE	METHOD	RESULT	EXAMPLES
Zealots	Revolt Force Revolution Hostility	Combative	Fight	Lunacy	Suicidal	Far extreme religious right and left
Sadducees	Compromise Collaboration Pragmatism Expedience	Conforming	Imitate	Liberalism	Shaped by others	Liberal religion
Essenes	Withdrawal Retreat Isolation	Cocooning	Ignore	Legalism	Irrelevance	Amish
Pharisees	Separation Moralism Draw Lines	Corrective	Condemn	Legislation	Condemnation returned	Religious subculture

Jesus Christ

When Jesus entered the scene, all the contemporary kingdom approaches were called into question. In fact, it wouldn't be long before His popularity incited jealousy and invited trouble with all of Israel's spiritual guides.

When Jesus was a boy, Judas of Galilee led a revolt among the Jewish people to not pay taxes. He ended up on a cross, but the people loved him for this. Jesus, however, stated unapologetically that people should render to Caesar that which was Caesar's. He willingly paid taxes. One time He said a certain Roman centurion had greater faith than anyone in Israel. In one of Jesus' sermons, He suggested that a proper response to "impressment" might include carrying a soldier's bag a second mile. The same sermon declared that prayer would be a superior response to our enemies rather than seeking revenge. Which group would these actions tick off? The Zealots. They were not happy campers with Jesus.

One day Jesus took a whip and with holy fire in His eyes chased the moneychangers out of the temple. He didn't want to reform the temple system but rather replace it. He hated the exploitation, the price tag for forgiveness, the power plays and money laundering techniques that lined men's pockets. Jesus taught that heaven's availability was universal and that resurrection followed death. Who

Disaster

was offended by this audacity? The Sadducees. Obviously, Jesus' first priority did not include winning friends and influencing people.

Constant ceremonial cleansings didn't impress Jesus. Instead, He touched lepers. He taught that legalism and withdrawal into religious subcultures opposed the kingdom of God. He called God's people to be in the world. Who wrote Him off? The Essenes.

Read about the seven woes found in Matthew 23. You can't help but wince. Jesus called people out by name. He used harsh words such as "blind guides, fools, hypocrites, and whitewashed tombs." He said in Matthew 21:31 that tax collectors and prostitutes have a greater chance of entering the kingdom of God than the religious elite of the day. Jesus dined with tax collectors and allowed prostitutes to touch Him. He broke the religious elite's customs, traditions, and rules while refusing to jump through their hoops. He seemed to do it with gusto, knowing He pulled their chain. Unbelievably, Jesus embraced His reputation as a lawbreaker and friend of sinners. Who hated this Jesus? The Pharisees.

For Jesus, the revolt, withdrawal, violence, and compromise methods were wrong. His call was not to slit throats or damn sinners. Instead His commands to turn the other cheek, confront injustice, and question blind patriotism drove people crazy. He said to love rather than hate. He invited all to join His side. He said "Follow me" to Simon the Zealot (Luke 6:15; Acts 1:13) and Matthew the tax collector—and then asked them to "room together." He also picked Nicodemus, the Pharisee, and invited revolters, withdrawers, collaborators, legalists, doubters, devotees, sexually trapped, and the self-righteous to His team. No one had ever seen anything like this. This wasn't just another revolutionary. This was a new kind of revolution.

Jesus spoke of the kingdom of God everywhere He went. He addressed it forty-nine times in Matthew, sixteen in Mark, and thirty-eight in Luke. He proclaimed that the kingdom of God was at hand, but people couldn't believe it. They bought in to the need to eject Rome first, reform or drive away prostitutes and sinners, or embrace a military messiah. The kingdom now? No way. Yet Jesus insisted that the kingdom of God existed now and not yet, present and future.

According to Jesus, the kingdom of God finds expression within a person and is available for everyone to live under the reign and rule, power and presence of God. It was the offer of a lifetime. Jesus made it clear that His kingdom was not of this world. He owned no bank accounts or soldiers and claimed no headquarters. His only crown became a crown of thorns. Jesus ushered in the kingdom, but not in Rambo style. Jesus' kingdom was on a crash course with the pseudo-kingdoms of this world.

Indeed, Jesus didn't get crucified for being nice or for teaching religious ditties, but because He threatened the power base of powerful people. As a King with a kingdom, He said, "Follow Me." He was no Mr. Rogers figure and everyone knew it. He couldn't be tamed and wouldn't fit anyone's mold. Nobody could control Him, though they tried. Every time leaders tried to trap Him, they came out with black eyes. A provocateur to the powerful, Jesus disturbed cultural norms. For those bent on removing Him, crucifixion provided the perfect solution.

Shocking, outrageous, and scandalous was the message of Jesus, the Shalom of God available to all through Jesus. Life through Jesus would be new and different. It would be true life as God intended. Jesus built a movement of followers, not a religious institution. Jesus' way turned everything upside down. It declared that service modeled greatness, the first shall be last, and the last shall be first. Living meant dying, forgiveness defeated violence, joy came through sorrow, strength came in weakness, and to conquer you must be conquered!

The Jesus Approach

Jesus called His people to enjoy the world, engage the world, and evangelize the world, resulting in transformed individuals from the inside out one life at a time.

> In a musical play about the life of Christ entitled *The Choice,* the handsome young Roman centurion named Marcus, who's single, takes notice of a somewhat spunky Jewish maiden named Hannah. While both guard themselves against falling headlong in love, they enjoy talking to each other and matching wits. One

day Hannah coaxes Marcus into going along to hear the itinerant from Nazareth, who is speaking on a nearby hillside.

On the way, they get into a brief argument about whether Roman justice is fair and what role a Messiah might play in Israel's political future. Then, in one of the most insightful lines of the play, Hannah says, "I don't pretend to be wise...but I do know that Jesus is special. He's different. He's not changing governments, Marcus. He is changing people."[2]

Jesus was after a quiet, non-forced revolution inside the human heart. He was different from many religious types who try to clean the fish before they catch them. Jesus didn't believe there was a political solution to everything. He didn't bully, write letters of protest against the disgraceful antics of politicians in high places, or suggest if only we got so-and-so in office the time of infamy would be reversed. Somehow He believed that a revolution of love and transformation one heart at a time was superior and more effective. Jesus called people not to anxiousness, apathy, alarm, or anger but to the hope that He is the real King on the throne and He is at work.

The key to change is nothing less than the life-changing power of the gospel of Jesus Christ. When it impacts an unconverted soul, the ripple effect will touch lives, worldviews, and eventually salt public policy and culture. C.S. Lewis said, "He who converts his neighbor has performed the most practical Christian political act of all."[3]

Truly remarkable and counter-cultural, Jesus' approach was not exclusive but inclusive. In the world, everyone divides into camps. You are either a good guy or a bad guy, in or out. Most of us find comfort and contentment living in our personally designed boxes. My box is:

Christ-follower
Evangelical
Conservative
American
Southerner

It's easy to build a box. It's easy to exclude. It's easy to draw lines in the sand, but it's hard to build bridges. How did Jesus do it?

> 1. Jesus knew where to draw lines in the sand and where not to.
> 2. When Jesus did draw lines in the sand, they were precise, absolute, and unchanging.
> 3. Jesus crossed every single line and loved people on the other side.

Uncompromising on God's views of sexual morality and loose living, He still enjoyed the company of adulterers and prostitutes. Jesus' huge heart for the poor, marginalized, and disenfranchised did not prevent His friendship with their oppressors, the tax gatherers. The embodiment of holiness, Jesus still seized each day to befriend sinners. He lived in an occupied land yet loved the occupiers.

Does it make sense? Only if you look at things through Jesus' kingdom lenses. The more you hang out with Jesus, the more you see people through new eyes, the more you want to draw proper lines in the sand, blow up manmade lines, and build bridges to all people. Truthfully, I like my box, but I know Jesus wouldn't spend as much time in there as I do. Only Jesus' approach can turn the world upside down, one person at a time.

Jesus heard the musings of philosophers and poets. He walked by Roman bathhouses, theaters, and gymnasiums. Jesus engaged with the woman at the well (John 4), the Roman centurion (Luke 7), a leper (Matthew 8), the woman caught in adultery (John 8), and a tax collector named Zaccheus (Luke 19). Remember tax collectors were the Bernie Madoffs of their day. Jesus was never fearful of contamination. He planned to rub off on others rather than them rubbing off on Him. He never said, "Make yourself clean and I will eat with you," but rather "Eat with me and I will make you clean."

If you've only tried a tamed Jesus, you've simply tasted a counterfeit Jesus. No one comes into contact with the real Jesus and remains unchanged. Don't settle for Jesus-lite—great taste, less demanding. Don't settle for a non-discipling Christianity. Dorothy Sayers said, "We have very efficiently pared the claws of the Lion of Judah, certified Him 'meek and mild,' and recommended Him as a fitting household pet for pale curates and pious old ladies. We love the Lamb of God, but we have discarded the Lion of Judah."

Jesus' way includes danger because Jesus is dangerous. He was the most subservient guy to walk the planet, but He is also the greatest game-changer and paradigm-shifter. T.K. Glover said, "The early Christians out-thought, out-lived and out-died their pagan counterparts." G.K. Chesterton said, "The Christian ideal has not been tried and found wanting, it has been found difficult and left untried."

Could it be that in the midst of seismic cultural shifts, God is raising up a new kind of follower? One who:

- Discerns good from bad and truth from falsehood
- Engages confidently without fear of being sucked into wrong thinking
- Appreciates an opposing perspective
- Works with others gladly in places of common ground rather than condemn
- Displays grace rather than demonization
- Proposes solutions to corruption as opposed to disgust, judgmentalism, and boycotts
- Works toward a future of beauty, justice, restoration, grace, and love rather than act offended and withdraw
- Creates a better future in arts, media, government, education, church, aged, marketplace, disabled, unborn, marriage, and urban renewal
- Brings the Shalom of God to all peoples
- Majors on the majors and not on the small stuff
- Shares the Jesus of the Bible and the hope that is in the soul with grace and truth

A.D. 30 Again

Some suggest that Christians need to hold the line against evil personally or Christianity cannot advance. The theory is well meaning, but it doesn't square with the Scriptures or with history. The gospel is powerful in both friendly and hostile cultures. It is simply a powerhouse.

What is the fastest growing religion in the world? Did you guess Islam? The answer is Christianity.[4]

1. China

Christianity had about 1 million adherents in 1949 when Mao Tse-tung and the Communists came to power. Persecution reigned. Missionaries were forced to leave the country. Pastors were killed, churches shut down, and Bibles scarce. Some thought, "That's the end of the movement of God in China." Today it's not easy being a Christian in China, but Jesus is doing much. Best estimates claim there may be as many as 100 million people following Jesus in China, and 30,000 a day are coming to Jesus.[5]

2. Sub-Saharan Africa

Africa was said to be 3 percent Christian at the beginning of the last century. In spite of AIDs, civil war, poverty, competition from Islam, and struggling economies, the gospel is on the move! Growth of the faith is estimated at 20,000 converts per day.[6]

3. Latin America

Despite governmental corruption, poverty, drugs, and hardship, the conversion rate is estimated at 10,000 a day.[7]

4. India

Estimates are that 7-10 percent of the population today has converted to Christ and that 40,000-50,000 are coming to know Christ daily.[8]

5. Indonesia

Post-tsunami there has been a movement of God. Things are changing in this Muslim nation.

Leith Anderson, president of the National Association of Evangelicals, says, "We read the book of Acts and celebrate the fact that on the Day of Pentecost, three thousand people came to Christ. Today, if you combine Mainland China, sub-Saharan Africa, and Latin America, *There's nearly a Pentecost every hour.*"9

In 1900, 80 percent of Christians were white, lived in the Northern Hemisphere, and were of Western culture. Now, 80 percent are non-white, non-Western, and not of the Northern Hemisphere. The kingdom of God is advancing powerfully. As Reggie McNeal says, "It's A.D. 30 all over again!"

Chapter 7

Where Is God When Things Go Wrong?

Where was God on 9/11?
Why Columbine?
Why didn't God prevent the Holocaust or at least stop it?
Where is God in earthquakes, volcanoes, floods, hurricanes, tsunamis, fires, famines, and other natural disasters that kill and hurt?
Who is to blame when disaster strikes?

When tragedy hits, our questions range from the theoretical to the personal, from the intellectual to the emotional, from the theological to the curious. Natural calamities or personal crises dominate our conversations. Life is fragile. We yearn for a way to process such things and discover a foundation on which to stand. It was no different in the first century after the news of a massacre and tower collapse. In Luke 13 you can almost hear people asking, "What about the eighteen killed in the accident, Jesus? Where was God during the massacre, Jesus? Are the dead in heaven or hell?"

Jesus replies, "Do you think that these Galileans were worse sinners than all the other Galileans because they suffered this way? I tell you, no! But unless you repent, you too will all perish. Or those eighteen who died when the tower in Siloam fell on them – do you think they were guiltier than all the others living in Jerusalem? I tell you, no! But unless you repent, you too will all perish" (Luke 13:1-5).

Jesus' response provocatively points out that the real question is not "What about them?" but "What about me?" Think of your own condition, for if today were your last day (as it one day will be), are you ready?

Let's unpack Jesus' words so we don't miss the significance. Jesus deals with two disasters that were the "breaking news" events of His day. The first was the Galilean atrocity involving Pilate and the Galileans. Galileans were known as the rebellious types by Rome. Many were Zealots who advocated the violent overthrow of Rome. Apparently, Pilate discovered the plot and waited for these seditionists—terrorists in his eyes—to come to Jerusalem to worship at Passover. While the Galileans were offering up their animal sacrifices, Pilate's operatives struck them down in the temple. In fact, their blood flowed into the sacrificial animal blood. This was a sacrilege; it was appalling that Gentiles would be in the temple. Can you imagine a government-sponsored surprise killing today at St. Peter's Cathedral, the Dome of the Rock, or the Taj Mahal? Murder in a place of worship! You can imagine the buzz on the street, in the editorial pages, and around the kitchen tables. Surely everyone had his or her own spin on this story.

The second disaster involved a famous tower in Jerusalem, the tower of Siloam. The tower collapsed and crushed some people who were in the wrong place at the wrong time. They probably weren't Zealots but simply ordinary, garden-variety folks. Again, everyone knew the news of this disaster.

Stories of Disaster Raise the Question "Who Is to Blame?"

Do you suppose these Galileans were greater sinners? (Luke 13:2) Do you suppose these eighteen were worse culprits? (Luke 13:3) The answer in the heads of most people would be yes!

The word "sinners" can refer to a non-observant Jew. Maybe they didn't keep a kosher table or neglected the required feasts or Sabbath observances. Heaven help them if they were tax collectors. Jesus may have been asked, "Do you think God judged them because they didn't keep the rules?" You can almost hear the crowd say, "Amen! They must have been big-time sinners who got what they deserved."

The phony doctrine of retribution is the way most people intuit the world. It goes like this:

Goodness   ⟶   Blessing/prosperity

Wickedness   ⟶   Suffering

In other words, it's "you get what you deserve" thinking. Take Job for instance. Before disaster hit, Job married a pretty girl, had ten great kids, built a dream house, led a successful enterprise, and was prized in the community. When catastrophe hit, Job's friends interpreted his loss as the direct punishment for some hidden wickedness.

Eliphaz	The innocent do not suffer	Job 4:1-3, 7, 12
Bildad	Lost ten kids, you had it coming	Job 8:1-3
Zophar	Your sin caused this loss	Job 11:13-14

In Job 22:4-11 the friends paint a picture that Job must have accumulated a debt so great that God had to punish him. Who is to blame for the calamity? Job. He deserves it. Their philosophy is when disaster happens it can always be traced to the sin of those impacted.

This same phony doctrine of retribution can be seen in Jesus' day. "And as He passed by He saw a man blind from birth. And His disciples asked Him, saying, 'Rabbi, who sinned, this man or his parents, that he should be born blind?'" (John 9:1-2). In other words, who has the big secret sin debt—was it the kid's sin or his mom or dad's sin that caused the blindness? Don't the disciples know better? Shouldn't we? Yet this thinking goes on in spades in our day.

In the "disaster zone" these questions become the hot potato questions. Immediately after Hurricane Katrina wreaked havoc in the Gulf, a Middle Eastern man, after finding out I was a pastor, wanted to know if Katrina was God's judgment on the French Quarter and New Orleans for wickedness. This kept coming up, and I found out it wasn't just being asked locally but nationally. I was asked to be a guest on a number of national radio programs. When the programs allowed for callers to ask questions, without exception callers asked, "Who is to blame? Is this God's judgment?"

New Orleans Mayor Ray Nagin entered the theological fray with his explanation for Katrina, saying, "God is mad at America." One person said, "Katrina was a judgment on the entire nation for our mistreatment of Israel." Even prominent religious leaders blamed the worldliness of New Orleans. Years of corruption, debauchery, and promiscuity were now being paid for they surmised. I couldn't help but question the dogmatism of those pointing the finger and seemingly having such direct revelation of the mind of God.

When I went to a flooded New Orleans just days after the devastation, I saw churches destroyed. Poor, God-fearing families faced utter ruin, yet the French Quarter was largely dry. Had God missed His target, or were the prognosticators off target completely?

Why is it that after 9/11 nationally known Christian leaders said the attack was brought on by sin—not the sin of the terrorists, but sins of the people in this country—and that these leaders knew exactly which sins God was punishing us for? Why is it that the list involved the exact agenda these leaders most pushed? How we love neat and tidy packages to explain complicated issues that point the finger at our foes. Anne Lamont said it this way, "We know that we have created God in our own image when we are convinced that He hates all of the same people we do."[1] We all need to be careful of adopting the phony doctrine of retribution.

Jesus loves to blow up false doctrines and take people to another level of thinking. He settles the issue once and for all that disaster and tragedy are not always directly linked to hidden sin of the individual. Had God whacked the Galileans (as killed by Pilate) and the hapless victims of the tower collapse because they had accumulated more sin debt than all the rest? Jesus says, "I tell you, no. Emphatic no!"

He blew up all the conventional wisdom. He wanted to set the records straight and correct shallow theology and runaway urban legends. People's minds were spinning. Those who lost their lives in the disaster were no guiltier than you, me, or those in the crowd. Fasten your seat belt because what came next rocked people's world. He said, "But, unless you repent, you will all likewise perish" (Luke 13:56).

Jesus says that the amazing thing is not that the tower fell on eighteen, but that it didn't fall on all sinners including you and me. The amazing thing about life is that anyone is still sucking air. The amazing thing is that amazing grace is still available. In the middle of disaster, it is easy for all of us to play the blame game – blame God or someone else. God is put on trial rather than ourselves. We forget about the goodness of God. It's easy to focus on the "why" of Noah's flood and forget the 120 years Noah preached an invitation to the world. It's easy to question the plagues of Egypt yet forget each was designed to communicate the shallowness of Egyptian theology and point them to the better way. The invitation to apply the Passover blood was open to all.

In every calamity you can run to grace or away from it, embrace the cross or shun it. The horrors in life can bring us closer to God. Will we refrain from putting God on trial? This is the graduate-level course that Jesus wants us to enroll in.

Jesus invites us to think of disasters as a great "wakeup call" in which we examine our lives and make sure we are right with God. C.S. Lewis said pain is "God's megaphone to rouse a deaf world"[2] If resurrection is the door into heaven, then repentance is the key to that door. Without repentance, the door is locked.

Repentance means a change of mind that results in a change of action and direction. It means to turn around because you were going in the wrong direction. You turn and trust Christ as the way, the truth, and the life (John 14:6) for no one comes to the Father but through Him. Have you trusted Jesus Christ?

Jesus goes on to tell a sobering parable in Luke 13:6-9. Through the metaphor of a fig tree, a vineyard owner, and a gardener, Jesus reminds us that God is a God of grace, the God of the second chance, third chance, and many chances, but at some point He is the God of the last chance. God wishes none to perish but all to come to repentance (2 Peter 3:9). Disaster, in part, should humble us and remind us of the uncertainty and brevity of life. It should lead us to get right with God.

Disasters, in part, are giant object lessons to all. What if you knew that one week from today a tower would fall on you or a hurricane would sweep you away? Would you be ready to meet your Maker?

I love how one man found Christ through his harrowing experience with Katrina. The storm was indeed his spiritual wakeup call. The family decided to ride out Katrina in their sturdy, raised home. Despite the ferocity of the hurricane, they thought they had survived. The storm's violence subsided and they went outside to enjoy the calm and survey the damage. For a few moments they experienced euphoria, but that soon gave way to fear. They realized they were in the "eye" of the hurricane and the backside of the storm was coming with a vengeance.

The water started rising a foot every few minutes. Soon their boat tied to the lower level of their home was up 12 feet or so, and they needed to get in it fast or the water would overtake their home. In the middle of the hurricane, they maneuvered up the river. The only problem was when they got to the first bridge, the water was almost bridge-high and the boat could not go under it. So they docked and got onto the bridge.

After a few minutes they noticed something big coming downstream. It was their house! It slammed into the bridge shattering into a million pieces. They realized that the water would soon go over the bridge. Their only hope was a mad dash back into the boat to try to maneuver to the other side of the river and onto a sturdy-looking tugboat. Because of the winds and currents, they didn't know if it was possible to make it.

They can't explain the last leg of the journey, but in their words, God got them on that tugboat and they rode out the storm. The man said, "I never thought about God before Katrina, but now I think about Him all the time." He trusted Christ and started weekly to attend church.

I ask you, if a hurricane gets a man connected with God, was the hurricane God's justice or His mercy? I say mercy for his life now and his eternal destiny are forever changed. The worst thing in the world is not dying, it's dying without Christ.

Titanic took 1,516 people to an ocean grave. When the news reached the shores, relatives had to be informed whether their loved ones were among the dead or the living. In Liverpool, England, at the ship's station, a huge board was set up with columns that read "KNOWN TO BE SAVED" and "KNOWN TO BE LOST." Crowds gathered to watch the updates. The travelers of *Titanic* started as first, second, or third class but ended up either "saved" or "lost."

In this world we have our ways of differentiating people, but on judgment day there will be only two categories: saved or lost. There is only heaven or hell. Jesus says, "Unless you repent, you will perish." Disasters should lead us not to point the finger of condemnation at others but to check our own heart.

A true story is told about a man who had saved money for a number of months to buy something he had wanted to purchase for years. It was a very expensive barometer. He had seen it in the Abercrombie & Fitch catalog. When he finally saved enough money he sent off for it, and the barometer came several weeks later. When it arrived, he opened up the box and discovered that the needle seemed to be stuck in the sector marked "Hurricane." He took out the barometer and thumped it with his fingers a few times to try to get the needle to move. It wouldn't budge. He banged it on his desk to get the needle to change. It didn't work. Finally, he became so upset that he wrote a scathing letter to the store, and the next day on his way to work in New York City he mailed the letter.

That night when he got home to Long Island he found that his barometer was gone, and so was his house. The month was September, the year 1938—the day a hurricane leveled Long Island. We consider a man like that to be a fool. To see information like that, to see it squarely, and choose to ignore it, react against it, and find out later that it is true.

Man is wise when he sees information and responds properly. God's Word is His message to us. It warns us of judgment if we do not repent. Wise men call upon the Savior.

Chapter 8

The God of the Resupply

Meet a woman who marries and thinks she has the world by the tail. Imagine the hopes and dreams she and her husband cherish. A baby boy soon adds to their joy. Then disaster strikes.

- Her husband dies
- She is a widow
- She is alone without an extended family support system
- She has no bank account or insurance policy
- She has no job

With everything already going against her, an extended drought rocks the economy. Everything turns brown and dies. She scrapes and claws out a living, but finally she and her son come down to the last of the flour and oil. One more meal and they will starve to death.

Interestingly, a stranger comes along. It happens to be Elijah, the prophet of God. Elijah had been public enemy number one of King Ahab. He was living as a fugitive, hiding out by a ravine and being fed by ravens (1 Kings 17:4). What a life! Every day he depended on the ravens to come. Every day he awaited God's supply. Every day divine supply followed divine placement. Just when Elijah must have thought he had God all figured out, the brook dried up and the ravens stopped bringing food. Elijah was driven back to his Source.

It's easy to seek God's hand and not His face, easy to trust a method and forget God is the Source. God decides to resupply Elijah through a widow living in town (1 Kings 17:9). Elijah may be thinking, "Yes! I hope she's got a big house, a pool, and a lot better setup than living in a ditch!" Instead, he finds a poor single mom from Zarephath in the heart of Baal country, and you recall Baal worshippers weren't fond of Elijah. She refers to "your" God and not "our" God (1 Kings 17:12).

What comes next is amazing. Elijah says, in essence, "I know I'm a stranger and probably thought of as your enemy, but give me your last meal. If you do, you will meet the God who will resupply your cooking products miraculously until the famine is over" (1 Kings 17:13-14).

What a crazy request, yet she does it. She discovers not mountains of flour and barrels of oil, but enough — enough for the day, and then the next day and the next (1 Kings 17:15-16). God is the God of the resupply. He's the God of manna. He's the God who gives daily bread. In fact, as her story unfolds, she ends up with her son in an above-average-size house and Elijah's God as her God. She found it was impossible to out-give God. She had met the God of the resupply.

It's hard to explain the math sometimes, but something happens with God. I have personally been introduced to and visibly seen the hand of the God of the resupply.

A friend of mine wrote the following words to me: "Gather in all that has happened since August – would the mighty wind of the Holy Spirit be seen like it is right now without the disaster? Would you have witnessed the mighty unstoppable hand of God like you have without the hurricanes? Would Trinity Church have become 'Jesus with skin on' without a community desperately in need of His arms, His strength, His love? A community that suddenly had nothing but Him?"

"Nothing but Him"...what a great statement and apt description of who we have been. People have been scattered, houses destroyed, jobs lost, keepsakes ruined, and futures left to uncertainty. All the props of life were kicked out from under us, yet in all our devastation, brokenness, weakness, and finiteness, we can still say, "He is able."

Days into the Katrina chaos, I wondered how we would survive. Jim Snyder of the EFCA TouchGlobal flew in and told me, "Michael, you are going to have to learn to receive." For the first time in my life I was truly desperate. I had to learn and learn I did. God's daily provision came as a new kind of manna from heaven. This manna came in the form of water, food, RVs, Bobcats, work teams, truck shipments, and lots of the love of Jesus displayed through His hand-picked instruments. This miraculous supply appeared before our very eyes.

Miraculous Church Provision

At Trinity Church, people were initially scattered across the country with only a remnant left. We didn't take an offering for a number of weeks, and I wondered how we'd survive, yet survive we did. Instantly manna came:

- On one of the first Sunday gatherings, a newcomer showed up from Mexico. He brought a bundle of pesos and presented them to the church. The pesos came from a small church on the Mexican border from the kind of community in which many people live in cardboard box homes. The pesos amounted to $90. These dear folks gave out of their poverty because they wanted to help us in the aftermath of Katrina. I was undone. This was incredible.
- We received communication from a group of churches in Czechoslovakia. They heard about our plight, took up an offering, and sent it to us. Trinity received a letter and gift from a man who leads worship at a Christian home where one-third of the participants were in wheelchairs and most were on Medicaid. He assured me many had very little money, yet their generous hearts produced a check for $550. What a blessing from those with so little. These correspondences were a modern-day retelling of 2 Corinthians 2:8-9. The generosity of God's people is amazing. This same thing was repeated hundreds of times.

- A stranger, maybe twenty years old, came into the office and said, "I want to pay my tithe." We didn't quite understand, so she explained, "My church in New Orleans was totally destroyed. This morning I said to God, 'The first church I see, I am going to give them my tithe.' So I was coming down Highway 190 and I saw the Free Food/Free Water Trinity sign, and I came in to pay my tithe." God provides! His hand is unmistakable.
- In our service I read the letter from a woman from Michigan who sent us a $5 gift certificate though she only made $130 a week with no hope for career advancement. She wanted to help people in Louisiana who had far less than she did. This modern-day woman with "two mites" blew us all away with her extreme generosity and desire to send more when she could save another $5. After the service, someone left me with an envelope to send to this dear saint of Christ. It contained $100. Our bookkeeper sent off the $100. The woman sent another letter. It was a thank-you note, and she indicated that she was out of money and had an unexpected expense. The $100 was God's miraculous supply for what she needed. In the letter she sent a new $10 gift card to be used for the relief effort. The next Sunday I read her letter to the church family. After the service, people kept putting $20 bills in my hand and pockets and whispering, "Send this to the $5 lady." By the end of the morning, I had a wad of bills that totaled $1,040. We sent a check off to the "$5 lady." You can't out-give God. Genesis 12 says that God blesses us so we can bless others, and the whole world gets blessed in the process. I would have loved to see the expression on the face of this new friend when she opened up the envelope.

Provision for Crisis Response

God's provision for the work of ministry started ten minutes after I got back from being a refugee. I sat in my office alone, realizing I didn't have a clue what to do. I had never been trained in seminary what to do in the event of the greatest natural disaster in U.S. history! Enter God. Just after the hurricane hit, two Trinity Seminary students, Seth and Ryan, headed our way from Chicago. They pulled into what was left of our devastated town looking for the church. They got me on my cell phone and said, "God told us to come to Trinity Church."

I thought, "He did?" Wow! These two valiant workers for Christ pioneered what would turn into almost twenty thousand volunteers. When Seth returned home, he told his parents, "All I want for Christmas is a plane ticket to Trinity Church." God provided and he was back at Christmastime.

- Early on someone contacted us at Trinity Church asking if we could use a church organ. That was an incredibly generous offer; however, we are more of a praise team style church and couldn't use the organ. Following the call, someone walked into our free store. The woman was a pastor's wife from the little town next to ours. Her husband had died in the aftermath of the hurricane along with two other family members. Their church suffered from Katrina and she casually mentioned what they really needed was—you guessed it—an organ! That led to a time of praise like you wouldn't believe. These new friends were "praising God" just like they did in Acts 2. God is God, and He cannot be stopped or contained.
- A pastor gave me this account: a sixteen-year-old girl named Elizabeth came in with her dad and her sister. Their home was gone. She had no extra clothes. And so she was taken to a team that helped her get some shirts, but there were no pants there. A woman who was working there said, "My daughter gave me a pair of pants when she heard that I was coming to New Orleans, and I'll give them to you." They were just the right size. And then this woman (Karen) looked at the girl's feet and saw that she had no shoes. She had a pair of sandals that had been ruined by all the muck, but no shoes. Karen asked Elizabeth, "What size are your feet?" They were the same size as Karen's feet, so Karen took off her boots. She had a really cool pair of boots. She knelt down and took a basin and a towel and washed the feet of that sixteen-year-old girl. Then she said, "Here, you take my boots." Elizabeth knew the vol-

Disaster

unteers were church people who were working in Jesus' name, and she said afterwards, "I am an atheist." The workers told her, "That's okay. Atheists need shoes too."
- A man named Steve prayed in the Trinity office for maps of Slidell, Louisiana. A few minutes later a work team returned to the church office. "Hey, as we were leaving the workplace today, a guy gave us ten maps of Slidell. Anyone need them?"
- Gene from Montana needed certain tools. A few minutes later someone walked in with the exact tools.
- The local hospital ran out of juice for patients. A few of us thought, "Could it be that juice bottles will come on our next truck?" What came on the truck? JUICE BOTTLES!
- One team member was amazed and undone by God's ability to provide. He had come to Louisiana without the cord to recharge his cell phone and couldn't locate the right cell phone store in the area to get a new one. After his team completed a major tree-clearing job, the team went deep into some bushes/tree area and, oddly, there was a cord hanging from a bush. As they took a closer look, they were dumbfounded to realize it was the exact cell phone recharger this man needed. Coincidence or divine appointment? Had it gone through the hurricane? How did it appear in the middle of nowhere? The fingerprints of God? I say "Yes!"
- Our office staff needed an additional staff person immediately, and prayers went up to God. Unbeknownst to them, a volunteer broke his foot in several places and all he could do was office work. He called his employer back home and the boss said he had full disability coverage and could stay here six weeks and work in our office. God provides.
- A fireman from Illinois wanted to bring a "Sawzall" to Trinity with their team. They didn't have one. The next day he was driving down Main Street and found one in the middle of the street. Apparently it had fallen from a truck. He put an ad in the lost/found section of his local newspaper, but since it wouldn't appear in the paper for a week, he figured God was letting him borrow the tool for a week to use in Louisiana! When he got back from Trinity, the owner of the tool called and came to

pick it up. When he heard the story of how his Sawzall was used in Louisiana, he was delighted. He gave the fireman $20 and told him to send it to Trinity. He was amazed his tool went to help with Katrina. If you don't know what a Sawzall is, don't worry, neither do I. However, I rejoice in God.
- Early on, Jenn, a choice and extremely capable young volunteer from California, coordinated all the teams who come to Trinity. She shared how she has learned to trust God for His supply of cooks for the teams. She told about how at first a man from Texas named Jay came out of nowhere to cook for us. Jay said, "I have to leave next Wednesday," and Jenn said, "No, you can't leave." Everyone was wringing hands, saying, "No, you can't leave." Jenn was told, "Don't even worry about it. God is going to give us cooks. You just believe it. It's God's deal." After Jay left, Crystal came, and then God provided another and another. By then, Jenn's job description included scheduling cooks. One week she wondered who would cook. Thursday, no time to look. No cook coming next week. Friday, no time. Saturday was her day off. She thought the world would not stop revolving if she took her day off. Sunday, no cook. Sunday afternoon she played the piano and had a quiet time with the Father, and He gave her a peace that He would provide a cook. Sunday evening she was calling churches to confirm some information and had temporarily forgotten the need for a cook. She contacted a Virginia church and got the information she needed, and the person said, "By the way, we have a guy who would love to cook." Jenn replied, "Of course you do." The cook was at Trinity the day he was needed. Jenn says, "This is God's gig, not my gig. It wasn't my job to figure it out, only to put it on the calendar."
- A brother and sister drove eleven hundred straight miles from Wisconsin to Trinity. They heard about our need to house key staff volunteers and decided to donate their fully furnished RV to us. With joy they dropped it off and headed home. God provides! A man came down with a beautiful new truck with a sign on it that read "Trinity Disaster Relief." We have needed

transportation for longer-term volunteers. He gave us the new truck. God provides!

Crisis Response Center

From the early days after Katrina, God planted a dream in a few of us to set up a permanent Evangelical Free Churches of America (EFCA) Crisis Response Center to serve on the Gulf Coast and across the United States. This center would be a resource center, staging base, and headquarters to respond to crises wherever possible with the life-giving ministry of Jesus Christ. This dream only intensified over time as we witnessed firsthand the powerful ministry of transformation in the midst of disaster not only in New Orleans, but also in disaster areas around the world. As seeds were sown, many areas became fertile ground for multiplication and church planting. Our challenge, however, was the price tag of $300,000 to build the ministry center.

Big problem for us, but no problem for God! One day a few folks from Hope Presbyterian Church showed up to check out our ministry. They spent ten minutes with me and more time with Mark Lewis, our director. They were quick studies. They couldn't promise anything but asked us to dream big in communicating what we needed. Mark put together a one-pager of options, from a $10 hammer at one end to a $300,000 Crisis Response Center. A few weeks later they informed us that they would fund the ministry center, no strings attached. Only God!

Today the Crisis Response Center is a reality with 6,000 square feet of space inside and 6,000 outside. The center is always buzzing with activity and is amply stocked with God's miraculous manna of equipment and supplies. One day we prayed for a forklift, believing it is only natural for a warehouse to have such a piece of equipment. As soon as we finished praying, Mark's phone rang and a group in Mississippi wanted to know if we could use a donated forklift. We needed a backhoe. This was a "big ask" as good backhoes cost $40,000 and up. In another state, one of our volunteers bumped into someone in the post office and in casual conversation mentioned the need of a backhoe. The woman had a backhoe and decided to donate it for the work. Only God! This stuff happens all the time.

People say, "If I only saw a miracle..." I can tell you there are miracles if you want to see them. One of the biggest is the miracle of generosity and the miracle of resupply.

Almost immediately after our disaster, we not only adopted the motto "Betting the Farm on God" but also "Unless God shows up, I am in big trouble." From the start we were in over our heads. In fact, I didn't know one person, not one, who wasn't up to their eyeballs in stress, pressure, and the demands of life. Between pastoring and relief work, for several months every day was an eighteen-hour day from 6 a.m. to midnight, seven days a week. Donna, besides helping me with the ministry, had the seemingly unending task of coordinating construction workers, painters, tree removal, and fighting the insurance company. We lived "Unless God shows up, I AM in big trouble." That He did—in faithful ways, over and over, for five years, often in ways that could not be explained apart from the supernatural.

We experienced for a time what the early church (Acts 2:44-45; Acts 4:32-39) lived. They owned stuff but stuff didn't own them. It salted everything and people were changed. One mayor we worked with said, "All my life I thought Christians were hypocrites. Now I'm starting to think differently." Another man (teams rebuilt his building and helped to reestablish his connections with the community week in and week out for nine months) said, "I've been trying to figure out their angle for nine months. I've finally found it out... they have no angle."

Thousands of times we helped people for free, wanting nothing in return. People wonder, "Why are you doing this? How much will it cost?" They are amazed when the answer is, "No cost...we are only doing this out of the love of God for you!" Sharing wasn't forced but was lived as a way of life. When we come to grips with "it's all God's stuff," it changes attitudes, behaviors, and lifestyles profoundly, so why do we hold on so tightly?

Our natural reaction is to clutch, claw, fret, and hold on to things. It changes everything when believers realize, "The earth is the Lord's and everything in it, the world and all who live in it" (Psalm 24:1).

I remember when my son, Jonathan, was young. We were at an athletic event and he wanted some money to get some candy from the snack shack. I gave him a dollar and he came back with some M&Ms. They looked so good I said, "Jonathan, give me a few M&Ms."

My dear, sweet, beloved son said, "No, they are MINE!"

I paid for them! I had enough money in my pocket to buy all the M&Ms from the snack shack, and I was big enough at that time to take the M&Ms from Jonathan, but he said, "They are mine!"

He said that only because he was young, right? All the rest of us mature adults would never say "mine" right? Yet, don't we say "mine" to God all the time?

The early church knew the God of the resupply and practiced generosity, despite the challenges. Times were tough all over with crisis, persecution, and economic downturns.

Rodney Stark, in his classic book on early Christianity, reminds us that the ancient world was difficult. In fact, infant mortality was at 50 percent. Epidemics sometimes wiped out 25 percent of a city. The water system was corrupt. No waste management or garbage management. No running water. It was often like the slums of Calcutta. Catastrophes, disease, and dependency abounded. He writes, "Any accurate picture of Antioch in the New Testament times must depict a city filled with misery, danger, fear, despair, and hatred. A city where an average family lived a squalid life in filthy and cramped quarters, where at least half the children died at birth or in infancy and where most of the children who lived lost at least one parent before reaching maturity. A city filled with hatred and fear rooted in intense ethnic antagonisms and exacerbated by a constant stream of strangers."[1]

Despite the times, an outrageously generous people saw their stuff as God's stuff. They yielded their possessions to the rule and reign of God. They got out of the accumulation game and leveraged what they had for the kingdom of God. They gave "no strings attached" and ended up turning the world upside down:

> All the believers were together and had everything in common. Selling their possessions and goods, they gave to anyone as he had need.
>
> Acts 2:44-45

All the believers were one in heart and mind. No one claimed that any of his possessions was his own, but they shared everything they had. With great power the apostles continued to testify to the resurrection of the Lord Jesus, and much grace was upon them all. There were no needy persons among them. For from time to time those who owned lands or houses sold them, brought the money from the sales and put it at the apostles' feet, and it was distributed to anyone as he had need. Joseph, a Levite from Cyprus, whom the apostles called Barnabas (which means Son of Encouragement), sold a field he owned and brought the money and put it at the apostles' feet.

Acts 4:32-37

It's easy to operate from a scarcity mentality: the more we give, the less we have. Not true in the kingdom of God. In the kingdom, the more you give, the more you have. The less you give, the less you have. Be generous and you win one way or the other. Your heart will grow bigger and bigger for God and the things of God. Be stingy and your soul will shrivel and your joy diminish. If you have a generous heart, you can't out-give God. He is the God of the resupply. I'm not talking about prosperity theology. If you give to get, you have wacky theology. But if you give to give, God will be the God of the resupply.

We, God's people, will tell stories of resupply, but we will have to take a risk. Step out in faith, just like the widow who made the loaf for Elijah and saw God resupply. Join the adventure! Look up, for God will write new stories. Where God leads, God supplies. It's a promise. Remember, "And my God shall supply all your needs according to His riches in glory in Christ Jesus" (Philippians 4:19) and "Yet, I have not seen the righteous forsaken, or his descendants begging bread" (Psalm 37:25b).

Chapter 9

Our Jesus

Somebody clued me in to a YouTube video link and the story of a violinist named Joshua Bell. As a four-year-old, Joshua attached rubber bands to dresser drawers and played classical music, adjusting the pitch by opening and closing the drawers. His parents saw the fingerprints of greatness and started music lessons. Today he is perhaps the greatest violinist in the world and plays the greatest instrument in the world, a $3.5 million Stradivarius violin hand-crafted in 1713.

Someone asked this question, "What if Joshua Bell were to take that Stradivarius, play some of the most gorgeous air, *Ave Maria*, the most transcendently beautiful music unannounced, unbilled in a metro station in Washington, D.C., at rush hour? What do you think would happen?" When musicians were asked, they said, "Even if he didn't get billed, music like that is going to draw a crowd—that's going to touch people's hearts. Might want to do a little crowd control. Things could get pretty bogged down. They would give him tons of money if his case was out there." Got the picture of what's coming?

It is 7:51 a.m. on January 12, 2007, as Joshua Bell, in jeans, a T-shirt, and baseball cap, opens his violin case, throws a little seed money into his case, and begins to play the violin in the L'Enfant Plaza Subway Station in Washington, D.C. Remember, this is the world's greatest musician playing the greatest violin and greatest music. In 43 minutes he plays six classical songs and 1,097 people pass by him. No one claps, not even one. Only seven people pause for more than 60 seconds. Only days earlier, Joshua had played at the Boston Symphony Hall. He can command up to $1,000 a minute for his performances, yet he only got $32.17 in his violin case at the metro station. Only one person recognized him. This was the chance of a lifetime, but all but a few people walked on by. More than 1,000 didn't even pause. Virtually no one noticed or listened. There was too much to do. Rush hour was on as crowds raced to work, to meetings, or to buy lotto tickets and a newspaper. No one expected majesty, greatness, and grandeur shoehorned into the ordinary. Who had time for anything transcendent amidst the hustle, bustle, and busyness? Everyone had things to do, places to go. Yet the master was at work.[1]

I wonder how much we marvel at the mechanical and miss the magnificent. I suspect at times we miss the work of the Master. I guess worry, hurry, and busyness mess with our spiritual ears and eyes and too often hinder our God sightings. But I don't want anyone to miss Jesus. I don't want anyone to miss the Master.

Sometimes it's easy to miss Jesus because I think I have God all figured out. After all, I've been in church almost since the time I was born. I've been a Christ-follower for over thirty-six years. I've had eleven years of formal seminary education. I've passed an ordination exam. I've got a doctor's degree. I've been a pastor for twenty-seven years. I love studying Scripture and theology. I read at least a book a week.

It's easy to have my theology structured in a nice, tidy box. However, I keep finding over and over that Jesus does not fit into my boxes. The Jesus of the Bible refuses to fit into the molds I conveniently design for Him.

My childhood picture of Jesus sprang from a Sunday school image of Him with long flowing brown hair. Jesus was handsome and striking as He cradled a small lamb in His arms. Jesus was nice, passive, gentle, almost Gumby-like. Over time I've encountered many caricatures of Jesus: prosperity-Jesus, my buddy-Jesus, get-out-of-hell-free-Jesus, feel-good-Jesus, cultural-warrior-Jesus, stay-on-the-cross-Jesus, legend-Jesus, therapist-Jesus, and more. My seminary view of Jesus included didactic truths to be believed and attributes to be learned. I was more aware of Jesus historically, biographically, and theologically. J.I. Packer in his book *Knowing God* writes a challenge:

> We need frankly to face ourselves at this point. We are, perhaps, orthodox evangelicals. We can state the gospel clearly, and can smell unsound doctrine a mile away. If anyone asks us how men may know God, we can at once produce the right formula—that we come to know God through Jesus Christ the Lord, in virtue of His cross and mediation, on the basis of His Word of promise, by the power of the Holy Spirit, via a personal exercise of faith. Yet the gaiety, goodness, and unfetteredness of spirit which are the marks of those who have known God are rare among us—rarer perhaps than they are in some other Christian circles where, by comparison, evangelical truth is less clearly and fully known. Here, too, it would seem that the last may prove to be first, and the first last. A little knowledge of God is worth more than a great deal of knowledge about Him.[2]

Time, and I trust growth, has made me yearn not just to know the Jesus of my boyhood or book learning but to know the Jesus of the Bible experientially, personally, and intimately. Like Paul I can say, "That I may know Him and the power of His resurrection, and the fellowship of His sufferings, being conformed to His death" (Philippians 3:10) and "I count all things to be loss ... count them but rubbish in order that I may gain Christ" (Philippians 3:8).

The more I learn of the real Jesus, the more difficult it is to pigeonhole Him. He is anything but predictable. He cannot be tamed or domesticated; the clergy of His day tried to bust Him for hanging with the wrong crowd. In His first recorded miracle He turned water into the best 180 gallons of wine ever tasted. He worked a miracle and told the grateful recipient to keep a lid on it. He rebuked His best friend with a "Get behind me, Satan." Unlike the antiquated pictures of Jesus where He looks like He just swallowed vinegar, He was in fact the most joyous person who ever lived.

Dorothy Sayer's comment about the church's effort to take the Lion of Judah and turn Him into a "fitting household pet for pale curates and pious old ladies" was incredibly insightful. Jesus called the reigning monarch a fox, a poser, a wannabe, and said His locust-eating cousin was the greatest of all. His family tried to take Him away forcibly, having deemed Him insane. The demons recognized exactly who He was, and Jesus told them to "shut up." The disciples were often clueless and the crowds confused. His claims kept Jesus at the center of controversy. His love dumbfounded the multitudes and ticked off His critics. His message of grace was scandalous. His clearing the commodity traders from His Father's house with a whip leaves us with a "huh?" or a "wow!" He offered not a formula or a bunch of hoops to jump through but an invitation to know God through Him. He came not to make bad men good or good men better but to make dead men – live.

Jesus taught in a way that turned everything upside down. You must die to live. You must lose to gain. Weakness is strength. Pray for your enemies. Up is down. A servant is the greatest. The first will be last and the last first. These things weren't politically correct, trendy, cool, or faddish, but they made everyone think. One thing was for sure: you were never the same after being with Jesus. No one ever heard God's heart taught with such depth, clarity, and ability to pierce the soul. The crowds were amazed, always.

Jesus is revolutionary. He amazes, confuses, shocks, and sometimes offends. He drives religious types crazy when He won't play by their rules.

Most of the affluent and popular of His day wanted little to do with Jesus. In fact, He was accused of being a drunk, a glutton, and a Samaritan full of demons. He clashed with all who wanted to wear His crown. Yet outcasts loved Him, as well as prostitutes, tax collectors, and the marginalized. He embodied holiness and yet the riff-raff flocked to Him. Explain that. Only Jesus. Walter Wink said, "If Jesus had never lived, we would not have been able to invent him." Why do we so often try to reduce Jesus, to domesticate Jesus, to edit Jesus? Is it that we want to control Him—our God in a box?

Jesus had no army, no weapons, no well-oiled political machine, no connections to Caesar or the Sanhedrin. He was not a likely candidate to change the world. His followers were relatively uneducated and on no one's VIP list, yet Jesus is the most revolutionary person who has ever existed. He has a kingdom, though not one of this world. He gives an invitation to all to live under the reign and rule of God. He is committed to advancing His kingdom in the hearts of people everywhere. His revolution is not for the faint of heart. It isn't comfortable. In fact, it may cost you everything. Jesus says, "Follow Me." Following Jesus may get you killed, may make you squirm, and most surely will be hard, but it is the opportunity of a lifetime.

Pearl of Great Price

Jesus' invitation captivates people like nothing else. Matthew 13:44-46 says:

> The kingdom of heaven is like treasure hidden in a field. When a man found it, he hid it again, and then in his joy went out and sold all he had and bought that field. Again, the kingdom of heaven is like a merchant looking for fine pearls. When he found one of great value, he went away and sold everything he had and bought it.

Jesus told stories everyone can relate to. This story illustrates the desire to get rich or hit it big. It's where you'll do just about anything to get it. An Internet story goes this way. I'm not sure if it's true:

> A man meets a woman at a party, and he is stunned by her beauty. He thinks to himself, I cannot let this woman get away. I've got to figure out some way to create a connection, so he says to her, "You know, I may not look like much, but my father is a very wealthy man, and he's in bad health. He's an old guy. He's not going to live more than two years at the outside. And when he dies, I will be worth fifty million dollars." And you can tell the woman is impressed. And she asks for his business card. And three days later, he gets a note that she is now his stepmother.[3]

In the parable of the pearl of great price, Jesus is saying that the kingdom of heaven is like that. It's the opportunity of a lifetime. The kingdom is worth paying any price. Abandonment to Jesus is a real opportunity.

Having the pearl of great price, Jesus, is like winning the lottery. It's like a kid trading in an old toy for a trip to Disney World. It's like giving up a bottle of Coke for ten thousand shares of stock in the Coca-Cola company. It's not that it's so noble a choice; it's just the only commonsense thing you could possibly do. Abandoning other allegiances for Jesus is not done grudgingly—you have to go this way. You didn't sell everything and say, "Oh, this is so hard." No! There is only joy. You laugh and high-five each other.

Many people, when considering greater commitment to Jesus, think of the decision in negative terms, not positive. The calculation is *what will I lose – fun, control, status, and freedom?* The parables of Jesus remind us that this decision is positive. You have to have Him, you can't go another way, because life in the kingdom is not just noble but the smartest decision you could ever make. It's not just good. It's the best—it's deliriously blessed.

With every passing year I find Jesus more compelling than ever, more surprising, interesting, shocking, confusing, attractive, awesome, mysterious, stunning, and fascinating. I'm not ashamed to tell you He changed my life. He's the One I most admire, respect, and follow. He's not a legend or a fable. He's the greatest Person you could ever know. The truth is you can't get close to the real Jesus and be disappointed.

I can say without a doubt I want to know Him more and more. I'm convinced He is absolutely revolutionary and irresistible. If you encounter the real Jesus you will love Him or hate Him. There is no middle ground, no sitting on the fence. It's almost impossible to ignore Him. He has this way of cutting through the crowd and forcing people to choose. You will be forced to give your allegiance to Him or cast Him off. The problem is not that Christianity is untrue; the usual problem is that it's left untried.

Tough, sturdy fishermen found Jesus so compelling they dropped their nets and gave up their occupations. Simon the Zealot gave up his resistance movement and became part of something more powerful. Matthew the shark in the marketplace left his cash register wide open and followed the opportunity of a lifetime. Jesus' hands were callused. He had some serious forearms, His fingernails were not manicured, His appearance was nothing to brag about, but men and women flocked to Him. Wealthy, poor, religious, and unreligious fishermen and prostitutes ended up saying, "I've got to have Jesus. Whatever it takes. I've got to follow Him."

Jesus: One of a Kind

Ralph Waldo Emerson writes, "The name of Jesus is not so much written as it is plowed into the history of the world." Jesus was born some two thousand years ago in an obscure village to an insignificant couple. Very few people in history actually heard Him speak. He didn't travel far and wide. He never published a book. He didn't lead an army or lead a nation. He didn't have a home or possess much money.

A recent survey of top bestselling Christian books revealed that almost 50 percent covered topics of parenting and family, and the rest were mainly focused on self. Only four were about Jesus.[4] It's easy to get away from what's most important. There's such a need to get back to a fresh biblical Christology. Jesus Christ can be known, loved, experienced, and pursued. He is supreme, brilliant, and wonderful. We must get past a once-a-week Sunday Jesus who is merely a mascot. The focus is not about us. It's about Him. As an old Franciscan said, "Once you come to know the love of Jesus Christ, nothing else in the world will seem beautiful or desirable."[5]

Who is Jesus? He is the King of Kings. He is the Lord of Lords. He mastered life and conquered death. He is the hope of the world, the hinge of history. He extends the greatest gift ever offered. He sparked the greatest movement the world has ever known. That's Jesus.

Scandalous Message

Our message is Christ crucified. Our message is a bloody cross and empty tomb. It's the old, old story that one man could die on a piece of wood, on an ancient hill in an obscure part of the world, and thereby shape the destiny of every person who ever lived.

So many people want to make the message look good, sound good, and be cool. They want to make Jesus fashionable. However, the cross is foolishness to those who are perishing. To those who get it, it's the power of God. The world is looking for a Savior with pedigree, not someone from the hick town of Nazareth who was born in a cattle trough. No way. It's moronic, scandalous. It's an oxymoron – crucified Messiah.

The gospel of Jesus is an invitation to know God. Remember:

- ➢ God is not an energy force or an abstract concept.
- ➢ God is not a belief in which you give assent.
- ➢ God is not a system you operate out of, nor even a theological system.
- ➢ God is not a doctrine.
- ➢ God is not a program. He has a name. His name is Jesus.
- ➢ God is not a set of principles. God is God.
- ➢ God is a person. As one fully alive, you can live in His presence, enjoy His ways, and enter into His purposes. And when asked "Do you believe there is a God?" you can declare, "No, I do not believe there is a God; I know there is a God."

We are not presenting people with a "program" but with a life. We are introducing people to our friend Jesus, the everlasting Savior and Lord. Jesus says, "Follow me." We can apprentice with Him as His disciples.

The Grace Plan

Recently I illustrated the gospel message from an encounter I once had with a group that wasn't necessarily going to be friendly to my topic of "Jesus Christ and the Bible." Indeed, in the room were people with leanings toward many worldviews and religious backgrounds. They would have little understanding of "why the human condition is so desperate" and "why a Savior is so necessary." Without understanding their need, they would probably be uninterested in a solution.

I decided to engage them in a thought-provoking exercise. I asked them to think about this question, "Outside of biblical figures, who are the worst and best persons who have ever lived?"

The worst person was easy for the group. Who do you think they said? Hitler. It was unanimous. The best person question created quite a discussion. Someone yelled "Gandhi!" Others immediately chimed in with Martin Luther King, Mother Theresa, and Billy Graham. One person even said, "My mother."

I said they needed to narrow it down to one person. After a long discussion they settled on Gandhi. Then I said, "Let's set up a goodness scale of 1 to 10. Hitler is a 1 and Gandhi is a 9." They agreed that none of their candidates for best person was perfect.

Next, I asked the group to put themselves on the goodness scale based on how they've lived their life. I encouraged them not to be too hard on themselves. No one would be down with Hitler, but probably none of us would be up there with Gandhi, Mother Teresa, or Billy Graham either.

"How good are you?" I asked. "What's your number?"

It was fascinating. There were 4s and 5s, some 6s and 7s. One guy said, "I'm a 7.5." He was the best guy in the room, at least by his self-analysis.

I had one more question for the group. "Where does God draw the line when He decides who goes to heaven and who goes to hell? What number does God require if you are to merit heaven on your own goodness?"

The room turned silent. They were thinking now. I had them where I wanted them. They were all ears. Secretly, they were hoping I would say a number just under their self-analysis number. They longed now for a God who would grade on the curve. I held back a little and let the significance of the question sink in. Finally I gave the answer. "The Bible says for a person to merit heaven—to merit a personal relationship with God, to have earned eternal life—a person has to be a perfect 10."

This brought a gasp from the room. Instantly the question came up, "Who can be saved? Is there any hope?"

Bingo!

Disaster

In understanding the bad news, they were ready for the good news. What we could never do for ourselves, God made possible through Jesus Christ. His Son died on a cross for our sins so that, through faith in Jesus, we could stand before a holy God, not on our merits, but on the merits of His Son, Jesus. By placing faith in Christ, our sins would be forgiven and we would receive spiritual life and eternal life. Think of it – a personal relationship and peace with God comes through faith in Christ, not by our works or religion. Jesus said, "I am the way, the truth and the life. No one comes to the Father but through me" (John 14:6).

At this meeting, many trusted Christ. The same thing happened many other times when I shared this illustration. If you haven't trusted Christ and are still relying on your own good works and righteousness, I urge you to abandon the performance plan and trade it in for the Jesus plan. Trade in the works plan for the grace plan. Quit climbing the ladder of good deeds to try to earn your way to God. Only Jesus can stand in the gap for you and make up for your goodness deficit. Right now you can trust Jesus Christ by faith. He will see your heart and hear your prayer for a Savior. Today can be your day of salvation. The grace plan is God's offer to you. Listen to John 3:16, "For God so loved the world, He sent His one and only Son, that whosoever believes in Him, will not perish but have eternal life."

Pick Your Pearls

The story is told of a little girl with a string of cheap pearls she wears around her neck. They are plastic and yellowed, but she is so proud of them. One night her dad comes into her bedroom and says, "Will you give me your pearls?"

"No, Daddy," she says. "You'd look silly in pearls."

The next night he asks the same question, "Will you give me your pearls?"

"No, Daddy. They are mine and they are special."

This goes on for three or four nights. The daughter finally gets upset and gives the pearls to her dad and says, "If you really want them, you can have them."

Her dad pulls out a case and opens it. Inside the case, sitting on black velvet, is a real set of glistening pearls that are beyond anything the daughter has ever seen.

Is there anything crowding out the best in your life? Are you wearing any fake plastic pearls? Anything you need to hand over to the Father so you can enjoy the pearl of great price? Consider: "Again, the kingdom of heaven is like a merchant seeking fine pearls, and upon finding one pearl of great value, he went and sold all that he had and bought it" (Matthew 13:45-46).

Part Three

Overcoming Knockout Punches

Chapter 10

Surviving Bouts with Doubts

The call went out something like this: "Michael, can we get together and talk? I see so many people around the church who have such a strong faith that I feel like I don't fit in. I have faith, but I have doubts and sometimes more questions than answers. Do Christians have doubts? Can you relate to any of this? Am I the only one?"

The caller was a bright, articulate, sincere leader in the community who would become a key leader in the ministry—especially in the wake of Katrina, when our mission was truly to be "Jesus with skin on." We met, we talked, and I found his honesty not alarming but refreshing. He didn't suppress his doubts but faced them squarely.

One of the things I have sponsored several times is "Doubt Night." This is a time when people are free to voice their questions, struggles, and doubts honestly, no matter how shocking, raw, or arrogant. Doubt Night always brings some interesting conversation. The truth is you can divide Christians into three groups:

1. Those who have doubted.
2. Those who haven't doubted yet, but will.
3. Those who are brain dead.

Without question, one of the least talked about struggles in Christianity is doubt. Christians often don't talk about it, are ashamed of it, feel guilty about it, beat themselves up over it, and in the extreme think doubt is the unpardonable sin. The truth is that doubt is part of the human condition. If you are a thoughtful Christ-follower at all, if you take seriously truth and the call to follow Jesus, then you will experience doubts, questions, issues, concerns, uncertainties, hesitations, theological squirmings, waverings, and wrestlings to some degree.

Perfect faith is not the ticket for admission with God. Let me be clear — you can have strong faith and still have doubts. You can be heaven bound without having every uncertainty settled.

Have You Ever Experienced Any of These?

Feelings:
- God, am I on the wrong road?
- God, where are You?
- God, do You care?
- God, why are You silent?
- God, can You really forgive me?

Understandings:
- Where is God's goodness and omnipotence in disaster?
- What about the mystery of suffering and evil?
- What about sovereignty and free will?
- Why the injustice? Why do bad people get ahead so often?
- Why are so many people starving in Africa?
- Why death?
- Why cancer?
- Why SIDS?
- Why is the world so cruel?

Let's deal with some huge myths about doubt that confuse and tear down. Hopefully, the myths can be blown up and done away with.

Myth #1 — God-fearers and Christ-followers don't have doubts

You may be surprised to learn that many of the "spiritual giants" from the Bible had their own doubts.

John the Baptist

John was the cousin of Jesus and the prophesied forerunner of the Messiah. Pointing to Jesus one day, he said, "Behold the Lamb of God who takes away the sin of the world" (John 1:29). John baptized Jesus and heard the Father say, "This is my beloved Son in whom I am well pleased." John said, "I have seen and I testify that this is the Son of God."

However, weeks later John finds himself awaiting execution in a dirty, dark prison for the terrible crime of telling King Herod the truth on a moral issue. Tired, discouraged, lonely, as John sits in prison questions arise. He is not so sure about Messiah anymore. John arranges for two of his disciples to track down Jesus and ask Him pointblank, "Are You the Expected One, or shall we look for someone else?" (Matthew 11:3). In other words, "I used to be convinced but now I wonder."

How did Jesus respond to John's honest doubt? Slam-dunk John? Shame John? No, Jesus provides evidence that He is indeed the Messiah. Jesus said to them, "Go and report to John what you hear and see! The blind receive sight and the lame walk, the lepers are cleansed and the deaf hear, and the dead are raised up, and the poor have the gospel preached to them" (Matthew 11:4-5).[1]

How did this bout with doubt impact Jesus' view of John? Jesus said, "I tell you, among those born of a woman, there is no one greater than John" (Luke 7:28a). Quite a compliment for a doubter.

The Disciples

But the eleven disciples proceeded to Galilee, to the mountain which Jesus had designated. And when they saw Him, they worshipped Him; but some were doubtful. And Jesus came up and spoke to them saying, "All authority has been given to Me in heaven and on earth. Go therefore and make disciples of all the nations, baptizing them in the name of the Father and the Son and the Holy Spirit, teaching them to observe all that I commanded you; and lo, I am with you always, even to the end of the age."

Matthew 28:16-20

Most will recognize this passage as the Great Commission. Most are aware this was originally written to the disciples, the original eleven: James, John, Peter, and the rest of the gang. The disciples saw Jesus perform miracles, studied under Him, followed Him, and beheld His resurrection. Notice the last words used in Matthew to describe the disciples – *some were doubtful!*

Matthew doesn't gloss over it, tear it down, or cover it up. In fact, the passage says they were worshipping doubters. Biblical scholar Frederick Dale Bruner says, "The Christian faith is bi-polar. Disciples live their life between worship and doubt, trusting and questioning, hoping and worrying."[2] Jesus' response to doubt was not to be furious with His disciples because they weren't 100 percent convinced. Rather, He gives them the Great Commission – "You go, you honest doubters, step out, take a risk, change the world!"

Jesus uses people who have bouts with doubt.

The Honest Dad

It's hard to imagine a more desperate dad. His mute, demon-tormented son suffers convulsions and destructive behavior. You can bet over the years he's tried every imaginable medication, potion, and healing technique. The dad even let the twelve disciples give it a shot. The dad ends up disappointed again, the crowd surely rolls their eyes, and the disciples are embarrassed and arguing with each other. Jesus asks what all the hoopla is about, and the dad basically says, "I brought my son to You for help but Your disciples jumped in, couldn't do a thing, and ended up in a big fight."

Jesus says, "O unbelieving generation, how long shall I be with you? How long shall I put up with you? Bring him to me!" (Mark 9:19). The dad brings the lad to Jesus, explains the history, and says, "But if you can do anything, take pity on us and help us!" (Mark 9:22)

Disaster

Do you notice the word *if?* The word *if* indicates doubt. Understandable doubt. This dad has prayed for years; he's been to every holy man he's ever heard of with a reputation for spiritual healing. He's gotten his hopes up so many times and been let down. He'd learned to say *if.*

Jesus picks up on the *if* and says, "If You can! All things are possible to him who believes" (Mark 9:23). The honest dad doesn't say, "Yes, I believe. I'm with you with all my heart." Rather he says, "I do believe, help my unbelief" (Mark 9:24). In other words, "I believe and sometimes doubt. I pray but sometimes waver. I ask but sometimes worry."

He's so real, so human, so like us. Jesus isn't insulted or shocked. He doesn't walk away but understands our *if's*. Jesus heals the boy, who will now grow up and grow old and love his dad. Jesus helps bouts with doubt.

Thomas

We find Thomas three times in the Gospel of John, and he's always a skeptic. It's no wonder he is affectionately known as "Doubting Thomas."

John 20:25 says, "The other disciples, therefore, were saying to him, 'We have seen the Lord!' But he said to them, 'Unless I shall see in His hands the imprint of the nails and put my finger into the place of the nails, and put my hand into His side, I will not believe.'" Thomas couldn't get into the resurrection hoopla. He didn't want to be taken for a fool. He wondered if he'd wasted three years of his life. The cross was so painful. Now the dream was over. His friends must be lying or delusional. He said, "I'd have to push my fingers into the wounds and examine the gash in His side before I'll accept that Jesus is risen."

A few days later Jesus appears to the disciples. Everyone remembers Thomas' diatribe, and now they think, "Thomas is in for it. He will regret opening his trap." Jesus doesn't say, "What's wrong with you!" or "Straighten up!" or "Drop dead!" Instead He says, "Touch me" (John 20:27). "Touch me, and do whatever it takes to discover I am real."

Myth #1 needs to go. Every Christ-follower I know has doubts, a crisis of faith, wrestling with private calamities, even hopelessness at times.

Myth #2 – Doubt is the same as unbelief

There is a vast difference between doubt and unbelief. Doubt is a person in the dark grappling for understanding. Unbelief is a person in the light choosing to say no to God. Unbelief is not simply one who doesn't believe, but one who won't believe.

Unbelief is not uncertainty but rather a refusal to trust as a choice of the will. In unbelief, you do not want to come under the reign and rule of God. Unbelief doesn't want to believe and will always invent an argument to justify not believing.

God doesn't ask us to manufacture certainty but rather be faithful to what we know.

One time I met regularly with a delightful seeker who enjoyed exploring the Bible and working through tough intellectual issues. He was easy to talk to and could summarize the essence of the gospel and basic truths about Jesus. Finally, one day I asked him if he had crossed the line of faith. His intellectual issues and emotional issues of faith had all been clarified or resolved. He said, in all candidness, "I guess it's just a matter of the will."

Honest doubt doesn't exclude certainty on some things. Not at all! Honest doubt leads or should lead to truth. "You will know the truth and the truth will set you free" (John 8:32). Some things can be known with certainty. First John 5:13 says, "These things I have written to you who believe in the name of the Son of God, in order that you may know that you have eternal life."

Did you catch the word "know"? We can grow to know many things with rock-solid certainty. After all, "the secret things belong to the Lord, but the things revealed belong to us" (Deuteronomy 29:29).

Therefore, can't we live with commitment and curiosity, dilemmas and dedication? Doesn't a healthy skepticism enable us to wrestle through contradictions in the human experience, superficial viewpoints, and erroneous fixed interpretations? Doesn't an unexamined theology lead to being misguided? Faith that has been refined on the firing line of doubt will end up stronger, surer, and confident. Thoughtful questions and contemplation develop a more substantial faith and in the long run a greater certainty.

Doubts, rightly honored, should strengthen and confirm our faith.

Myth #3 – Doubt is always damaging
Many people want faith and life to be nailed down into ultra-safe fixed boxes, even if the things nailed are to a false or unbalanced foundation. To be honest, extreme people who are dead certain about everything frighten me! Legalism tends to reveal people who are often the most insecure inside.

Does anyone but God have all the answers and no questions? Could a good dose of honest doubt be good for a growing faith? People who never question, never wrestle, never battle, never struggle, or never have a bout of doubt often remain shallow or sometimes set themselves up for a spiritual blowout down the road. Beware of a naïve faith that has never been tested in battle. Yearn for a faith that has struggled with doubt and encountered the firing squad of error, a faith that has been refined, purified, and deepened.

Frederick Buechner: "If you don't have any doubts you are either kidding yourself or asleep. Doubts are the ants in the pants of faith. They keep it awake and moving."[3]

Quaker pastor Rufus Jones: "A rebuilt faith is superior to an inherited faith that has never stood the strain of a great testing storm. If you have not clung to a broken piece of your old ship in the dark night of the soul, your faith may not have the sustaining power to carry you through to the end of the journey."[4]

Francis Bacon: "If a man will begin with certainties, he shall end in doubts; but if he will be content to begin with doubts, he shall end in certainties."[5]

In my younger years, I was too quick to hurry people through their disasters. It's easy to be unnerved by the tension uncertainty brings and to manufacture a spiritual reason for a speedy healing and a painless transformation process. Sometimes God wants us to linger with questions and even darkness for a season, even as we yearn for Him to speak clearly. Why? Sometimes this is where we are most ready to listen.

The Scripture calls us to test all things (1 John 4:1). What if David Koresh's followers had questioned his bizarre end-times teachings and exotic behaviors? What if Jim Jones' followers had honest doubts about his teachings and the Kool-Aid?

Wouldn't asking good questions and being honest before God create a more wholesome, balanced, deeper faith? What if Paul, as a Pharisee, had not reevaluated his preconceived notions of the Law and the kingdom of God? The presence of honest doubt never diminishes faith, but it often enhances it.

You can have strong faith even if you have doubts. These words might be the words you need to hear. Go ahead, breathe easier, and keep on keeping on for God.

Myth #4 - The tension can be removed from every question and the "mystery of God"

The truth is that we will not have all the answers on this side of heaven, but we can know the One who has all the answers. Sometimes we will get an answer, sometimes we will get a glimpse of an answer, and sometimes we must live with "Will Be Explained Later" answers. On this side, we see through a glass dimly (1 Corinthians 13:12a). The secret things belong to God, and His ways are higher than our ways. We cannot understand everything about an unlimited God.

The temptation, if we are not careful, is to replace the mysteries of faith with spiritual formulas. The temptation is to manufacture simplistic solutions to complex problems and give nickel answers to $10,000 questions. The temptation is to go for the "God in a Box" approach like Job's three so-called friends.

Job is a book filled with white-hot doubt in the midst of the loss of family, fortune, and health. Job is tormented as he tries to understand the calamity. At times, Job doubts God's character (Job 19:6) and God's goodness (Job 6:4; 30:20). His friends react with shock,

"Stop feeling this way! Shame on you! This is scandalous!" They play God and act as if they stand in God's shoes. They overestimate themselves and speak too much about God for thirty-seven chapters.

Finally, God appears in a whirlwind and rattles off dozens of questions like, "Where were you when I laid the foundation of the earth... Can you send forth lightning?" Job and the others are silenced before God. I wonder how often I speak too much, too definitively, too absolutist with an authority that is beyond mine to offer. In the end, God holds up Job as the hero and not his friends (Job 42:7) who seemingly had God all figured out.

For years I thought it was my job to defend God, present an unwavering spiritual front, never ask a question, and always have the answer. No more. I don't know about you, but I don't want a God anymore who I've got all figured out. In fact, the moment we think we have God all figured out, we are no longer dealing with God but rather a god made after our own image. By definition, that is an idol.

I don't want a God who is predictable, who thinks like me, and who fits in a box. I find in Scripture a God who is mysterious and unfathomable. He has no limits. He won't be caged and can't be domesticated. He is wild at heart, yet always true and good.

Oh, for a faith that allows for questions, doubts, and mystery. A faith that forever knows there is more to know. A faith like the psalmist's, who asked why with honest, disturbing, befuddling, unsettling, and candid questions. A faith like Mary's, who upon discovering she was with child said, "How can this be? I am a virgin." A faith like Jesus', who said, "My God, my God, why have you forsaken me?" A faith that allows us to be awed, silenced, messy, dumbfounded, or filled with wonder and amazement.

Oh, for the mystery of God and a faith that may be, but doesn't always have to be, clean, tidy, and black and white. Oh, for the mystery of God that does not repel us but moves us to bow our knee before Him.

Myth #5 – Overcoming doubt leads to a faith that cures all problems

Doubt is prevalent today because many have bought the fool's gold that if we have enough faith we can do anything, fix anything, and cause all our dreams to come true. We name it and claim it. We speak it, visualize it, count it as done, and it will be like magic. Faith is the king-sized ibuprofen that eases all pain. The formula works like this: God is obligated if we doubt not and have faith.

It's amazing how man makes a system that tries to trump the sovereignty of God. When this thinking gets etched into a believer's conscience, it's a setup for a fall and great disillusionment.

Hebrews 11 presents a much more realistic view of faith in the real world. In this Hall of Fame chapter, we start with the victories of Noah, Abraham, Joseph, Moses, and the twelve others. Kingdoms are won, lions are overcome, flames are quenched, and the dead are raised. Faith works…but the chapter continues as believers are torched, jeered, flogged, imprisoned, stoned, sawed in two, mistreated, persecuted financially, impoverished, and speared.

We forget this section of Hebrews 11. When I get a little wimpy or fall into self-pity, I often read this chapter and remember I have not suffered to the point of shedding blood. The second half of Hebrews 11 isn't politically correct and doesn't preach too well in America – "Come to Jesus. It may be hard; you might be hated by family, jailed, or even killed." It's too bad we settle for a lesser message, often fool's gold. Rather, we should remember that (Hebrews 11:39) the so-called winners and losers were all commended for their faith and applauded by God.

Myth #6 – Doubt is reduced by unrestrained venting at God

Today in some circles it is popular to promote the idea of venting at God. A popular episode of the television show *The West Wing* shows the fictitious president, played by Martin Sheen, lashing out at God after the death of his beloved long-term secretary caused by a drunken driver. After the funeral at the National Cathedral, the president orders the doors sealed and he starts a tirade with God. "She bought her first car and you hit her with a drunk driver. That's supposed to be funny? Have I displeased You? You feckless thing!" The anger continues in Latin with the words translated, "Am I really to believe that these are the acts of a loving God? A just God? A wise God? To hell with Your punishments!" With contempt, the president lights a cigarette and crushes it on the church floor. The reaction to the diatribe was wide-ranging, from blasphemous to celebration of such brutal raw emotions.

Certainly, honesty with God is a good thing. Verbalizing feelings of anger, frustration, grief, sadness, and lament are authentic and often modeled in the Psalms. God's people can admit to being mixed up or troubled and certainly can ask "why?" ("Why" appears 430 times in Scripture.) Rather than stuffing our feelings or pretending they don't exist, we are invited to tell God about our pain, to tell Him how weary we are, how hopeless or discouraged. Please forget the poetry and clichés and cry out to God. Your words won't surprise Him, diminish Him, or threaten Him.

Too often in the church we ask people to play the "quiet game." Pretend it doesn't hurt. Show how strong you are by silence. Hydroplane over wounds. Thus losses are never mourned and tears are never shed. Fear, sadness, disappointment, and pain are buried, stuffed, deep-sixed. Unfortunately, the cork will one day pop and the toxic junk will splatter all over.

All this being said, we should not sit in judgment of God, accuse God, or chastise God. Ecclesiastes 5:1-3,7b says,

> Guard your steps as you go to the house of God, and draw near to listen rather than to offer the sacrifice of fools....Do not be hasty in word or impulsive in thought to bring up a matter in the presence of God. For God is in heaven and you are on the earth; therefore let your words be few...fear God.

It is possible to sit in judgment of God and say too much. Reckless speech doesn't make a situation better and cause doubt to dissipate. Isn't it better to get past the clenched fist and open your hands and receive His peace?

Which Will It Be, Redwood or Squash?
After months of nonstop crisis response work, I felt like I was losing strength. I was beat-up and overwhelmed. Maybe you can relate. For me, God provided a gift after a speaking assignment and I was able to go for a walk in a redwood forest. Some of these redwoods were 2,500 years old, meaning they were around when Jesus

walked the earth. The size was incredible. It was the kind of upward gaze that leaves you with a crick in your neck. Redwoods can grow to 360 feet tall, and some are 16-18 feet in diameter. Together, these fabulous creations create a canopy that results in a cathedral feel in the forest. In this outdoor church, there is a vibrancy of flora, sunrays, fog rising up, birds whistling, and squirrels playing, yet a stillness that compels attention to the voice of God.

"What would God speak to me?" I wondered. I reveled in the tenacity of a tree that could survive twenty-five centuries. I admired the thick bark that created an almost fireproof shell. My initial reaction was that it seemed nothing could hurt a redwood.

How wrong I was! The end of my journey in "redwood land" concluded with a downed redwood with its inner rings exposed. This tree was illustrative of every tree in the forest. Some rings showed years of great growth. Others revealed years of drought and insect infestations. There was a spot that disclosed an almost devastating forest fire and another spot that declared a lightning strike. Light rings revealed good times which were the growth years. Dark rings were the hard times which produced strength. Scrutinizing the rings shows the reality of the ups and downs of life.

If we could look inside at the rings of our lives, much would be revealed. Our stories may include dark rings of tragedy, hardship, suffering, loss, grief, sadness, and doubt. The rings may likewise show rings of growth, prosperity, gladness, and fruitfulness. It is interesting how often suffering is the instrument God uses to prompt a growth spurt.

God is at work growing us up. It's hard to speed up the process if our goal is His goal. If you want to take a shortcut, just remember that He can grow a squash in a few short months. But it takes a long time to grow a redwood.

Your choice: redwood or squash.

Chapter 11

Sustainability — Surviving for the Long Haul

Has it ever cost you for having your RPMs too high? It sure has for me. One day as I drove across Lake Pontchartrain via the Causeway to New Orleans, I approached the end of the 24-mile bridge and noticed the speed limit change from 65 to 35 mph. I had a choice — tap the brake or coast. Seeing no other cars around, I decided to coast and let my speed decrease. Within moments I was being waved down by a police officer and received a ticket for going 22 mph over the speed limit.

My eighteen-year-old son thoroughly enjoyed every minute of it. He reiterated to me every lecture he had ever received from yours truly. I was reminded several times that he had never had an accident or ticket. *"And you're supposed to be a pastor!"* he teased. Even my dear wife, Donna, had a little snicker and some words of instruction. Ouch, yet not the end of the story.

A few days later, our family was traveling to Texas. Donna was driving and I was asleep in the backseat. All of a sudden I sensed that we were slowing down, and I heard Jonathan say something like "He's coming after you." Sure enough, a police officer was soon at Donna's window asking about her speed. She had accidentally missed a sign in this little rural town. The Texas Ranger kindly gave her a warning. Of course, my son had a field day with this infraction

Disaster

as well. I confess, I couldn't help at least smile a little—but I held my tongue. Yet not the end of the story.

A few days after we returned from Texas, I was looking out the window of our home as Jonathan pulled into the driveway. Behind him was—you guessed it—a police car. I walked outside and the policeman informed me that my son had not fully stopped at the stop sign next to our house. The officer said, "Do you want to give him the medicine, or do you want me to?"

Everything in me wanted to say, "After all I've been through, you give him the medicine. Give him a big ticket. Put him in the back of the squad car, take him down to the station, and get the mug shot."

But I said, "I will give him the medicine."

Are you laughing at me? Be careful. I don't know if these things ever happen in your house, but these things really happened in ours. The men in blue with badges had certainly gotten our attention, and the common thread was "slow down."

After Katrina hit, I was moving at the fastest pace of my life, virtually sixteen- to eighteen-hour days every day for the first three months. The needs were great and the demands endless. I constantly juggled competing time demands in the midst of great opportunities: pastor/shepherding, community outreach, prayer, preaching, building teams, administration, new building, staff oversight, recruiting (I lost four staffers), networking, radio interviews, capital campaign, communication, crisis response, family, etc.

Though my body got weary at times, my spirit was vibrant, alive, and exhilarated through the entire initial response endeavor. The grace of God was unmistakable as I was created for such a time as this. The strength I had to persevere came from God. Yet we all realized that our staff could not maintain the pace. It would eventually kill us. The Spirit of God was pulling me over to the side of the road and saying "slow down."

My calling in life is not to be a NASCAR driver, zipping in and out of the lanes of life to gain some elusive checkered flag this world offers. There is a better RPM level that creates a right rhythm for life and fulfillment of calling.

Disaster

Disasters and crises naturally create insane scheduling. To some degree, RPMs ramp up in changing or catastrophic times. It's unavoidable. When you get deployed to Afghanistan, when the lawsuit hits, when your son is diagnosed with autism, when aging parents are demanding or simply needy, when the new business launches, when you are suddenly a single mom... These stressful times warrant much attention. They necessitate the best of our time for a season. People depend upon us. We step up to our responsibilities and give it our all.

On top of the extraordinary rigors of crisis days are the other issues, the everyday pace-of-life things. Many drive too far and too long in the fast lane, swerving and honking as a way of life. Author Richard Swenson helps those in the fast lane see ourselves as he writes, "Take a look at our lives. We send packages by Federal Express, have a long distance company named Sprint, manage our personal finances on Quicken, schedule our appointments on a Day-Timer, diet with Slim-Fast, and have swimming trunks by Speedo."[1] Our words show our addictions to speed: time crunch, fast food, rush hour, frequent flyer, rapid transit, and others. One Christian survey asked, "What is the #1 obstacle you face as Christians?" The #1 answer was, "I'm too busy."

Do you suffer from the hurry syndrome? In our culture this 24/7 hurry syndrome often keeps us from a fullness of life and life in Christ. It can be so insidious it kills health, shrivels hearts, wrecks marriages, cripples families, eats away joy, murders friendships, and stifles callings. We must realize God is not pro-exhaustion.

Recently I have been asking groups of people, "What are the signs of burnout, soul neglect, and busyness? What tends to emerge in the life of a person who neglects his or her soul? What symptoms creep in?"

The lists looked something like this:

- Fatigue, irritability
- Loss of vision, impatience, mentally sluggish, noise
- Anger
- Anxiety, headaches, body aches
- Loss of joy, no belly laughs, emotions flat-lined

- Escapist behavior, feeling like one's missing out on life
- Spiritually dry, apathetic, drifting
- Preoccupied, shame, not fully present in the moment
- Isolation, limited time for relationships, Sabbaths, vacations
- Growing weary, chronic sense of not enough time
- Compassionless
- Self-focused
- Sin looks more appealing

What a list, a sad list. We turned the page of the flipchart and I asked, "What emerges when your soul is healthy and deeply connected with God?" A new list emerged, quite different from the first:

- Love
- Joy
- Peace
- Patience
- Focus
- Vision
- Trust
- Creativity
- Energy
- Enthusiasm

Flipping to the first list, I asked the group, "Who votes for this list?" There was laughter and no hands raised. Flipping the page back, I asked, "Who votes for this one?" Everyone got the point. Then I said, "The truth is, you vote for one or the other every minute of every day."[2]

Our souls are such that they can thrive or shrivel. They can be healthy or unhealthy. We all need to pay attention.

Spiritual Anchor – Be a Finisher
Galatians 5:7 says, "You were running well, who hindered you?" There are countless reasons why Christ-followers burn out, drift, get disillusioned, and drop out. I've been through real burnout once and almost a second time. It's no fun. When it comes to personality

testing, I have been an upbeat person all my life. In fact, I'm off the charts in optimism, positivity, and cheerfulness. Yet life can throw you a whole lot of curveballs, and it's easy to want to throw in the towel. It's easy to run the 50-yard dash and hard to run the marathon.

I've found it helps to verbalize a commitment to want to "finish well." I want to go out with my boots on. I yearn to be a finisher. Virtually every year I'll be in something that is over my head, or I'll find myself in a state of self-pity over something and I'll turn to Hebrews 11:36-38, which states, "And others experienced mocking and scourgings, yes, also chains and imprisonment. They were stoned, they were sewn in two, they were tempted, they were put to death with the sword; they went in sheepskins, in goatskins, being destitute, afflicted, ill-treated (men of whom the world was not worthy, wandering in deserts and mountains and caves and holes in the ground." As I read, the Spirit of God almost always reminds me, "Michael, you are not serving to the point of shedding blood. Get back to work and get over it." Endurance and perseverance return.

I love the truth of Proverbs 4:4, "Where no oxen are, the manger is clean, but much increase comes by the strength of the oxen." To be a finisher, I need right expectations. If the goal is a clean manger, there is no need for oxen. But if you desire to make a difference, you have to be willing to clean up some do-do now and then. If you're afraid of messes, you'll never get anywhere.

Do you have the goal to be a "finisher"? You are not crazy. This is a worthy desire. Verbalize it. Make it known. Stand by it. "Be steadfast, immovable, always abounding in the work of the Lord, knowing that your toil is not in vain in the Lord" (1 Corinthians 15:58).

Your Calling: Fall Back on It

God chooses. God calls. God equips. God unleashes. This calling stuff isn't just for pastors. In fact, people across the board are becoming increasingly aware of a purpose-driven life and calling.

Many of the Reformers and Puritans spoke of their vocations as callings from God. Luther wrote that the work of monks and priests was to God "in no way whatever superior to the works of a farmer

Disaster

laboring in the field, or of a woman looking after her home." What dignity there is in the breadth of callings!

We were made for a purpose and should feel God's good pleasure in it. God saved us to serve and we "are His workmanship created in Christ Jesus for good works" (Ephesians 2:10). Who are you? You are a plainclothes agent in the Jesus Revolution, the only revolution that will ultimately endure. You are a full-time servant of God who happens to bring home the bacon by being a carpenter, sales associate, banker, or whatever.

Getting the concept of calling motivates and promotes sustainability, particularly when it's easy to quit. I've heard Gordon MacDonald help people understand this sense of calling by sharing a story from his days while pastoring in New York City. Over the years, Gordon befriended many city bus drivers and occasionally had a few over to his home for breakfast. One driver commented how Gordon had an interesting job helping people, but all bus drivers do is drive dumb buses. Gordon replied,

> I have an idea for all of you...Look, I believe that God will make any job interesting if we believe He wants to use us. Now here's what I suggest. Tomorrow morning before anyone gets on your buses, close the door, face all the empty seats, and say loudly, "In the name of Jesus, I declare this bus a sanctuary for the next eight hours. And I declare that all the people who enter this sanctuary will experience the love of Christ through me, whether they realize it or not."[3]

At first the drivers thought Gordon was crazy, because isn't it peculiar to think of New York City buses as sanctuaries? But after the shock one by one each of the drivers affirmed they would give it a try. When Gordon saw his friends over the coming months he'd ask them what they were driving, and they'd always smile and say, "A sanctuary, man, a sanctuary." One bus driver commented that this new sense of call had changed his life and perspective. He said,

> "Well, you know, this sanctuary stuff. I've been doing it. And it works. Each day I've been turning my bus into a sanctuary,

and it's made all the difference in the way I do my job. Why, the other day a guy got on my bus, and he was so mad at me because I wouldn't let him off at a stop that was illegal. He cussed me out something awful. And you know what? There was a day when I think I would have gotten up and let him have it. But not in a sanctuary." "So what happened?" "I let him off at the next stop and said, 'Hope you have a good day, sir. Nice having you aboard.' And a lady behind me said, 'Charlie, how can you be so nice to a jerk like that?' I just muttered to myself that it wasn't hard if you were driving a sanctuary and not a bus."[4]

Gordon has told this story many times over the years. He has discovered that some pilots fly sanctuaries instead of 747s for Delta, and some surgeons operate in sanctuaries and not operating rooms. Callings change people's lives and perspectives.

Stay above the "Empty" Line
Sustainability is not possible apart from slowing down and spending time with God and His Word. "I am the vine, you are the branches; he who abides in me and I in him, he bears much fruit; for apart from Me, you can do nothing" (John 15:5).

Have you ever had the Holy Spirit remind you, "What part of nothing do you not understand?" I have!

I want to stay committed to drink regularly, not from a stagnate pond but from the One who is a running stream. I want to practice being a lifelong learner. I want to carve out space for God and practice being still. I listen for His whispers. I want to be careful not to skim with Him in the midst of crisis-mode living.

What a difference it would make today if Christ-followers were self-feeding Christians. The danger is many want to be spoon-fed. What happens over time is the pastor or church subtly becomes the SOURCE for people's spiritual life rather than the RESOURCE. Of course, this never works. Over time spiritual stagnation leads to complaints, blame, and often church hopping rather than taking personal responsibility for growth by self-feeding, study, solitude, and listening for the whispers, nudgings, and promptings of God.

Months into the Katrina recovery effort, Donna and I attended a retreat for pastors and their wives. While we were there, trying to rest and get our batteries recharged, our leader, Bob Blahnik, explained some things about trout that amazed me. For example, if trout stay in the current all the time, they end up swimming on their backs (dead) due to exhaustion or smashing against rocks. They need to periodically swim behind big rocks, find quiet waters, or discover deep spots so they can rest and catch up.

So do we. If we don't, we slip below the "empty" line and lose any chance of sustainability.

Watch Bitterness

Unresolved conflict, bitterness, and seeking revenge are powerful agents that sap strength, drain joy, and exhaust emotions. These struggles are huge after a life disaster. Maybe you can relate. The truth is if you live long enough, sooner or later you will get hurt. Little things happen and you forget about them, but some things are not so easy to forget, like betrayal, abuse, abandonment, divorce, unfaithfulness, lying, injustice, etc. These things are heavy, hurtful, and hard and often lead to bitterness, resentment, and a preoccupation that tends to color everything.

Are you holding a grudge, pointing a finger, and replaying a tape over and over? Is anybody on your dartboard? Are you "rotisserizing" certain people by turning them over and over in the flame of your mind?

About a year after Katrina, I had the opportunity to speak at Hershey Evangelical Free Church. Afterward I went out to lunch with Pastor Dave Martin. There was buzz in the news that week about *Time* magazine's 2006 "Person of the Year." They chose YOU, which meant people everywhere were nominating themselves and others for certain actions taken. Dave explained that their Pennsylvania paper selected a person of the year – the Amish.

They picked these people for teaching the world about forgiveness in response to the horrendous shooting at the Amish school where all those children were killed. For five hundred years, the value of forgiveness has been burned into the DNA of the Amish. They have learned that it is often complicated, difficult, and painful, yet they choose to forgive as an act of the will, giving up the right to hurt back or seek revenge, and this allows the emotions of forgiveness to catch up over the coming months or years. Note that this does not mean approval, excusing, justifying, or denying evil and wrong.

Here is what is amazing: as money came into the Amish families from outsiders who wanted to show their support, the Amish in turn gave an equal portion to the shooter's widow and children. I learned that half of the people at the shooter's funeral were Amish! And what's more, all of the Amish families who lost children had the shooter's family into their homes. What an example of Ephesians 4:32: "Be kind to one another, tender-hearted, forgiving each other, just as God, in Christ also has forgiven you."

I went through a hurtful time once that I couldn't shake easily. I ended up talking to a counselor/pastor type who focused me on Ephesians 4:25-32. He asked me to read *Total Forgiveness* by R.T. Kendall. He then suggested I write out my loss in a letter, share my heart and hurt, and make a declaration of forgiveness as an act of my will. The counselor said I should take the letter and release it. He told of how one person burned a letter like this, another flew it as a paper airplane from a mountaintop, and another let it go in the ocean.

I carved out some time and carefully wrote a letter and made a choice to forgive. I took that letter to an old abandoned cemetery with tombstones dating back to the 1800s. I read the letter before God, tore it up, and placed the pieces under a broken tombstone. While I was walking out of the cemetery, I saw "danger" signs for a Wasp Research Testing site being conducted by a university, so I kept my distance. It was like the Holy Spirit was telling me, "Don't come back here or you'll get STUNG." I went home feeling free. Forgiveness does that.

Remember the old Andy Griffith show and the town drunk, Otis? Otis would be put in jail and the keys would be placed right outside the cell door. Any time he wanted to leave, he could let himself out. God does the same with bitterness. We lock ourselves in our own jail, yet God leaves the keys of forgiveness right by the door so we

Disaster

can let ourselves out and be free—if we want to. Do you need to reach for the key?

Recognize There Are Dangerous People Out There

Some people have the gift of criticism. They seem bent on draining, exhausting, and frustrating you, repeatedly crossing relational lines. You must maintain the health of your soul, and that means you must practice discernment with people. Proverbs 9:7-9 says, "Whoever corrects a mocker invites insult; whoever rebukes a wicked man incurs abuse. Do not rebuke a mocker or he will hate you; rebuke a wise man and he will love you. Instruct a wise man and he will be wiser still; teach a righteous man and he will add to his learning."

I once saw author/counselor Henry Cloud draw the following chart,[5] highlighting three kinds of people you find described in this passage:

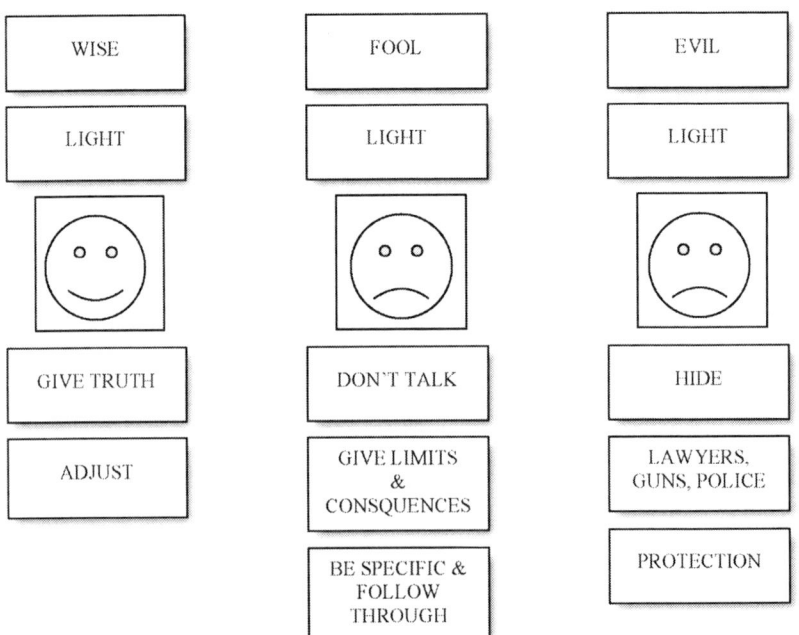

The wise, by definition, are not necessarily the most talented or the smartest, but they smile in response to the light (truth). When truth is presented, they adjust their life to it. As they dial in to the Word of God, they are instructed with more truth.

The fools frown for light hurts their eyes. They respond with defensiveness, blame shifting, and attempts to shoot the messenger. They always have an excuse. Fools don't try to hurt you but simply want to avoid responsibility. Fools need limits, consequences, and deadlines.

The evil person is blinded by the light and hates it. Their intent is to harm so you need to hide. Proverbs 22:3 says, "The wise man sees evil and hides himself. The fool proceeds and pays the price." In extreme situations, evil people act in ways that require you to call the police, use guns for self-defense, or call a lawyer. Limits and distance are required in most of these situations.

As a friend once said to me, "How many times are you going to stick your hand into the bee's nest and think you're not going to get stung?" The helpful point of the proverb is that we need to practice discernment in dealing with people. This protects our souls as well as our lives. Boundaries—personal property lines that mark us off as individuals—sometimes need to drawn to help us sustain energy and promote living.

Portfolio of Friends

It hit me like a ton of bricks. As I led a sharing time in a service packed with people, a young woman stood up and in tears described the value of a significant friendship with another woman. She told of how they carved out a weekly time for sharing and praying for each other.

The instant I heard the story, I knew that was what I needed. The old saying is, "In the ministry you are everyone's friend, sort of, but no one's friend, really." Though I had many friends, I realized I was largely on the giving side of things and not allowing others to build into my life. I wasn't actively cultivating relationships that would go to deeper levels of authenticity, openness, and sharpening.

With fear and trepidation, I approached a few friends and told them what I was thinking. I half expected them to think I was turning wimpy, but each said, "That's what I need as well." We met once a week. It wasn't a Bible study but a roundtable conversation where we addressed the following questions: "What's going on with God, spouse, kids, money, job, and your soul?" We took a chance, banned together, and it was life-giving for almost ten years.

Do you know the value of the right kind of friendships to your soul? Interestingly, the Gospels record only thirty-one days of ministry in the life of Jesus. What happened in the other days? Lots of walking, talking, time by a fire, hanging out with friends. They learned the value of friendship. Who's your mentor? Who listens? Who replenishes you? Who protects you? Who makes you laugh? Who will confront you? Who is the friend you can call at 3 a.m. in an emergency? Who plays with you? Who?

Proverbs 18:24b says, "There is a friend that sticks closer than a brother," and you need that in your life.

Play Hard, Pursue Hobbies

The most classic burnout case study in the Bible is found in 1 Kings 19. The shrewd, ambitious, and power-hungry Queen Jezebel is outraged and orders Elijah killed within twenty-four hours (1 Kings 19:2). Elijah responds and says, "It is enough; now, O lord, take my life" (1 Kings 19:4a). Basically, Elijah says, "I'm done, I'm dead meat, I quit, I'm a failure, and I don't want to be alive!" It's the classic case of an over-adrenalized, overextended, emotionally depleted, lowly, disappointed, burnt-out prophet.

God's "get well" approach to burnout is a pattern that will serve all generations well, particularly those in crisis. God never says, "Snap out of it, get with the program, try harder, run faster, pray longer, preach better, or shape up." Rather, God preciously recharges our batteries. Elijah's spiritual and relational batteries get recharged at the end of the chapter, but it's interesting that God recharges the physical and emotional batteries first. God gave Elijah rest (1 Kings 19:5a) and then nutritious food and water, and another nap (1 Kings 19:56-58).

God doesn't allow us to bypass being human. Maybe God's application for you reading this chapter is simply to hear the message "Take a nap" or "Go to bed early!" Maybe some of you are nodding off right now! At times, in counseling, I say, "The single most helpful thing you can do this moment to live like Jesus and deal with your crisis is to get a good night's sleep." Lack of sleep over the long run leads to exhausted, critical, drained people.

Next God gave Elijah exercise and relaxation. The prophet had been running for so long, but now God slows his pace down. God has Elijah travel two hundred miles over forty days to Horeb, the mount of God. That is an average of five miles per day. He walks two hours a day and rests for twenty-two hours a day.

You may be thinking, "What does this have to do with spirituality?" Lots! God wired us up with a rhythm of working six days and resting one (Exodus 34:21). The Bible says, "Bodily discipline is only of little profit, but godliness is profitable for all things." Notice that He didn't say bodily discipline is of no profit.

What's more, consider these: "A cheerful heart is good medicine" (Proverbs 17:2a); "A joyful heart makes a cheerful face" (Proverbs 15:13a); "… who richly supplies us with all things to enjoy" (1 Timothy 6:17d).

Exercise, relaxation, and laughter are biblical and beneficial. We need to think through what replenishes us. We need to enter into these things without false guilt. For me, it's basketball. It helps me keep my sanity. What is it for you—tennis, gardening, stamp collecting, genealogy studies, reading, travel, or something else?

Dallas Willard said, "The responsibility of every Christ-follower is to celebrate so life inside the kingdom is supremely better than life outside the kingdom. Without enough celebration the Christian life becomes so heavy and arduous sin starts to look good."[6] We need to celebrate enough so that sin looks bad! Selfishness is unhealthy. Proper self-care is healthy.

Caution: when times are tough and we've been working hard, it's easy to reward ourselves in ways that eventually cross the line and lead to addictive cycles. It's easy to say, "I'm serving, I'm sacrificing, and therefore I deserve _____." You may be serving and you may be sacrificing, but if you are tired, you may think you deserve something you would normally never consider, so be on your guard.

Handling Discouragement with the Sovereignty of God

In a sin-stained world, you can always count on "zingers" coming your way that hit soft spots. Do you remember hurtful words you were called as a kid or the less than flattering nicknames you were given in junior high—or the word missiles from last week? I think back and remember the people who said:

- I hate you
- You are not God's man
- Get out of town
- You don't teach the Bible faithfully
- Compromiser...of the devil
- Michael is trying to turn the church into a Bible church (I took this one as a badge of honor)

Everyone has a list. Jeremiah the prophet sure did. I can't wait to meet Jeremiah in heaven. He spoke for God in the power of God but got blank stares and yawns for forty years. Four decades and no response that we know about! He was falsely accused, slandered, under appreciated, laughed at, rejected, beaten, imprisoned, and nearly assassinated. He moved from idealism to optimism to realism to disillusionment to despair, yet he didn't quit.

Finally, the Babylonians invade, butcher, and haul most of the Israelites off to captivity. Instead of saying "I told you so," Jeremiah becomes the weeping prophet and writes Lamentations. "The Lord's loving kindnesses indeed never cease for his compassions never fail, they are new every morning. Great is thy faithfulness" (Lamentations 3:23).

The sovereignty of God makes the difference in our discouragements. When we stake everything on God's faithfulness, we look for a better day. Leith Anderson gives this account that reveals the benefits of understanding sovereignty:

> In 1994, television networks featured the fiftieth anniversary of the allied invasion of Normandy, called D-Day. They rebroadcast actual film footage and commentary from the decisive battle. The advantage of a fiftieth anniversary is that viewers know who won; the original films, radio tapes and commentaries could only report current events and future hopes.

Part of the anniversary celebration was a reenactment by former soldiers who took part in the invasion. The celebrations were likely the last public expressions of memories for men now in their seventies and eighties ... Some wore their half-century old uniforms. Others parachuted out of vintage aircraft to relive old memories of fear, courage and glory.

One telecast ran two interviews. The first was with a soldier who fought the battle on the ground. "I was convinced there was no way we could possibly win," he reported. The other interview was with a pilot, who saw a much wider view of the conflict. "I was convinced," he said, "there was no way we could possibly lose."[7]

When we are caught in life's crises and are told there's no way we can possibly win, we need God's aerial perspective and His voice that says, "There is no way you can possibly lose."

Enjoy Life
Many people are aware of the exhortations in Ecclesiastes to fear God, to know that everything under the sun is vanity, and to avoid taking seven hundred wives and three hundred concubines. We've all heard these exhortations and perhaps chuckled at them, but sadly most of us have missed the exhortations to relax, eat and drink, seize life, enjoy the ride, laugh our butts off, and smell the roses. But that is exactly what Solomon calls us to do. Listen:

Seize life! Eat bread with gusto,
Drink wine with a robust heart.
Oh yes–God takes pleasure in your pleasure!
Dress festively every morning,
Don't skimp on colors and scarves.
Relish life with the spouse you love
Each and every day of your precarious life.
Each day is God's gift. It's all you've got in exchange
For the hard work of staying alive.
Make the most of each one!
Whatever turns up, grab it, and do it. And heartily!

This is your last and only chance at it,
For there's neither work to do nor thoughts to think
In the company of the dead, where you're most certainly headed.
Ecclesiastes 9:7-10 MSG

Joy is serious business. Without it, we will simply be sad sacks who look like we just swallowed pickle juice. Life is intense and complex, so we occasionally need to chill out, hang out, lighten up, celebrate life, and throw a party. Have a good meal with some buddies. Get a triple dip of Rocky Road ice cream. Quit thinking it's a sin to enjoy life.

My professor Howard Hendricks said the faces of most Christians would make a great cover for the book of Lamentations.

Instead, we should remember these words:

"The glory of God is a man fully alive." Irenaeus

"Live to the hilt every situation you believe to be the will of God." Jim Elliot

"Making the most of your time..." (Ephesians 5:16a)

Ann Wells of the *Los Angeles Times* records the paradigm shift she experienced when her sister died unexpectedly. Her brother-in-law pulled from a dresser drawer a tissue-wrapped, silk, handmade, lace-trimmed slip with an astronomical price tag on it. This lingerie had been purchased in New York City eight or nine years earlier and was being saved for a special occasion. Now it was being sent with some other clothes to the mortician. Ann was riveted to the words of her brother-in-law as he lingered over the never-worn silk slip and said, "Don't ever save anything for a special occasion. Every day you are alive is a special occasion." Ann ruminated upon these words and writes,

> I'm still thinking about his words, and they've changed my life ... I'm not "saving" anything; we use our good china and crystal for every special event—such as losing a pound, getting the sink

unstopped, the first camellia blossom ... "Someday" and "one of these days" are losing their grip on my vocabulary. If it's worth seeing or hearing or doing, I want to see and hear and do it now ... I'm trying very hard not to put off, hold back, or save anything that would add laughter and luster to our lives. And every morning when I open my eyes, I tell myself that it is special. Every day, every minute, every breath truly is a gift from God.[8]

Give yourself exuberantly to life. Don't hold back. Have fun, be grateful. Redeem the time.

Choose One

Are you on the path to sustainability? Will you survive for the long haul? In which of the arenas discussed in this chapter do you need to give reflective thought, make a decision, or create a new pattern?

After reading this chapter, saying you are too busy to make one application is not allowed. Slow down, my friend, and live well.

Chapter 12

When Sheep Act Like Wolves: Revealing the Dirty Little Secret in the Body of Christ

The carcass lay lifeless in the valley. It was just below the wolf den filled with wolf cubs chowing down while the wild pack roamed in the sage above. A magnificent bald eagle perched on the tip of a bush looking upon the scene, as did I. The kill made the scene soberingly real. These wolves were trained killers whose cunning speed and strength put them at the top of the food chain. They mastered a full range of techniques to get what they wanted: observation, testing, stalking, dividing and conquering, and active fighting. The scenery was stupendous, the day spectacular, but I couldn't get over the carcass in the valley.

After twenty-six years of ministry, and a fast-moving and tumultuous last five years, Donna and I decided to get away for a week. The plan was to enjoy God's creation in the Grand Tetons and Yellowstone National Park. The mountain ranges, lakes, waterfalls, and valleys were breathtaking. Observing bear, elk, moose, bison, fox, beaver, coyote, pronghorn, osprey, and deer can't help but make you smile. Then, unexpectedly, came the black wolf, and the next day the den of gray wolves, and even a white cub near another den.

These events introduced me to arguably the greatest wildlife experiment of the twentieth century, the magnificent story of the reintroduction of wild wolves into Yellowstone National Park after decades of absence. I was spellbound by these untamed killing machines on this wild frontier.

The pristine, splendid world of the national park with its lofty peaks, wildlife, and star-studded nights differed vastly from my world in New Orleans, yet the wolves resonated with something in my spirit, reminding me of an aspect of ministry almost never talked about. In fact, many wouldn't admit its existence. I'm talking about the dirty little secret we dare not voice in polite church company: when sheep act like wolves.

Now, let me quickly clarify what I am talking about. I am not referring to the need to stand guard against wolves in sheep's clothing as Jesus mandated. Indeed, the call to vigilance against false teaching and heresy by those who appear to be sheep yet are ravenous wolves remains (Acts 20:28-31; John 10:12). Likewise, I am not calling a true sheep a wolf. Not at all!

Sometimes, however, true sheep practice "wolf-like" behavior. We all are capable of this. Too often in the family of God we shoot our wounded, suffer from friendly fire, and smite faithful shepherds and faithful servants. Good people do bad things. Good people can create toxic speech, power plays, politics, control tactics, comparison games, and simply lack the fruit of the Spirit. We bite, devour, and maim in the name of advancing Christ while secretly fulfilling agendas, and it's killing us. This has to stop (or at least become rare) or we will suffer in mission and woundedness.

If you don't believe me, ponder these five observable and alarming trends among Christ-followers:

1. ***Pastoral Change*** – the statistics for pastoral longevity are roughly 18 months for a youth pastor and 3 to 4 years for a pastor. Every month in the United States, 1,300 pastors are fired or forced to resign. One study showed that 70 percent of pastoral resignations resulted from the pastor being forced out regardless of church size. In either case, the church members are left wondering, "What happened?"

   One-third of all pastors minister in a church that either fired their previous pastor or forced them to resign. Of all current pastors, 23 percent have been forced out at some time in their ministry life. Of those who have been forced out, 13 percent were terminated, 29 percent were pressured to resign, and the remaining 58 percent were forced to resign.

Sixty-two percent of ousted pastors were forced out by a church that had already, at least once in the past, extended the foot of Christian fellowship to another pastor. At least 15 percent of all U.S. churches have forced out two or more pastors. Ten percent of all U.S. churches have forced out three or four pastors.[1] The sudden resignation of long-term, faithful pastors is rarely sudden but is in fact often the product of years of digs, disappointments, and frustration. Pastors don't have to be contestants on *Survivor* to know what it feels like to be "voted off the island." What is especially disturbing is that on average 18,000 pastors annually resign or are fired and never return to vocational ministry.[2]

2. *First-Assignment Pastor Road Kill* – 80 percent of seminary and Bible school graduates who enter the ministry will leave the ministry within the first five years.[3] Many of them will never give pastoral ministry another try. In the church we often eat our youngsters.

3. **Pastoral Health** – "80% of pastors and 84 percent of their spouses are discouraged or are dealing with depression."[4] Twenty-eight percent of pastors thought seriously about leaving church ministry in the preceding year.[5]

A CBN fact sheet titled "Pastor Burnout: Combating a Churchwide Epidemic" reported:

"What might be called a spiritual virus is stalking the homes and pulpits of America's pastors. Each year, thousands of clergy walk away from their ministries, suffering from burnout brought on by frantic schedules and unrealistic expectations... The clergy is like the *Titanic*—it is sinking fast. Fifteen hundred ministers every month drop out of ministry. That's an epidemic. Even more sobering is that nearly

6,000 Southern Baptist ministers annually fall victim to burnout, depression, marital problems, and even suicide."[6]

4. *Spectatorship and Dropouts* – More and more Christ-followers are choosing simple attendance over active participation because of wounds inflicted during ministry service. Others are choosing to drop out. They haven't given up on Jesus but have come to the end of the road with the church. They have concluded that church doesn't equal Jesus. Friendly fire incidents result in disillusionment, hurt, loss of cohesion and morale, anger, resentment, lack of trust, and suspicion of those in spiritual authority. You know how it goes: you belong…you invest…you are a band of brothers and sisters…then you get hurt and everything changes. This hurricane seems to blow you away. Pain. Rejection. Disappointment. Loss. Loneliness. Cruelty. Infighting. Is this you?

These disenfranchised servants are not simply in the category of babes, fainthearted, or ungrounded but are increasingly solid, mature leaders who have made difficult choices regarding their church attendance. When I first heard of the likes of Larry Crabb, John Eldredge, George Barna, William P. Young (*The Shack*), and others making this choice, I was dumbfounded and, to be honest, angry. How could they? I read books like *Quitting Church*, *Life After Church*, *So You Don't Want to Go to Church Anymore?*, and *Revolution*. It was chilling and perplexing. Now I wonder if their choices resulted from too much friendly fire or "wolf-like" behavior that has sapped leaders' strength and driven them to take cover.[7]

5. *Evangelistic Ineffectiveness* – The number of adherents to Christianity (in the United States) is declining significantly. Only 17.5 percent attend church on a given Sunday (Gallup), 94 percent of churches are in decline, and 5 out of 6 Americans don't think church is relevant to finding growth or experiencing God. More Americans claim "no religion" now than

all Presbyterians, Methodists, Lutherans, and Episcopalians combined. Every year 4,000 churches close and 500,000 members leave. George Barna's research reveals that nearly 4 in 10 unchurched people (37 percent) in the United States avoid church life because of bad experiences in the church or in relation to churched people.[8]

These five trends are real. "Wolf-like" behaviors seriously contribute to each dangerous trend. A failure to acknowledge the existence or seriousness of "wolf-like" behavior is no different from families denying domestic issues ranging from lack of respect, toxic behaviors, and extreme issues of abuse. Caution lights need to be lit during times of chaos and upheaval. **"Wolf-like" behavior, to one degree or another, almost always presents itself during times of disaster and crisis.**

I have spent my life in extraordinary churches. My training taught me well how to expect suffering and endure hardship and even persecution from outside the family of God. Yet I wasn't prepared to anticipate and respond well to the stream of challenges from within. Over the years I have been tested with politics, gossip, unsigned notes, screaming, power plays, betrayal, intimidation, out-of-control anger, hurtful words and actions, threats, "they said," "I hate you," and several spiritualized financial incentives. Arrows in the chest are one thing, but arrows in the back are quite another. Again, this is in the context of mostly great pastoral experiences. If you don't believe these things happen, ask any veteran leader or long-term servant in the active body of Christ and you will hear about more hurt and train wrecks than you can imagine.

My last five years of ministry in New Orleans were crazy, exciting, and God-blessed in the midst of the greatest natural disaster in the history of the United States. Kingdom history was written in the aftermath of Hurricane Katrina. In the sovereignty of God, our nice, safe, comfortable, suburban, God-fearing church overnight was transformed into an uncomfortable, dangerous, moment-by-moment, Holy Spirit-dependent mobilization center for the kingdom. The supernatural hand of God revealed itself. The church of Jesus Christ was often at its very best, but in some cases at its worst. To be honest, sometimes it's easier to endure a hurricane than "wolf attacks." Sometimes God has to save us from ourselves.

During these five years our church became the great recipient of a God-ordained revolution of volunteerism that descended upon New Orleans to help rebuild homes and lives for Christ. Thousands of volunteers from forty-two states and seven countries traveled to New Orleans, most sleeping on the floor of our worship center, and were deployed one week at a time. The worship center also served as a dining hall for these pastors, leaders, and laborers.

The devastation of Katrina led to many talks, often nightly, with leaders about ministry hurt, pain, loss, and secrets. In these talks, I was unprepared for the number of conversations that revealed painful "wolf attacks." I never knew. Honestly, I never knew. Only the unusual, disastrous conditions of Katrina caused leaders and laborers to open up and share their stories. I daresay stories of "wolf-like" behavior are more common than any of us know.

A Plea to the Body of Christ

If indeed my observations ring true, what can be done? There are no magical solutions or simplistic answers. However, a dialog needs to begin as we admit to and tackle the issues of sheep that turn into wolves. I offer a starting point for discussion:

1. **Pastors/leaders need to talk more about these realities with one another.** Veterans need to tell stories wisely and appropriately. Great strength resides in the stories of pastors and leaders who realize "I am not the only one" when it comes to wolf bites. Dialog should be affirmed because "wolf-like" behavior usually has a field day in the midst of secrecy. Pastors and leaders are too often trained to "tough it out" alone, be the nice guy, be optimistic, and believe for the best even as we trust God. "Wolf-like" behavior must be brought into the light or it will thrive in the darkness.

2. **Seminaries must better prepare, train, and equip the next generation of leaders.** If they don't, who will? In my seminary master's program, I can't remember one warning

to watch out or one chapel speaker telling their horror story. We can do better. Students must understand the dark side of the church: church politics, control battles, and manipulation. Young shepherds must learn the art of perseverance, spiritual and emotional health, and dealing with a broken heart and woundedness. Also, pastors need to get the 701 course on how not to be a weenie.

3. **Churches must be aware of the ever increasing numbers who have been hurt by toxic behavior and dropped out or are present but perplexed, disillusioned, and hurt.** Many attend but no longer lead or serve for fear of another episode. Who will minister to the strays? Who will care for the hurting? Who will bring people to Jesus…the real Jesus? Great sermons will probably not heal these wounds, but ministries of listening, mercy, care, drawing near, and trust rebuilding will help.

4. **The "elephant in the room" must be named: sheep can act like wolves.** Yet I wonder, is anyone outraged? Who should trumpet the warning? Where are the voices? I hear voices against legalism. I hear voices against an inward-focused mission orientation. I hear increased voices against sex trafficking, creation abuse, discrimination, universalism, and even gay bashing. But are there voices in the assembly calling out "wolf-life" behavior? Will we choose to name, challenge, and act for Jesus' sake?

5. **Honor faithful leaders** – Too many leaders suffer from the quandary of multiple and conflicting expectations. Some sage penned the resume of the perfect preacher:

    The Perfect Preacher

    After hundreds of years a model preacher has been found to suit everyone. He preaches exactly 20 minutes and then sits down. He condemns sin, but never hurts anyone's feelings. He works from 8 am to 10 pm in every type work from preaching to custodial service. He makes $400 a week, and wears good clothes. He buys good books regularly. He has a good family. He drives a nice car and gives $60 a week to church. He also stands ready to give to any and every good work that comes along. He is 26 years old and has been preaching for 30 years. He is tall, dark and handsome, thin and short, heavyset and good-looking. He has one brown eye and one blue. His hair is parted in the middle, left side dark and straight, the right brown and wavy. He has a burning desire to work with the young people and spends all of his time with the older folks. He smiles all of the time with a straight face because he has a sense of humor that keeps him seriously dedicated to his work. He makes 15 calls a day visiting church members and spends all of his time evangelizing, yet is never out of his office...the perfect preacher.

We laugh, but we often hold leaders to unrealistic expectations. Faithful leaders need honor; some are worthy of double honor. Most pastors I know pay the price for God and for others. No one knows the silent load they carry. They carry on despite dark nights of the soul, only to have their legs cut out from under them come morning. They pray, serve, and deeply want to follow Jesus fully. During times of crisis – insufficient finances, lack of numerical growth, a popular ministry up the street, criticism, economic struggles, and change – firing the coach presents the easy fix. Occasionally this is the will of God, but many times this quick fix only keeps a ministry from discovering its deeper problems, exacerbates its troubles, and masks its real issues. Honoring leaders leads to longevity, which often leads to the good success of an organization.

Here is a starter list to honor leaders:

- **Be Responsive**

    "Be responsive to your pastoral leaders. Listen to their counsel. They are alert to the condition of your lives and work under the strict supervision of God. Contribute to the joy of their leadership, not its drudgery. Why would you want to make things harder for them" (Hebrews 13:17 MSG).

    With God, dictatorial, narcissistic, self-serving leadership is out and servant/shepherd leadership is in. The response to God's leaders is to be responsive – obey, don't make them sad in the work, and don't overburden them. First Thessalonians 5:17 says to honor, appreciate, be thoughtful, and pay proper respect to leaders. When these actions are present, it brings benefit and advantage both to the pastor and to the flock.

- **Grow Spiritually**

    Nothing motivates a pastor more. Nothing! Don't stay baby Christians who live on milk rather than solid food (Hebrews 5:14). Become self-feeders and grow in devotion to Jesus.

- **Be Encouragers**

    The apostle Paul repeatedly wrote about the value of "refreshment" (Philemon 1:7). Pray for your pastors and tell them you uphold them. Send a note, email or call. Do something totally unexpected, unexplainable, yet extremely helpful. Remember tangibly the pastor's wife and kids.

- **Be a Friend**

    A 2006 Barna Research Group study revealed that 61 percent of pastors have few close friends. What a gift if a pastor has a few friends he can take off the collar or pastor's "hat" with. What a gift to be able to talk at deeper levels: share feelings, wounds, dreams, struggles, and fears. Laugh together and often. Sometimes a pastor needs to be the receiver and not the giver. A pastor realizes God knows the pressures, but it is nice to know someone with skin on knows the pressures also. The gift of just being one of the guys at times helps restore emotional equilibrium and keep one sane.

6. **Live an apologetic called love** – American Christianity is seemingly falling behind in spite of having greater resources and a vast array of methodologies and techniques. Could it be that we need to pay more attention to the apologetic called love? Jesus said, "They will know we are Christians by our love" (John 13:35), and in His Gethsemane prayer He yearned that we would practice oneness so the world would know God sent the Son (John 17:21). Years ago Sheldon Vanauken said, "The best argument for Christianity is Christians: their joy, their certainty, their completeness. But the strongest argument against Christianity is also Christians – when they are somber and joyless, when they are self-righteous and smug in complacent consecration, when they are narrow and repressive, then Christianity dies a thousand deaths."[9]

    Perhaps our "churchianity" tendencies and internal wars do more to alienate seekers than all the bestselling books by angry atheists combined. I cannot prove this, but it warrants thoughtful evaluation. Perhaps we need to hire shepherds and not CEOs, be a family rather than an enterprise, and love insiders and outsiders with an amazing graciousness. Who knows, it may turn the world upside down once again.

A Plea to Those Who Have Been Hurt

Maybe you have not been back to church in years, except for weddings and funerals of course. Possibly you say, "I wouldn't go back to a church without a bodyguard and a lawyer on retainer." Perhaps you float from one place to the next, fearful to put down roots or get close to anyone. Could it be you always hide in the back row of a mega-church so no one will ever know your scars, hopes, or dreams? Might you choose Charles Stanley on TV as your church? Do you say, "All I need is God"? Please, please consider the following:

1. **Allow for Healing Grace**

   Do not rush past your pain but rather slow down and let the Holy Spirit cut you open and do surgery. Listen for His voice. Allow Holy Spirit salve to be applied to your most pronounced cuts, bruises, scrapes, and gashes in the depth of your being. The Spirit will guide you into green pastures and beside quiet waters and restore your soul. Let Him lead you into His custom-designed gracious healing.

2. **Forgive**

   Do not let the sun to go down on your anger for one more day (Ephesians 4:26). Forgiveness is always a choice. It is not an emotion or a feeling but it is saying, "I know what you've done and it really hurts. But I choose to forgive you. I do this because of the example and power in Jesus." Forgiveness releases bitterness that suffocates joy and sours much. Forgiveness is never easy. In fact, the only thing more costly than forgiveness is not forgiving.

3. **Live the 50/20 Rule**

   What is this? In Genesis 50:20 Joseph says after so much betrayal and hardship, "You intended to harm me, but God intended it for good to accomplish what is now being done." Joseph grasped that a higher purpose was at work. God can and does use stupidity, wounding, and hurt in redemptive ways. The bigger picture reveals that God turns stumbling into steppingstones that lead into destinies. God is always working behind the scenes. Who would ever have thought Joseph would become the prime minister of Egypt? Nothing stops God. Not opposition. Not sin. Not betrayal. Not "wolf-like" behavior. God never says, "Uh-oh. What's happening?" With God's sovereignty in mind, the choice remains either to run from pain or enjoy the scenery in life's zigzags as we squeeze out all He has for us. By faith, cling to the 50/20 rule.

4. **Reset Your Expectations**

Sometimes when our apple carts get turned upside down we need to make sure our trust is in God and not men. One reason we get so discombobulated is we say in shocking tones, "People can be so cruel." Yes, but we shouldn't be so surprised. The truth is Christians can be dangerous. We can all be monsters at times. Every Christ-follower has the capacity for moral splendor and beauty or disgusting acts of the flesh. Isn't it interesting how honest the Bible is? God doesn't cover up any embarrassment or utilize any sin damage control. He shows the good, the bad, and the ugly in His people. All Christians are works in progress. All Christ-followers were saved, are being saved, and one day ultimately will be saved (justification, sanctification, and glorification). Do not be surprised Christians are not perfect. If you expect perfection you will only end up disappointed.

5. **Step toward Trusting Again**

With all the hurt and wounds today from friendly fire many adopt the Love God/ Hate the Church mentality. Many rationalize, "I don't need to belong to the visible church, just the invisible church. I'm part of the capital 'C' church, and the small 'c' church is optional." Some say, "I do church on the golf course or at Starbucks with a buddy once a month." It is easy to fall into a privatized spirituality and abandon the assembling together of the saints (Hebrews 10:24-25).

Has hurt, heresy, power struggles, or controversy driven you to join the "church is lame" club? It is understandable. It really is, but don't give up on the church. The church is Jesus' bride. He loves the church and gave Himself up for her... warts and all (Ephesians 5:25). What Jesus loves we must love. Jesus is crazy about His bride, and He surely would not take kindly to anyone badmouthing her. It may be time to make nice with His bride. You can check it out for yourself. The New Testament knows nothing of an unchurched Christ-follower. Nothing. It is scandalous that solo Christianity thrives and such a low view of the church prevails. Here's what I suggest: take steps, even baby steps if necessary, in the direction of obedience and wisdom.

I remember working hard in seminary to secure a summer internship with what I considered the premier slot in the entire Washington, DC region. I would personally be mentored by a well-known veteran pastor of one of the largest churches. What an opportunity. What a good friendship. It was a great summer. Months later, it was discovered this beloved pastor, mentor, and friend was a fraud parading for years as a pastor and clinical psychologist. It was the ecclesiastical version of Leonardo DiCaprio's movie *Catch Me If You Can* (the true story about Frank Abagnale Jr., who conned his way as a Pan Am pilot, doctor, and legal prosecutor). When the truth came out, everyone was stunned and the church imploded. The man who first exposed the fraud was particularly disillusioned and withdrew. Months down the road, when he finally returned to a church, I met him at the front door. He said to me, "I don't think I can ever trust again." I understood. The situation was devastating. But I said, "Don't go the rest of your life never trusting again. You will miss too much. Go as slow as you need to. Test everything. Learn to trust again." Do you know what? He did! And he was glad. You can too.

A Plea to All

Back to Yellowstone...my intrigue did not lie in the story of the wild wolves as much as my introduction to and acquaintance with a community of precious souls known as "wolf watchers." Before dawn, a group of tightly bundled, coffee-toting, story-trading wolf watchers peer through spotting scopes and binoculars to look the untamed wolves right in the eye. Like teenagers dogging movie stars, these educated and respectful paparazzi know all the tricks of the trade to scan the valleys and hillsides for the wolves.

This phenomenon has spilled over to more than 200,000 amateurs seeing wolves every year in Yellowstone. The wolf watchers invited me to peer into the scope, listen to a wolf radio collar tracker to catch a directional signal, learn the way of the wolf, and become one of them. Morning and evening, every day of the year, the wolf watchers stand guard, ever watching.

While camping out late one night, it dawned on me that maybe a phenomenon will occur in the family of Christ where thousands, morning and night, will choose not only to stand guard against the wolves on the outside, but also against our own "wolf-like" tendencies from within.

This is my prayer:

> May we be transformed Christ-imitators who stop shooting our wounded, who say NO! to friendly fire and YES! to authenticity, civility, respect, love, truth, and unity. May the church truly represent the body that Jesus called it to be. Indeed, a light sitting on a hill. May the number of carcasses in the valley diminish and the health of the body of Christ soar. May it be so for Jesus' sake and for His bride's. Amen.

Chapter 13

Spiritual Warfare

"High-ranking demons have been assigned to your church," he said. Normally I would have blown off those words as kooky and bizarre. Too many people today are obsessed with the unseen world, infatuated with superstition and a gospel that seems to focus more on demon binding, devil chasing, and deliverance than on Christ. A lot of extremes, nonsense, and downright heresy get presented in the name of spiritual warfare. However, these words, spoken by a godly pastor two months into the Katrina disaster, seemed not only plausible but real.

When Katrina hit, the leaders of a solid, Bible-centered megachurch gathered quickly to decide how they could help us after watching our catastrophe from their Northwestern perch. What should be done? Who should go? Being compelled to respond, all options were on the table. Should a large house-gutting team or a chainsaw team be sent? Should the mission's pastor go to scope things out or several staff members?

The leaders' impressions from the Holy Spirit were different from anything they had anticipated. First, they decided they should not come immediately but should come on day sixty—not day fifty-nine or day eighty-four, but day sixty. Second, the person to come was not to be the mission's pastor, youth pastor, or a team, but the senior pastor.

Disaster

Unbeknownst to everyone, day sixty was the day I had to make a huge decision. Katrina, crisis, and ministry challenges had brought me to a fork in the road. A decision had to be made that would cast a long shadow and have enormous ramifications.

Leadership was weighty and lonely until my day sixty surprise showed up. This seasoned senior pastor was a veteran of many spiritual battles. He prayed, listened, served, and helped me weigh options. A series of bizarre and ominous circumstances alerted us that we were not merely dealing with detailed ministry decisions but were involved in deeper spiritual realities, including spiritual warfare.

The truth is whenever you push against evil, evil pushes back. Resistance comes from the powers of darkness, and a battle rages. Wise words had come from a volunteer named Tom at day thirty. He said: "Please know that I will be adding you to my prayer list. The enemy always seeks to take out the leaders first. In wartime a strategic tactic is to break up the opposing forces by attacking the men at the top. This will confuse the 'troops' and paralyze efforts. You are a marked man, and the leaders in your church are in the sight of the enemy. The hectic schedules, endless needs and avalanche of ministry opportunities can take godly men off course. Fight from your knees."

Much was at stake, including honor, ministry, and unity. I can tell you that of all the Katrina challenges, God's interventions at this crucial point were nothing short of miraculous to make a way in the middle of an impossible situation.

Spiritual warfare is needed in every disaster and crisis. When the fighting is fierce, when the storm engulfs you, when the battle is hot, temptations will come and you will be most vulnerable. What is at stake could be your marriage, your kids, your integrity, your job, your lifelong friendships, your future, and/or your finances. Your life, future, and soul are on the line.

I'm grateful for the reminders that there are powers dedicated to steal, kill, and destroy (John 10:10). There are five things you need to know about spiritual warfare when you are in the midst of a disaster:

#1—Know a war is going on

It's easy to think Christianity is played on a playground rather than on a battleground. We forget we are in a war zone. The apostle Paul speaks as if he were a commanding general on steroids motivating the troops at the conclusion of the book of Ephesians. It is a high-octane set of marching orders. The war's ultimate outcome is secure. The victory has been fought and won, not on San Juan Hill or Hamburger Hill, but on Calvary's Hill. We are on the winning side, but the battle still rages.

Some say, "You don't need to fight the enemy. Let Jesus do it for you." This is unbiblical. Passivity is nonsense. It's like a soldier in Afghanistan saying, "My commander will fight for me. I don't need any weapons."

To be ignorant of spiritual warfare is naïve and dangerous. It's like walking into an al-Qaeda outpost wearing a T-shirt that reads "I Love the U.S.A." It's like having your body smeared with blood while swimming with great white sharks.

Paul says, "Put on the full armor of God, that you may be able to stand firm against the schemes of the devil. For our struggle is not against flesh and blood, but against the rulers, against the powers, against the world forces of darkness, against the spiritual forces of wickedness in the heavenly places" (Ephesians 6:11-12). We face a God-hating, human-hunting, soul-bashing enemy that is at war with us. Stand firm. Don't be gullible or naïve. The battle will rage and intensify as long as you are living on your adversary's turf. Hold the high ground at all costs. Refuse to retreat.

#2—Know who your enemy is

As a seminary student years ago, I remember getting angry at a cricket. The bug was loud, obnoxious, and hidden next to my normally quiet office at my home. "CHIRP! CHIRP! CHIRP!"

How do you get anything done when a bug is bugging you? After a few hours of chirping, I declared war. I got on my knees and searched and searched for the intruder. Finally I isolated the culprit. The cricket was in a hole in the floorboards. My weapon was a sharp scissors blade that I repeatedly jammed through the hole to pierce my nemesis. I sprayed hairspray in the crack to euthanize the monster. Rubbing alcohol was poured in the hole to drown the annoyer. A hanger could turn corners to root out the cagey creature. Silence came for a moment...but then more CHIRPING!

Being totally distracted from study, I finally brought in the heavy artillery – an exterminator who would spray the house. Still, it was "CHIRP! CHIRP! CHIRP!" Just when I thought the battle had been won, the chirping would start again. By the end of the week, after many sleep-deprived nights, I discovered the cricket was the smoke detector. It was faithfully chirping to let me know the battery was going bad. **The lesson: know who your enemy is!**

Our enemy is Satan and his demonic forces. Many laugh and conclude, "There is nothing to it." The word out on the street is that intelligent, well-adjusted people are too sophisticated to believe in spiritual attacks and evil forces. Once I was in a nationally known bookstore and overheard two teenagers looking for the Satanic Bible.

I asked, "Just out of curiosity, why are you looking for that book?"

One responded, "A friend of mine has it and says there are good things in it. We don't really believe in it but..."

I said, "Satan is real and can destroy people's lives."

They looked at me as if I were from Mars. After they located it, I heard one of the girls say, "Should I buy it or ask my mother to get it for me?"

Is there any evidence for an evil one? Is Satan real?

Think through your experiential knowledge. How do you explain the evil that goes on in our world? Why can't nations figure out how to get along? Why are there record numbers of arrests and record numbers of jails? Why do so many marriages feel pressure? Why is there so much self-destructive behavior? Why discrimination, genocide, poverty, abuse, addiction, and racism? Can you really explain it all with damaged chromosomes, a failed school system, or governmental inequities? Could part of the answer be something deeper, something more sinister? Someone perhaps who wreaks havoc in our world? Could evil and an evil one really exist?

Professor R.C. Sproul remembers asking his class of Western Philosophy students, "How many of you believe in a real, personal devil?" There were three yeses and twenty-seven who considered the devil a myth. Sproul asked the class, "How many of you believe in the existence of God?" Surprisingly all thirty believed in God. The next question went like this, "Why is it that you affirm the existence of a spiritual being who has the ability to influence for good, but you deny the existence of a spiritual being who can influence us to evil?" The basic response was, "Modern science has made it impossible for educated people to believe in the devil." Sproul challenged the point saying, "What discovery of modern science has made the idea of Satan no longer credible? Is it the second law of thermodynamics? Is it the laws that govern nuclear fusion or fission? What is it?" There was silence and no one could name a scientific discovery that applied. Finally, one student summed things up: "The idea of a devil seems to fit in the category of ghosts and goblins. How can anyone believe in a sinister fellow in a red flannel suit with cloven hoofs, horns, and a pitchfork?" In other words, it's politically correct to assume the devil is only a Halloween caricature or the product of a horror movie made in Hollywood.[1]

However, is that where the evidence points? You have to admit, if there really is a Satan he would surely want humanity to believe he did not exist.

According to the Bible, Satan is real. Satan is mentioned in seven Old Testament books and by every writer in the New Testament. The Bible clearly states Satan is an entity to be reckoned with. Fifteen times Jesus spoke of the devil. In fact, Jesus had a conversation with the devil while being tempted (Matthew 4; Luke 4). There is no question Jesus was convinced of the reality of the evil one. Satan has a vile bio and rap sheet. He was created by God as an angelic creature (Ezekiel 28:12b-15) with great beauty, strength, and authority. Unbelievable egotism and pride caused him to attempt a wicked insurrection (Isaiah 14:12-17). In his coup against God, one-third of the angels followed Satan (Revelation 12:4). These fallen angels are called demons (Matthew 12:26). Satan is powerful but not all-powerful, clever but not omniscient, mobile but not omnipresent. Satan's and the demons' destiny is hell (Matthew 25:41). His time is short. His names and titles give insight into his character.

The Names and Titles of Satan

- Satan means the adversary, opposer (Revelation 12:9)
- Roaring lion (1 Peter 5:8)
- The accuser (Revelation 12:10)
- The evil one (John 17:15)
- The tempter (Matthew 4:3)
- Angel of light (1 Corinthians 11:14-15)
- The deceiver (Revelation 20:10)
- The ruler of darkness (Ephesians 6:12)
- The lord of the flies (Matthew 12:24)
- The devil, the one who slanders (1 Peter 5:8)

As for me, I conclude there is a Satan. I've witnessed the destruction and ruin that crushed too many people's lives, marriages, and children. I believe the reliability of the Bible and the authority of Jesus Christ. What Jesus believes, I believe. I don't believe in being obsessed with the devil, seeing a demon behind every tree, attributing every mental, emotional, physical, or spiritual problem to him or thinking he makes people's heads spin around. However, I also don't want to underestimate him.

#3—Know the strategy of the enemy

In the book *The Gift of Honor*, John Trent and Gary Smalley recount a true story illustrating why Christ-followers are often unprepared and ill-equipped.

> Something took place in the fall of 1944 that can explain a major reason why many...are facing a losing battle today.... It was late October when an officer commanding a platoon of American soldiers received a call from headquarters. Over the radio, this captain learned his unit was being ordered to recapture a small French city from the Nazis—and he learned something else from headquarters as well. For weeks, French resistance fighters had risked their lives to gather information about German fortifications in that city, and they had smuggled this information out to the Allies.

The French underground's efforts had provided the Americans with something worth its weight in gold: a detailed map of the city. It wasn't just a map with the names of major streets and landmarks; it showed specific details of the enemy's defensive positions.

Indeed, the map even identified shops and buildings where German soldiers bunked or where machine-gun nests or a sniper had been stationed. Block by block, the Frenchmen gave an accounting of the German units and the gun emplacements they manned.

For a captain who was already concerned about mounting causality lists, receiving such information was an answer to prayer. Although the outcome of the war wouldn't be decided on this one skirmish, to him it meant that he wouldn't have to write as many letters to his men's parents or wives telling them their loved one had been cut down in battle.

Before the soldiers moved out to take their objective, the captain gave each man a chance to study the map. And wanting to make sure his men read it carefully, he hurriedly gave them a test covering the major landmarks and enemy strongholds. Just before his platoon moved out the officer graded the tests, and with minor exceptions every man earned a perfect score. As a direct result of having that map to follow, the men captured the city with little loss of American lives.

Nearly thirty years after this military operation took place, an army researcher heard the story and decided to base a study on it. The project began in France, where instead of a platoon of soldiers, he arranged for a group of American tourists to help him with his research.

For several hours, the men and women were allowed to study the same map the soldiers had, and they were given the same test. You can guess the results. Most of the tourists failed miserably.

The reason for the difference between these two groups was obvious—motivation. Knowing their lives were on the line, the soldiers were highly motivated to learn every detail of the map. For the tourists, being in the research study provided some motivation. But most of them had little to lose but a little pride if they failed the test.[2]

Are you a tourist or a soldier? Do you realize what is at stake? Paul tells us not to be ignorant of the enemy's tactics, methods, and strategies (2 Corinthians 2:11). We are told to stand firm against the schemes of the devil (Ephesians 6:11).

What Is in the Devil's Old Bag of Tricks

- He blinds people to the truth (2 Corinthians 4:4)
- He tempts (1 Thessalonians 3:5)
- He deceives (Revelation 12:9)
- He lies (John 8:44)
- He accuses (Revelation 12:10)
- He creates false spiritual experiences (1 Timothy 4:1)
- He stirs up disunity (Ephesians 4:27; 2 Corinthians 2:10-11)
- He steals, kills, and destroys (John10:10)
- He undermines God's goodness (Genesis 3:4-5)

#4—Know God's power

It makes all the difference in the battle if you've got someone Big, Powerful, and Able on your side. As a kid, I was skinny and without a whole lot of muscle. I'll never forget the day before sixth grade started. A gigantic mountain of clay with trenches was mine to explore near my home. All of a sudden two boys cornered me. Actually, they were giants! They turned me into their slave to enable them to build a fort. Escape seemed a real option, but just when I was ready to make my getaway, I encountered the sister of one of the boys who was a giant herself – 7 feet tall, and I could swear she had a mustache. Okay, I may be exaggerating a little, but these dudes were huge. Each could have beaten the life out of me. The enslavement seemed to last forever, and when it was finally over, it was an ordeal I never wanted to repeat.

The next morning I walked to school in anticipation of the first day. All the sixth graders had to line up. Guess who I had to line up between? The two giants! They had grown to be 9 feet tall. It was going to be a long year. Yet, miraculously, we turned into great friends. The biggest one was Charlie. We did all kinds of things together, like basketball, baseball, camping, and hiking. I went through sixth grade without any fear. Why? Because Charlie had my back. He was my friend. All I had to do was stay near Charlie or mention his name and no one would mess with me. I was confident, not anxious. I was convinced I was not alone.

Life is like that. Things are different when you are with someone BIG.

Well, Charlie is no longer around, but God is present 24/7 and He is bigger than Charlie and the sister. God is able for every situation. No wonder He says "fear not"!

Elisha and a servant found themselves surrounded by soldiers. In fact, it was an entire army. The servant frantically says to the prophet, "What should we do?" Elisha, bold as a lion, replies, "Do not fear, for those who are with us are more than those who are with them" (2 Kings 6:16). The servant must have thought the prophet was delusional, but Elisha prays, "O Lord, I pray, open his eyes that he may see. And the Lord opened the servant's eyes and he saw: and behold the mountains were full of horses and chariots of fire all around Elisha" (2 Kings 6:17). For a brief moment the stressed-out servant got a glimpse of the supernatural realm—angels, demons, and God's power. He saw God's forces at work on their behalf and realized the enemy was dramatically outgunned. Through the eyes of faith may we see the same reality!

The size of our God always determines the size of our faith. Big God = big faith. Little God = little faith. Our job is not to focus on the size of our challenge but to focus on the size of our God. General Paul says, "Finally, be strong in the Lord and in the strength of His might" (Ephesians 6:10).

You cannot be a conscientious objector in this war. There is no peace treaty to sign with Satan. No spiritual pacifism allowed. Our strength comes from the Lord. Daily we are to put on the full armor of God (Ephesians 6:13). Dress with all the equipment, not missing one or three pieces. Every piece of equipment is critical. Paul says to put on *all* the armor (Ephesians 6:13-20). Here is how it breaks down:

Disaster

DEVIL'S SCHEME	ARMOR	SPIRITUAL ARMOR	APPLICATION
Lies	Belt	Truth	Know the truth and the truth will set you free
Guilt	Breastplate	Righteousness	Stand on positional righteousness and walk in practical righteousness
Discouragement	Footwear	Peace	Live in peace with God, experience the peace of God.
Worry	Shield	Faith	Take God at His Word and obey.
Fear	Helmet	Salvation	Assurance of salvation.
Confusion	Sword	Word of God	Saturate your mind with the Word and speak it.
Isolation	Communication	Prayer	Live in moment-by-moment dependence.

#5—Know the unity of fellow soldiers

Mark Buchanan masterfully describes a scene from the movie *Gladiator*:

> General Maximus comes to Rome dirty and shackled. This is not the way it's supposed to be. Where's Rome's legendary pageantry to greet one of her war heroes—the heraldry, the burnished armor, the laurel crown? Where is the honor due him?
>
> Maximus comes as a slave.
>
> That's the premise of *Gladiator*. Through a maze of events, Maximus goes from celebrated warrior, favorite of one emperor, to despised traitor, nemesis of another. He becomes a fugitive, then caged slave, then unvanquished gladiator. His growing fame in the arena brings him to the sports pinnacle: Rome's magnificent Colosseum to face her elite warriors. They are marched out a dark passageway into brilliant sunlight and met with a roar of bloodlust.
>
> Maximus, their leader, shouts to the men: "Stay together!" He assembles them in a tight circle in the center of the arena: back to back, shields aloft, spears outward. Again he shouts, "Whatever comes out of that gate, stay together!"

What comes out of the gate is swift and sleek and full of terror. Chariot upon chariot thunders forth. Warhorses pull with deadly agility and earthshaking strength wagons drawn by master charioteers. Amazonian warrior princesses ride behind and with deadly precision hurl spears and volley arrows. One gladiator strays from the circle, ignoring the order, and is cut down. Maximus shouts once more: "Stay together!"

The instinct to scatter is strong. But Maximus exerts his authority and they resist that impulse. The chariots circle, closer, closer, closer. Spears and arrows rain down on the men's wooden shields. The chariots are about to cinch the knot. Right then Maximus shouts, "Now!"

The gladiators attack and decimate the Romans. Whatever comes out of that gate, stay together.[3]

These words echo the words of Scripture. Jesus prayed on the eve of His crucifixion that we would be one (John17:23). Paul warned us to watch out or we will be destroyed by each other (Galatians 5:15).

How ridiculous for an army to fight each other rather than the enemy. How crazy to have two soldiers in the foxhole who are trying to kill each other. It happens. Satan loves to divide and conquer. The longevity of organizations, families, sports teams, churches, and even gladiators is determined by the ability to harness the group into a unified front against an opponent. Family, friends, and teams must bring their shields together into a defensive wall and attack the enemy in concert.

The forces of hell will be thrown at us, especially during hardship and the storms of life. The temptation is to gossip, fracture, isolate, take sides, or fight...but the call is to know you are in a war, know who the enemy is, know the enemy's tactics, know God's power, and no matter what comes out of Satan's gates, stay together.

Part Four
Kingdom Building

Chapter 14

Be Dangerous

It has been more than sixty-five years since the Nazis hanged Dietrich Bonhoeffer for his attempt to overthrow Adolf Hitler. You have to wonder how the church of Luther, by and large, capitulated to the hellish, ghastly ways of Hitler. The answer, of course, is one small step at a time.

Prior to the Fűhrer rising to power, liberal Christianity, or "cheap grace" as Bonhoeffer coined it, was normative. No confession. No repentance. No discipleship. It is sad when there is no Christ in Christianity. It wasn't politically correct for a Jewish Jesus to be an Aryan hero. In 1930s Germany, a crucified Jesus was replaced with a Fűhrer, the Bible with *Mein Kampf*, and faith with secular totalitarianism. Bonhoeffer and a remnant (named the "confessing church") called for a "costly grace." Dietrich, at age thirty-nine, put it, "When God calls a man, He bids him to come and die." In standing up for the Jews, Christ, and sanity, these courageous Christ-followers were on a collision course with Hitler, and many paid the price.

Surveys show that the great majority of Americans are pessimistic about the future of America, and many think we are in store for some really bad times. You have to wonder, "What if?" What if one day we lived under a dictatorship where those who disagreed with the state are killed? How would we live? How would I? Would we live as Dietrich Bonhoeffer did, even if it meant paying the ultimate price?

God calls us, His followers, to take whatever hell throws at us. With guts and courage, the call is to venture into the danger zone, pain or no pain. Jesus trained His disciples to this high and holy calling.

Go

Jesus called His twelve (Matthew 10:1-4). He delivered the marching orders and outlined the risks. "Preach...heal the sick, raise the dead, cleanse the lepers, cast out demons" (Matthew 10:7-8). In other words, go to the diseased, the dying, the despised, and the dangerous. This is not the assignment we Americans are used to hearing, especially on our first venture, but this is how Jesus broke in His new recruits.

He calls us to go where the needs are, no matter what.

Go to Danger

Jesus said, "Behold, I send you out as sheep in the midst of wolves" (Matthew 10:16a). Imagine the look on the faces of the disciples. Sheep among a pack of wolves licking their chops is not a pretty picture, is it? Jesus was telling His recruits and you and me, "You will have assignments in dangerous places at times. Don't be surprised! It will seem crazy. You'll be way out of your comfort zone; but this is what it means to be My disciple."

David Platt, in his book *Radical,* writes on Jesus' call to go to danger:

> We don't think like this. We say things such as, "The safest place to be is in the center of God's will." We think, if it's dangerous, God must not be in it. If it's risky, if it's unsafe, if it's costly, it must not be God's will. But, what if these factors are actually the criteria by which we determine something is God's will?...What if the center of God's will is in reality the most unsafe place for us to be?"[1]

Jesus' teaching raises some profound questions for all of us. Are we willing to go? Are we willing to go out of our comfort zone? Are we willing to go into dangerous places? Of course, the courage to risk needs to be balanced with the wisdom to discern a call.

There is an old story about a man who appears before the pearly gates:

> "Have you ever done anything of particular merit?" St. Peter asks.
>
> "Well, I can think of one thing," the man offers. "Once I came upon a gang of high-testosterone bikers who were threatening a young woman. I directed them to leave her alone, but they wouldn't listen. So I approached the largest and most heavily tattooed biker. I smacked him on the head, kicked his bike over, ripped out his nose ring and threw it on the ground, and told him, 'Leave her alone now or you'll answer to me.'"
>
> St. Peter was impressed. "When did this happen?"
>
> "A couple of minutes ago."

Discernment is always needed between faith and foolishness. Jesus made this abundantly clear with these words to be street-smart, not gullible, not living with our heads in the sand. He said, "Therefore, be shrewd as serpents and harmless as doves" (Matthew 10:16b).

Paul was willing to be dangerous. One time (Acts 21:9-14) a prophet took Paul's belt and tied his own hands and feet like he was a roped steer. "This is what will happen to you, Paul, if you go to Jerusalem," he said. Everyone tried to convince Paul not to go. You can picture Paul saying, "Thanks for the visual aid, but I'm more than willing to be bound like an animal or killed for the gospel. Now give me back my belt."

In 1956, missionaries arrived in Ecuador to take the gospel to the tribe with the highest homicide rate of any group in history. The missionaries were:

- Nate Saint, age thirty-two
- Jim Elliot, age twenty-nine
- Roger Youderian, age thirty-one
- Pete Fleming, age twenty-seven
- Ed McCulley, age twenty-eight

Note the ages of these men and their deep convictions:

"Every time I take off I am ready to deliver up my life." – Nate Saint

"I owe to God. I would give my life for that tribe." – Pete Fleming

"He is no fool to give up that which he cannot keep to gain that which he cannot lose." – Jim Elliot

On January 8, 1956, all were confirmed dead. Their blood paved the way for the tribe to be reached for Christ. Danger didn't stop them.

Go and Be Persecuted

Jesus explained, "And brother will deliver up brother to death, and a father his child; and children will rise up against parents and cause them to be put to death. And you will be hated by all on account of My name" (Matthew 10:22-23a).

Do you think the disciples are perspiring a little more now? Family betraying you...friends becoming your enemies? There is a price to be paid for following Christ. This reality was shared years later with the disciples' disciple (Paul): "And indeed, all who desire to live godly in Christ Jesus will be persecuted" (2 Timothy 3:12)

Persecution may come from government, your family, your boss, a friend, or the religious subculture, but one thing is for sure: it will come. In fact, the more our lives conform to Jesus, the more we will be on a collision course with this world system. It goes with the territory of a disciple. If you are looking for a nice, safe, comfortable life, follow these guidelines precisely:

  #1 – Stay away from Jesus
  #2 – Don't think of yourself as a disciple
  #3 – Don't read Matthew 10
  #4 – Settle for cheap grace and routine religion
  #5 – Believe the gospel is simply "God loves you and has a wonderful plan for you."

However, what if biblical Christianity is far different? What if the reality is when you come to Jesus you find He has a difficult plan for your life? What if the call in your future includes suffering in one form or another?

The truth is, over the centuries, persecution has been the norm and not the exception for Christ-followers. Most people don't realize it, but the number of Christians martyred in the twentieth century outstripped the combined number of martyrs in nineteen centuries prior, and there is no sign of this bloodshed ending. We are told that Chinese Christians don't pray for a change in harsh government practices. They assume this is their lot and they can't imagine anything else.

In many parts of the world, persecution means verbal, emotional, and physical hostility that comes from bearing the name of Jesus. In America, persecution often means people saying, "No. I don't go along with that." It may mean being laughed at, passed over for a promotion, fired, rejected by family or friends, or called bigots or extremists.

In our beloved country, storm clouds are rolling. Steve Farrar says:

> When Christians are viewed as "threats," that ought to tell us something.
>
> In a recent poll of leaders across America (business leaders, government leaders, academics, priests, and rabbis, for instance), evangelicals came out the highest as a perceived "threat to democracy." Can you believe that?
>
> Thirty-four percent of academics rate evangelicals as a menace to democracy, compared with only fourteen percent who see any danger from racists, the Ku Klux Klan, and Nazis. So when it comes to the menaces of society you have your Nazis, your skinheads, the Ku Klux Klan, but leading the way are those dangerous Christians. That's why at the recent gay march in Washington, D.C., many of the marchers were shouting, "Bring back the lions." They weren't referring to the Detroit Lions, they were referring to the lions in Rome who would maul and eat the Christians in the Coliseum.

There seems to be a move to give everyone the right to say anything they want – except Christians.[2]

In the earliest centuries of Christianity, followers carved six hundred miles of catacombs beneath the city of Rome to flee persecution, worship secretly, and bury their dead. The catacombs are filled with a fish symbol and the inscription *ichthus,* which in Greek is an acrostic for "Jesus Christ, God's Son, the Savior." During intense persecution, Christ-followers would draw an arc in the sand with a walking stick or their toe. If the other individual drew a second arc opposite the first, forming a fish shape, they knew they could fellowship freely without threat of persecution. Do you realize the little fish symbols on the backs of mini-vans and trucks today are reminders of our Lord and the history of persecution?

Kingdom Safety

These words are encouraging: "Are not two sparrows sold for a cent? And yet not one of them will fall to the ground apart from your Father" (Matthew 10:29).

Our safety is found in the sovereignty of God, not our own protections. The child of God is invincible until the Father is done with him or her! Invincible! Therefore, Jesus says three times, "Do not fear" (Matthew 10:26, 28, 31).

Erwin McManus relates the story of his youngest son coming home from a Christian camp terrified from ghost, demon, and Satan stories. "Dad, please leave the hall light on. And don't shut my door all the way." His son struggled night after night with what might get him when the lights were out. One night the boy asked his daddy to pray that God would make him safe. Erwin said, "I will not pray for you to be safe. I will pray God will make you dangerous, so dangerous that demons will flee when you enter the room." And he goes, "All right. But pray I would be really, really dangerous, Daddy."[3]

In our world full of uncertainty, risk, and bad news, it's easy to live retreating rather than advancing. Risk-minimization colors everything. We choose less involvement in adventuresome activities, deploy the latest in surveillance and communicating equipment, say no far more than yes to our children and employees, and often opt for the comfortable over the risky. There is a lot to fear in our world, but living in fear is no way to live.

It was said of the early church that they "risked their lives for the name of the Lord Jesus Christ" (Acts 5:26). Epaproditus is a standout example of one who was "risking his life" (Philippians 2:30) for the cause of Christ. The word for "risking" is a Greek gambling word (*parabolani*) similar to horseshoes. The word was used more broadly "to risk oneself or to take a chance." This is what Epaphroditus did. In the years following, a group of Christ-followers challenged by Epaphroditus' example would call themselves the *parabolani*, the gamblers, the risk-takers for God, and they stepped into many dangerous situations.

Hudson Taylor, the missionary to China, said, "Unless there is an element of risk in our exploits for God, there is no need for faith." Someone observed, "Consider the turtle: he makes progress only when he sticks his neck out." A poster had the caption, "A ship in a harbor is safe, but that is not what ships are made for."

In baseball, you can't steal second with your foot on first base. You have to venture off the bag, take a lead, risk, and go. If you choose not to risk, you will never get anywhere. C.T. Studd, the great missionary, said, "The gamblers for gold are so many, but the gamblers for God are so few. Where are the gamblers for God?"

Aren't you glad Abraham left Ur rather than hang on to his retirement plan? Aren't you glad Jesus took the risk to come to earth? Is it time you prayed "God make me really, really dangerous, even as I rely upon You and Your armor"?

Kingdom Security

We must always remember, "But the very hairs of your head are all numbered. Therefore, do not fear, you are of more value than many sparrows" (Matthew 10:30-31). Our security resides in the God who knows every inch of us and who loves us profoundly. He takes care of His own. We can live in this supernatural care of the Father.

Yet given the choice of supernatural care and power as described by Jesus versus the power of fame, money, and status, for most it's a no-brainer. Fame, money, and status win every time. Even under the so-called umbrella of Christendom, many opt for the Prosperity Gospel of God-wants-me-healthy-wealthy-and-successful. It is the "vending machine" God and the "divine butler" Jesus.

The Prosperity Gospel is not gospel at all. It is self-centered, manmade, and temporal. The true gospel is trust in the biblical God who gives real security and peace, no matter the circumstances.

Kingdom Satisfaction

You won't find this in Sunday school curriculum: "Do not fear those who kill the body, but are unable to kill the soul; but rather fear Him who is able to destroy both soul and body in hell" (Matthew 10:28). There is a high probability that those words won't be included in any new seeker-friendly preaching series.

Yet Jesus boldly says to His disciples, who face great threats and challenges, "Don't fear people...the worst thing they can do to you is kill you."

What? Read it again; this is exactly what Jesus declares. You say, "I could never go on a mission trip or go to the inner city. I might get killed!"

Jesus says, "That's all?" Obviously, Jesus is saying this to comfort us, but how can this be so? It is only possible if:

- We fear God – not men
- We have already died with Christ
- We realize that death really is a gain

Consider this:

> John Paton (1824-1907) served 10 years in a Scottish church, but God began to burden his heart for the New Hebrides, a group of Pacific islands filled with cannibalistic peoples and no knowledge of the gospel.
>
> He set his heart on one island in particular. Twenty years earlier two missionaries had gone to that island. They were killed and cannibalized. So it was no surprise that many dissuaded Paton from even the thought of following in these missionaries'

footsteps. Paton wrote, "Amongst many who sought to deter me, was one dear old Christian gentleman, whose crowning argument always was, 'The Cannibals! You will be eaten by Cannibals!'"

John Paton replied to this man, "Mr. Dickson, you are advanced in years now, and your own prospect is soon to be laid in the grave, there to be eaten by worms. I confess to you, that if I can but live and die serving and honoring the Lord Jesus, it will make no difference to me whether I am eaten by Cannibals or by worms; and in the Great Day my resurrection body will arise as fair as yours in the likeness of our risen Redeemer."

The old man left the room, exclaiming, "After that I have nothing more to say!"

At the age of thirty-three, John Paton traveled to the New Hebrides with his wife. The journey was not easy. His wife and newborn child died within months after arriving, and he found himself alone, digging their graves with his bare hands. He faced threat after threat upon his life. But in the years to come, countless cannibals across the New Hebrides came to know the peace of Christ, and the church across Australia, Scotland, and the Western world was challenged to rise up and make the gospel known among the peoples who were toughest to reach.[4]

Our world today pushes us to taste, touch, dream, put down stakes, cling, and focus on the here and now. Jesus reminds people of faith of another reality:

"To desire a better country, that is a heavenly one" (Hebrews 11:16a).

"To live is Christ, to die is gain" (Philippians 1:21).

We are pilgrims, just passing through. This is not our home; the best is yet to come. Those who take some risks are not scared by the thought of heaven. May eternity be burned into our eyeballs. May we be so heavenly minded that we are of a great earthly good.

Think of Dietrich Bonhoeffer. In reality, his hanging was not a tragedy but rather a reward. As he said before he died, "This is not

Disaster

the end but the beginning." He closed his eyes on this side and he woke up and was home. He instantly saw the face of Jesus and the nail marks in His hands. Certainly, this servant heard a "well done my good and faithful servant." Bonhoeffer did not go from the land of the living to the land of the dead. He went from the land of the dying to the land of the living! In his dying, this martyr inspired countless others to take up the cross and follow Jesus.

You can be sure Bonhoeffer doesn't for a moment regret being obedient to Jesus. He knew that eternal life is to know God and Jesus, as John 17:3 states, "This is eternal life, that they may know You, the only true God, and Jesus Christ whom You have sent."

Eternal life doesn't start in the future. Rather, it starts now where we live under the reign and rule of Jesus and where we live in the sovereignty, security, and satisfaction of the Father. With this conviction, it only makes sense that we risk, obey, and are willing to sacrifice. The disciples caught this perspective. After the resurrection, Jesus' courage spilled out of them and they got dangerous. Peter was dangerous. James and John were dangerous. Stephen too. And all the rest. The kingdom became unstoppable.

In *Foxe's Book of Martyrs*, we discover the fate of Jesus' disciples[5]:

- Peter was sought by Nero. Jerome wrote that Peter was <u>crucified</u> in Rome with his head down and his feet upward because he thought he was unworthy to be crucified the same way as the Lord. Clement of Alexandria writes that prior to Peter's own crucifixion they made him watch his wife being crucified; his words were "Remember the Lord."
- Andrew, brother of Peter, preached the gospel in the Asiatic nations, but at Edessa he was <u>crucified</u> with the ends of his cross fixed transversely in the ground, hence the derivation of the term "St. Andrew's cross."
- James, the older brother of John, was <u>beheaded</u> in Jerusalem by the sword in A.D. 44.
- John, the "beloved disciple," was sent to Rome to be <u>boiled to death in oil</u>. Miraculously, he was not injured. Domitian

Disaster

- <u>banished</u> John to the Isle of Patmos. He is the only disciple to escape a martyr's death.
- Philip ministered in Upper Asia. At Heliopolis he was scourged, thrown into prison, and <u>crucified</u> in A.D. 54.
- Bartholomew preached in many countries, including India. He was beaten and <u>crucified</u>.
- Thomas preached in India and Parthia. He was martyred with a <u>sword thrust</u>.
- Matthew served in Ethiopia and Parthia and was <u>slain with a halberd sword</u> (a shafted weapon with an axe-like blade and a speared end) in Nadabah in A.D. 60.
- James, the son of Alphaeus, was <u>crucified</u>.
- Thaddaeus was killed by <u>arrows</u>.
- Simon the Zealot preached in Mauritania, Africa, and even Britain, where he was <u>crucified</u> in A.D. 74.
- Matthias was <u>stoned</u> and <u>beheaded</u> in Jerusalem.
- James, the brother of the Lord, was thrown from the temple roof, <u>beaten</u> and <u>stoned,</u> and had his brains dashed with a <u>fuller's club</u>.
- Mark was <u>dragged to pieces</u> in Alexandria.
- Luke was <u>hanged</u> from an olive tree in Greece.
- Paul was <u>beheaded</u> with a sword by Nero.
- Jude was <u>crucified</u> at Edessa in A.D. 72.
- Stephen was <u>stoned</u> outside Jerusalem.

These are not the kinds of stories you promote in your recruiting brochure for the movement, but people kept signing up. Tertullian said, "The blood of the martyrs is the seed of the church."[6]

The Reward

Jesus stated, "He who has found his life shall lose it, and he who has lost his life for my sake shall find it" (John 10:39). Revolutionary! Countercultural! Jesus' words defy the word out on the streets as dictated by the American dream and for that matter the standard, generic, "cheap grace" message of many churches.

You want life? Then lose your life. You want life? Then give up finding it in the security, safety, and satisfaction of this world. You want life? Then take up a cross.

Jesus said, "And he who does not take his cross and follow after Me is not worthy of Me" (John 10:38).

In our day, the cross is a piece of jewelry. We forget it was an instrument of torture and excruciating death. Imagine someone today saying, "Pick up your electric chair and follow me." Jesus' words were just as startling and provocative in His day. The Romans had perfected crucifixion to an art form. The first-century historian Josephus records times when the Romans would crucify more than 500 Israelites a day to deter rebellion. There was a road in Palestine called "the way of the cross" where Roman General Varus crucified 1,760 people 30 feet apart for 10 miles. Josephus said there were so many crucifixions they ran out of crosses for the bodies.[7]

What's more, the Romans deliberately left the bodies up on the crosses for days, months, and even years to send a message. Perhaps as Jesus said "take up your cross" He pointed to a skeleton nailed to a cross. Everyone knew what Jesus meant: "Be willing to die."

What a way to start a movement. What a way to attract disciples. Isn't this over the top? Does Jesus really want to mess with our comfortable lifestyles? Can't we soften His words?

Indeed, the Jesus way is different from the way of religion. It's scary how easy it is to substitute religion for following Jesus. Jesus says, "Give me all!" He doesn't say, "Give me a little money, time, and devotion."

Tokenism doesn't count for much with Jesus. The aim is to kill the "self way" and die daily (and voluntarily) to pride, plans, and convenience as a lifestyle. "Follow me," Jesus says, not religious activity, formulas, sin management techniques, etc. In fact, the evidence of being a follower of Jesus is following Jesus. The truth is Jesus doesn't come to take sides. He comes to take over. This is the glorious, impossible, beautiful news of the gospel. Impossible for us, possible through Him!

Will we risk where God leads, even if we face danger, whether in the inner cities, the diseased communities in Haiti, or the hostile regions of China? Will we seek more comforts or greater zeal?

Disaster

Let's not settle for lesser lives than we should and stories not worth telling. Let's choose the higher story. Let's leave the harbor, sail into the ocean waters, take on the storms, and enter the adventure we will not forget or regret—for the glory of God.

Chapter 15

Do Good Deeds

Slowly digest the following data to understand the challenges and realities of our emerging new world:

- The largest Christian church in the world is in Korea
- The second largest is in Nigeria
- The largest Buddhist temple in the world is in Boulder, Colorado
- The largest training center for Muslims is in New York City
- The largest training center for transcendental meditation is in Fairfield, Iowa
- The U.S. leads the industrial world in the percentage of:
    - single-parent families
    - teenage births
    - STDs
    - abortions
    - illegal drug use
    - prison population[1]
- Only 1% of U.S. churches are growing by conversion growth
- 80% of 350,000 churches surveyed in America are in decline
- 1,300 new U.S. churches will open this year
  3,750 existing U.S. churches will close their doors

- Tom Rainer, in the book *The Bridger Generation*, says that 65% of those 53 and older claim to have a personal relationship with Jesus.
  - 35% of those 35-53
  - 15% of those 25-34
  - 4% of those 6-23
  - When do most people trust Christ? 90% before age 18. Extrapolate this out 30 years and we may be like Europe (post-Christian).[2]
- Islam is the fastest-growing religion in the United States
- The fastest-growing ideology is humanism
- The highest number of non-Christians are found in:
  - #1 China
  - #2 India
  - #3 Indonesia
  - #4 United States
- Today, there are "almost twice as many Presbyterians in South Korea as in the United States."[3]
- South Korea sends more missionaries than any country but the United States. And it won't be long before it's #1.[4]
- "Currently over 3,700 Nigerians are serving as missionaries ... in more than 50 countries ... it's becoming a major missionary sending country." America is now a mission field of Nigeria.[5]
- 95% of church ministries in America are for members only. Many churches have no ministries for those outside their congregation.[6]

As you can see, the Christian world today has huge challenges. But they are no bigger than the ones Christ-followers faced in the first century. Those followers turned the world upside down for Jesus Christ.

Let me ask you, why couldn't it happen again? Isn't God still on His throne? Isn't Jesus still building His church? Isn't the Word sharper than any two-edged sword and the Spirit still able? When sin abounds, doesn't grace abound all the more? Shouldn't we pray for revival? Don't you want to be a part of it?

Let's go back to the first century and discover what ignited revival.

A History Lesson

July 19, A.D. 64, was the day Nero, the lunatic Caesar, torched his own city of Rome and turned it into a raging inferno. It was common knowledge among insiders that Nero hated the architectural layout of Rome. Narrow streets and dilapidated structures were embarrassing, and he was consumed with ambition to build a new Rome in the image of the model that his architects designed. But how could it happen unless fate or a well-placed match destroyed the city? Nero torched it.

Incensed, Roman politicians and citizens wanted retribution, and Nero needed a scapegoat to take the heat off his own neck. "The Christians burned Rome," he claimed, and Christians were arrested en masse as rebel-rousing enemies of the state. Christians were herded into the coliseums to face half-starved lions that devoured them to the delight of bloodthirsty spectators who loved the sport. Christians were arrested and dipped in oil and lit up as human torches to illuminate Nero's parties. Words of slander, ridicule, and hate talk occupied the public square. Enemies of Christianity spread rumors that communion services were orgies because they were called "love feasts," and participants were cannibals because they "ate the body and drank the blood of Jesus." Christians were labeled insurrectionists and seen as a threat to the empire because they refused to proclaim "Caesar is Lord." They were called atheists because they refused to worship multiple gods, accused of being haters of mankind for refusing to participate in pagan festivals, and labeled as "the evildoers" (1 Peter 2:12). How could you ever prove you were anything but an evildoer?

Throughout the empire, local government officials would blame Christians for natural disasters and all sorts of troubles, saying, "Christians have made the gods angry. We must get rid of them before judgment comes to all."

These tactics endeared local politicians to Rome and advanced careers. Christianity was officially declared illegal in A.D. 112. Imagine the pressure on Christ-followers. It made the spiritually curious think twice about answering an altar call. Believers were scattered (1 Peter 1:1) in caves, tents, and the catacombs (little tunnels under Rome, originally built for burial purposes). They left behind everything to live in pup tents.

Here's the million-dollar question that Baylor University sociologist Dr. Rodney Stark asks in the subtitle of his classic book, *How the Obscure Marginal Jesus Movement Became the Dominant Religion in the Western World in a Few Centuries.* Think about it. The Christian faith started with 120 followers in the upper room. By A.D. 40, Christians were about .0075% of the Roman Empire. However, Stark calculates that by A.D. 350 there were about 33 million, or 56% of the empire who named the name of Jesus. Christianity colored everything. This is an estimated growth rate of 40% per decade. It's staggering.

Again, the question is how did this persecuted, insignificant, marginalized, often uneducated group of Jesus followers, who were considered vagabonds, gypsies, or members of some cult, turn the world upside down? What accounts for the phenomenon?

Was it money? No.

Was it power? No.

Was it soldiers? Not a one.

Was it weapons? No.

Was it buildings? None existed for two centuries.

Was it an ability to out-argue? No.

Was it seeker-sensitive services, praise bands, or youth groups? No.

Stark concludes that the key to their success was a willingness to sacrifice themselves out of love for others. This sacrifice, such as the following, rocked the world:

- They treated slaves as human beings, sometimes liberating them.

- They elevated women and treated them with dignity.

- They reacted to persecution as martyrs, not terrorists.

- They loved neighbors, as one pagan said, "as if they were family."

- They offered charity and hope to strangers, orphans, losers, and the lame.

- Tradition has it that a Roman government official demanded St. Lawrence, the second-century treasurer of the church, bring forth all the treasures of the church. Lawrence showed up with orphans, widows, the blind, the lame, and the poor and said, "Sir, these are the treasures of the church," for which he was burned on a spit over a bed of coals.

- Emperor Julian despised Christians and tried to establish a pagan charity to rival the Christians' work. He complained in a letter that the pagans needed to equal the virtues of the Christians because their "moral character" and their "benevolence toward strangers and care for the graves of the dead" were causing their growth. He wrote, "The impious Galileans support not only their poor, but ours as well, everyone can see that our people lack aid from us."[7]

- Clement in A.D. 95 wrote, "We know of many among ourselves, who have delivered themselves into slavery in order to ransom others." Imagine you are a slave with no hope and no dreams. One day the master says, "You are free. Take off your chains. Someone has taken your place!" Clement said it happened many times! Some sold themselves into the salt mines to minister even though they would never see freedom again.

- In A.D. 65 and A.D. 251 massive epidemics killed a third of the population each time. Imagine in our day 100 million Americans dying of an epidemic that we had no control over. Imagine the hysteria. Imagine how people would be tempted to look out for themselves. The ancient writer Dionysus said of the fear this generated, "They pushed sufferers away and fled from their dearest, throwing them in the roads before they were dead and treated unburied corpses as dirt, hoping to avert disease." But when others fled, Christians nursed the sick and buried the dead, despite risk to their own lives. Many became Christians after they were nursed back to health. When family members who fled the disease returned to the cities and found their loved ones alive and well, it increased admiration for the faith. People remember those who treat them well in the worst of times. Historians say that the response of the early church to the epidemics and to other disasters like earthquakes, famines, floods, riots, and civil wars played a huge role in the spread of the Jesus Way in the ancient world.

- In the ancient world, infanticide was the most popular form of birth control. In one Roman pipe-well ninety baby skeletons were found inside. Roman law permitted moms and dads with unwanted babies to leave them in garbage dumps outside of town to die. Early Christ-followers rescued these babies and raised them as their own. Was it better to be born a boy or a girl in the ancient world? A boy. One historian declares: "Exposure of unwanted female infants (the practice of just abandoning them until they would die outside somewhere) was legal, morally accepted, widely practiced by all social classes in the Grecian Roman world. Notice the note a first-century Roman husband wrote to his pregnant wife: 'Know that I am still in Alexandria. I beg you to take good care of our baby son. If you are delivered of a child before I come home, if it is a boy, keep it. If it is a girl, discard it. You have sent me word, "Don't forget me!" How could I forget you? I beg you not to worry.'"[8] This Roman would think of himself as a good family man. That's the world in which Christ-followers stepped up and modeled that all life is sacred and prized. No one should be discarded. Furthermore, both male and female are one in Christ Jesus. Is it any wonder that women flocked to this new way, the Jesus Way?

- The ancient Roman world was very hierarchal and strictly divided into classes of people. The pecking order looked like this:

    Roman Senate
    Equestrian – wealthy and powerful
    Decurion – some wealth
    Citizens – had rights as Romans
    Free People – former slaves
    Slaves

Everything in the society was built around this caste system. Clothes showed what caste you were in. Citizens and up wore a toga. Equestrians and Decurions wore stripes on their togas to show their status. Slaves had to wear a tunic. Imagine a culture where the clothes you wore showed your class. In the ancient world, festivals abounded. At the festivals, guess who ate first? Guess who got the best food? Guess who got the worst food, if there was any left? Among the Jesus people, Equestrians and Decurions learned to serve free people and slaves food, the best food. Imagine an Equestrian washing the feet of a slave. If you were a slave, you were never served a day in your life. However, it was different in the Jesus Way. There was real community. It was transforming. This Jesus grassroots movement became something of irresistible influence. The pagans admired the steadfastness of these Christians to care. Good works were Exhibit A, Exhibit B, and Exhibit C to a watching world. It was unlike anything the world had ever seen, and it drew people by high morals, good citizenship, and sacrificial acts of love. The raging opposition was overcome. Good works won the day over a mocking world.

Persecution

Take this test: True or False...
1. The bloody butchering of Christians stopped with Constantine.

2. Instruments of torture and death – thumbscrews, stakes, and hanging ropes – are but relics of medieval intolerance.
3. Persecution of Christians has almost ended (except perhaps under Communist regimes).[9]

False, false, and false! Persecution has been normative for two thousand years, and it is a contemporary reality. In fact, as we've already mentioned, there were more Christian martyrs in the twentieth century than in any other century. Many missionary organizations train their missionaries in procedures for kidnappings and attacks. In the United States, a good-sized chunk of the media, Hollywood, and the music industry think Christianity is fair game to be mocked and ridiculed. Many Christ-followers are branded as evildoers if any conviction is expressed about Jesus, reproductive or sexual morals, the sanctity of marriage, or views brought to bear in the public square.

Some well-known individuals have stated publicly:

- "Christianity is a religion for losers." (Ted Turner)
- "When you see that fish symbol on the bumper sticker of the car in front of you, know that it is the enemy." (Musician Frank Zappa)
- "From my point of view, I would ban religion completely. Organized religion doesn't seem to work. It turns people into really hateful lemmings and it's not really compassionate." (Elton John)

This is to be expected. No football player goes onto the field and complains, "Hey, they are trying to tackle me! I wasn't expecting this. Time out!" Opposition comes with the territory.

So how do we make a difference and overcome our "evildoer" image? Peter gives us a clue: "Beloved, I urge you as aliens and strangers to abstain from fleshly lusts which wage war against the soul. Keep your behavior excellent among the Gentiles, so that in the thing in which they slander you as evildoers, they may on account of your **good deeds**, as they observe them, glorify God in the day of visitation" (1 Peter 2:11-12).

Disaster

The strategy: GOOD WORKS ... for even when the world stops listening to you, they will still watch you. Over time the visual aid helps people see the "Jesus Way" is the right way.

This "good deeds" strategy needs to be understood. There were two key words for "good" in Peter's day: *agathos* and *kalos*.

	Agathos	*Kalos*
Definition	Morally straight Personal righteousness Keeping the rules	Good works Visible, winsome acts Loving expressions
Essence	Good behavior	Good deeds
Function	Credibility	Curiosity Compelling, attractive
Scripture	Idea in 1 Peter 2:12a though *agathos* not used	Word "good" in 1 Peter 2:12b
Result	Not hypocrites	Observed by others Some "glorify God"
Feel	Rules Behaves Does right	Relationship Blesses Forgives those who don't

The word Peter uses is *kalos* and the call is to a life of Holy Spirit-led good deeds. A pagan may respect your morality, but attractive, loving, compelling deeds arouse curiosity among the resistant. When people are:

> ➢ served
> ➢ prized
> ➢ acknowledged
> ➢ listened to
> ➢ given a hand
> ➢ given a few bucks
> ➢ invited to lunch
> ➢ invited to a party
> ➢ given a cup of cold water
> ➢ treated with dignity

Disaster

... God opens up doors! I saw it time and time again in New Orleans. Nobody, regardless of their belief or lack of belief in God, could argue with the kindness, love, and sacrificial giving from those who called themselves Christ-followers.

The opportunity to share Jesus will come. In fact, Peter says, "But sanctify Christ as Lord in your hearts, always being ready to make a defense to everyone who asks you to give an account for the hope that is in you, yet with gentleness and reverence" (1 Peter 3:15). This means we share respectfully, winsomely, graciously, not arguing, not with contempt, or with a know-it-all attitude.

Kalos reminds us that the antagonistic world will probably not be impressed if we keep all the rules and say "darn" instead of "$#*%!" Most won't be impressed if we tithe, attend church four times a week, or can quote the sixty-six books of the Bible. The average pagan won't be impressed at all if we moan, "If only we were a Christian country." We had South Africa and its "Christian government" that required you to be a member of the Dutch Reformed Church to serve in government—and the church defended four million whites oppressing forty million people because they had the wrong color skin! It is tragic, as someone said, "when Christianity exists apart from Christ."

However, pagans will notice if the office really is a better place because Jesus-followers work there, or if the community actually would miss a church if it didn't exist. *Kalos* is the Peter strategy. Outsiders might take a look at Christianity if crime went down because the church worked with troubled teens. Waiters and waitresses might be curious about Christianity if Christians gave good tips and treated busboys with dignity. Businessmen might be curious if Christian executives were famous for their generosity and the creation of positive work environments.

Consider:

- Like it or not, we are "living epistles" read by all men.
- You may be the only commercial some people see.
- I'd rather see a sermon than hear one any day. I'd rather someone walk with me than merely tell me the way.
- People don't go where the action is, they go where love is.

- People don't care how much we know until they know how much we care (Floyd McClung).
- You know 90 percent of evangelism is love (Dr. Bob Smith)
- Love is "the final apologetic" (Francis Schaeffer)
- "A new commandment I give to you, that you love one another, even as I have loved you, that you also love one another. By this all men will know that you are My disciples, if you have love for one another" (John 13:34-35).
- Preach the gospel at all times; if necessary, use words.
- "Let your light shine before men in such a way that they may see your good works and glorify your Father who is in heaven" (Matthew 5:16).
- Let everyone see your good deeds (Matthew 5:16).
- Love your enemies, do good to them (Luke 6:31-35).
- It is more blessed to give (Acts 20:35).
- Overcome evil with good (Romans 12:20-21).
- Do good to all people (Galatians 6:9-10).
- Created to do good works (Ephesians 2:10).
- Do not grow weary of doing good (2 Thessalonians 3:13).
- Be rich in good deeds (1 Timothy 6:17-19).
- Engage in good deeds (Titus 3:8).
- Be eager to do what is good (Titus 2:11-14).
- Spur one another to love and good deeds (Hebrews 10:24).
- Be eager to do good (1 Peter 3:13).

A while back, as I sat in a Jacuzzi at a community pool, two guys stepped into the calming waters. All of a sudden one said that a friend of theirs had become a Christian, and they both broke out in laughter. The other said, "We're just going to watch him and see if it's for real. You know your actions speak so loud I can't even hear what you're saying."

That is instructive! I silently prayed that the new Christ-follower would practice *kalos*. Ours is an age of suspicion and cynicism. Everyone is selling, hyping, or spinning something. People have gotten burned too many times, so their defenses are up, even when it comes to spiritual things. *Kalos* breaks down the barriers.

At Trinity Church, teams have gone out two by two or five by five. Armed with truckloads of mops, the "bleach brigade" descended upon homes. Armed with a shoulder to cry on, women served in the free store. Armed with chainsaws and Bobcats, work crews cleared away. Armed with crayons and animal crackers, childcare workers freed up moms and dads to go to work. Armed with medical supplies and juice, our doctor and nurse assisted a hospital staff. Armed with truckloads of supplies, our drivers restocked orphanages, shelters, and churches. Day by day people asked, "Why are you doing this? Who are you? Who do you represent?"

The answer is Jesus. It is *kalos* time.

Christ-followers are often at their best when they are in the shadows, quiet, humble, and underground as they go about their stealthy acts of service, all while expecting nothing in return. These expressions of compassion usually don't grab the headlines, but they lead to changed lives. The weapons of the Jesus kingdom are brooms, rakes, visits, listening ears, open hands, and generous hearts. We are an army of bridge builders and love extenders. What evangelistic packages, intellectual arguments, political know-how, cultural relevancy, professional presentations, and good sermons can't produce, love has produced. Love has proven to be the indispensable element.

Chapter 16

Ripples

Only God could conceive a plan to drop a cannonball into a pond to create ripples in every direction. The cannonball impact point was New Orleans, and ripples went out nationwide through nearly twenty thousand volunteers.

Contagious Christ-followers were afflicted with Jesus' heart of compassion, and it created an irresistible influence that is still impacting the Gulf region.

The bigger story is that this ripple effect can happen in any church and community across our country through a revolution of compassion and service. Volunteers realize quickly that ministry is not rocket science and that it can be a way of life. God's ripples are people making visible the invisible kingdom for the glory of God. This is people getting outside the four walls of the church. It's servants who don't want to just go to church but want to *be* the church—to get out of the pew and put feet to faith.

Here is a sampling of the stories that ripple from New Orleans across the country:

>West Shore Evangelical Free Church in Mechanicsburg, Pennsylvania, has sent many wonderful volunteers our way. While speaking at their mission's conference, I heard how they were bringing compassion to their neighborhood through a life-giving Saturday. The goal is one thousand adults, youth, and children from West Shore "flowing deep and wide" into

their community by performing acts of service directly with people in the community. Their motto: "The Church has left the Building." Their theme verse, 1 John 3:18: "Let us not love with words or tongue ... but with actions and truth." They have over sixty project opportunities including outdoor/building cleanup, construction with Habitat for Humanity, food drives, gardening, music at nursing homes, kids outreach, cooking at soup kitchens and shelters, carnivals/parties in the inner city of Harrisburg, help at private homes of seniors and the needy, etc. All of this will be done in the name of Jesus and is designed as an annual event. This isn't a ripple but a tidal wave (www.becominglikejesus.org).

Evangelical Free Church in Hershey, Pennsylvania, has sent hundreds of volunteers to New Orleans. Upon returning home, some of these volunteers dreamed up a compassion support ministry. Requests come into the church and volunteers are deployed. Amazingly, one team member's heart was so touched on our super Friday in New Orleans that she went home, sold her nice, safe house in the suburbs, and moved into inner-city Harrisburg. She says, "God put the wheels in motion and I'm coming along for the ride." Ripples!

A volunteer from Hershey was out on a project near the French Quarter when he was approached by a heroin addict who said, "Give me some money." The response was, "I don't have any money, but I can tell you about the love of Jesus Christ." The man responded, "I'm an addict. I'm not interested in that." The volunteer responded, "I'm an addict who has been changed." The man wasn't interested, but the friend with him was. He said, "I've been in thirteen rehabs and they haven't worked." The gospel was shared and this man was referred to nearby Castle Rock Church. The story doesn't stop there. The volunteer, amazed by the boldness fueled in his heart for evangelism, returned to Hershey, and his pastor asked him to start a Celebrate Recovery ministry to help people with hurts, hang-ups, and habits. A year later, Rising Hope was founded, and it has been growing on a monthly basis. The volunteer said, "Praise God

Disaster

that He can use an addict like myself as an instrument to lead people to Christ." Ripples!

Christ Community Church in Waseca, Minnesota, started a Loving Through Serving ministry. Requests come into the church office and twenty volunteers are deployed one Saturday morning a month. Retired volunteers handle jobs during the week. These teams handle moving people, yard work, painting fences, gutting a basement that flooded, etc. Ripples!

Milica Evangelical Free Church in Minnesota had men return from Louisiana who didn't want to stop their ministry. They started a Helping Hands ministry. Requests from the community come in for snow shovels, painting, home or auto repairs, etc. Needs are matched to volunteers based on gifts and abilities. Ripples!

Crystal Lake Evangelical Free Church in Illinois started a HUGS ministry (Hearts United in God's Service) after returning from Trinity. They have done house makeovers and helped widows. Ripples!

Discovery Hills Church in California sent eight people last year, and they came back to their church and "testified on wings of the Holy Spirit" as to what God had done in their lives. One man was so touched he said, "The rest of my life I'm going to reach out to the community." The church started a ministry called "Discover your wings – reach out in God's love. Find a need and meet it." Ripples!

Valley Church from California returned home from New Orleans and spawned a compassion ministry called TouchLocal. Their pastor and teams designed this compassion ministry "to encourage Valley volunteers to reach out to their neighbors – to encourage them to a relationship with Christ and to get them into a nearby 'solid' church." The mission verses are James 1:17, 2:18 and Galatians 6:10. They call themselves the "James Gang" and have T-shirts, a logo, and business cards. The leadership team includes three directors and eight foremen. The three directors divvy up the responsibilities between organizing workdays, administration, and oversight. Workers turn out for a Saturday breakfast and go out to a project. Homeowners pay for the mate-

Disaster

rials for the projects unless the family meets a benevolence criterion. Projects get an interesting name to pique interest in the bulletin and website, and a photographer chronicles the projects. The church is accumulating tools and supplies and has a wiener wagon for the projects. The monthly projects have had between fifteen and sixty volunteers and meet the fourth Saturday of the month. Many home groups and the men's ministry are getting tied in. Projects have included a kitchen remodel, ministry to families of deployed soldiers at the local Air Force base, projects with the Alpha Crisis Pregnancy Center, and an inner-city park cleanup. They are tying in with the local disaster preparedness agency.

Their report is that "God is absolutely just a-heapin' blessings on us and we're loving it" ... "What is thrilling and exciting is that people come up and ASK me when the next work day is!" ... "God is good ... and you can bet the farm on that!" One of their leaders concludes this way, "What is currently exciting and gratifying and captivating me right now is this new and wonderful ministry. I can actually serve in my community! A dream I've had for years. It **never** occurred to me that it would surface in this venue. I'm learning, growing, doing ... being. And, I LUV it! It's a ministry that regenerates itself throughout our church – how cool is that!" Ripples!

One church told me how they went home from Trinity and started a Compassion Ministry to orphans and widows. On the third Saturday of the month a team goes out and ministers in practical ways. Get this – once they adopt an orphan or widow, it is for *life*. Each adopted person is visited at least once a month by at least one person on the team. This sounds like part of true Christianity as James 1 describes it. Another church leader told me his group has been set on fire with compassion ministry. Their goal is to go back home and complement the strength of their church in vertical worship and horizontal love inwardly, with a new outward focus. Ripples!

Compass Church (formerly Evangelical Free Church of Naperville) launched a compassion ministry called TouchLocal to give people the opportunity to serve in Jesus' name. Compassion without action is not compassion; it is simply a deep emotion. "When you serve compassionately and don't seek anything in return, actions are so powerful," said Doug Tobin, TouchLocal leader. "Preach the gospel at all times...if necessary use words." The new ministry will focus outside the church and into the local communities. Doug would like to help those who fall through the cracks.

He met with Pastor Dale Hummel about TouchLocal after working for the past three years on mission trips to New Orleans, cleaning up from the devastation of Hurricane Katrina. Doug asked himself time and time again, "Why did God put this in my heart to go there?" It was something he couldn't stop thinking about and couldn't walk away from. He traveled to New Orleans and led teams to reach out to those who lost everything and saw where God was working in unique and powerful ways. The question that kept coming up in his mind was why can't we serve locally like we've done in the Gulf Coast? "That is what this new ministry is all about. It is about the people and not the projects," Doug said. "Jesus came to seek and to save what was lost, so we make a point not to get lost in the work, but the people we are serving." TouchLocal Compassion Ministries is developing opportunities to serve in Jesus' name, building a leadership team, and seeking project leaders and volunteers to serve those in need.[1] Ripples!

A team member from Community Evangelical Free Church in Harrisburg, Pennsylvania, returned from New Orleans and said to our church elders, "We need a ministry like what is going on in Louisiana right here in our church." They agreed. They prayed for months, and on September 13, 2006, Partnering with a Purpose, better known as PWAP, was born The mission of this ministry is to scatter seeds in the community through simple acts of love and kindness. It has begun as an outreach to an elementary school, partnering with the school to identify children and families who have basic needs that can be met by the church. The leader said, "This ministry will continue as long as I have breath or HE RETURNS" (www.communityfreechurch.org). Ripples!

One church, while practicing good deeds, hands out a little Ripple Effect card that has the church's name and this quote: "What we do here today will echo into eternity." As one volunteer wrote, "We tell them the reason we wanted to serve them was to show that we care and that Christ loves them. We never take money for our service, and we never try to get them to come to our church. There are no strings attached. We just want people to experience the power of serving. Then we encourage them to create a ripple effect by serving someone else in their life." Ripples!

TouchGlobal Crisis Response Center in New Orleans

I'm absolutely convinced that God chose to raise up a disaster response ministry from the rubble of the Katrina disaster. Over many years, leaders of the Evangelical Free Churches of America, like President Bill Hamel and Jim Snyder, prayed that one day there would be an International Crisis Response Ministry.

When Katrina hit, we talked briefly about this dream. The need was great but the opportunities were greater. The problem was that no one seemingly had a "game plan." I never had a "disaster response" class in seminary. Likewise, my extensive pastor's library didn't have one resource that would get us started in the right direction. Whatever was going to happen would be made up one day at a time. We decided we would "bet the farm on God" and ask Him to show up. He did.

Disaster Response Teams

One of the first volunteers to arrive on the scene was an energetic, highly effective young leader named Mark Lewis. God told Mark to make his way to Trinity Church just after the hurricane hit to help for a few days. As it turned out, God was preparing Mark to move to our community to lead our Crisis Response Ministry, later named TouchGlobal. This wasn't a lucky break for us but rather part of God's master plan. God had been orchestrating this for years.

Years prior to his arrival on the scene in Louisiana, God had been building into Mark and his wife, Denise, a heart for ministry and compassion. Mark's vocation as a project manager in an engineering corporation provided him the skill sets that would prove ideal in leading a disaster response ministry. Denise amazingly had written her thesis on "disaster response" almost five years prior to Katrina and predicted there would be a need within five years. Was it a coincidence that this couple arrived at our doorstep or a divine appointment? I vote for a divine appointment.

Our goal was to learn the lessons God wanted to teach us so we would be able to help other churches in the future. God never wastes a hurt. In fact, through our sufferings, He created the "playbook" for disaster response in the future that will bring great glory to Jesus and extend the kingdom of God.

The Ministry Expansion

TouchGlobal expansion has been fast and furious. The Crisis Response Ministry branched out initially from New Orleans to help communities from Florida to the Midwest in the aftermath of tornados as well as drought communities in North Dakota. We helped flooding victims along the Mississippi and encouraged churches in the aftermath of the fires in Southern California. A complete mobilization center was set up after the hurricane in Galveston, Texas.

Internationally, the ministry established outreaches in China and Peru after their enormous earthquakes, and flood victims received help in Burma and the Philippines. Haiti and Japan are now at the center of major ministry initiatives in the aftermath of their devastation. God continues to do some of His best work in the wake of disasters.

Church planting, evangelism, and compassion ministry opportunities abound around the world. It often seems there is a new disaster every few weeks in the world. TouchGlobal has grown in five short years to become the International Crisis Response Ministry of the Evangelical Free Churches of America. TouchGlobal works with churches not only in the United States but also in Africa, Asia, Europe, Latin America, and the Middle East.

Desperate times such as wars, droughts, pandemics, floods, and hurricanes allow the tangible love of Christ to be shown. The healing salve is applied to physical and spiritual wounds, regardless of ethnicity, religion, or economic class. The International Crisis Response center is now fully operational in Covington, Louisiana. Ripples!

Visit www.efca.org/touchglobal to discover:

- How to send a team to New Orleans or other crisis response centers around the world
- Short-term and long-term opportunities
- Training for short-term teams
- Quick Start Guide to creating a ministry of compassion
- Timely updates on crisis hotspots worldwide.

Future Work

"What medical and educational missions were to outreach and advancing the kingdom of God in the 1800s and 1900s, international business and disaster-hazard response will be in the future," said an international missions director.

Natural and manmade disasters are something everyone is aware of now. The following list reminds us how varied these disasters may be. From 1976-1999, the Federal Emergency Management Agency (FEMA) issued 816 disaster declarations. The disasters continue to increase.

Natural Disasters

- Hurricanes
- Tornados
- Storms
- High water
- Tidal waves/tsunamis
- Snowstorm/hail
- Drought
- Earthquakes
- Fires
- Floods
- Extreme heat
- Volcanoes
- Rock/mudslides
- Typhoons
- Avalanches

- ➢ Wind
- ➢ Mine cave-ins

Technological Disasters

- ➢ Nuclear power plant emergencies
- ➢ Hazardous materials
- ➢ Terrorism
- ➢ Radiological accidents
- ➢ Pandemic diseases
- ➢ Accidents – marine, planes, trains
- ➢ Building and infrastructure collapse
- ➢ Bomb threats
- ➢ Oil spills
- ➢ Contaminated food supply
- ➢ Wars
- ➢ Electrical blackouts
- ➢ Arson
- ➢ Riot/civil disorders

Disasters in the Bible

- ➢ Tornado – Job
- ➢ Building collapse – Luke 13
- ➢ Wars
- ➢ Flood – Genesis 6-9
- ➢ Famine – Acts 11; Genesis 37-50
- ➢ Violence – Luke 10
- ➢ Sickness
- ➢ High water – Exodus
- ➢ Earthquakes – 1 King 19

Disaster Terminology

1. **Rescue** – Rescue from rising waters, fires, collapsed buildings, etc.
2. **Relief** – Initial food, water, shelter, clothing, etc.

3. **Recovery** – Repairs, rebuilding, etc.
4. **Restoration** – Emotional and spiritual.

The Role of Faith-based Organizations

President Bush said, "Because they are closer to the people they serve, our faith-based and community organizations deliver better results than government. And they have a human touch: when a person in need knocks on the door of a faith-based or community organization, he or she is welcomed as a brother or a sister." Franklin Graham noted, "Pastors usually know their community better than government officials do....While the government talks about systems and infrastructure problems, faith-based organizations are able to provide immediate assistance thanks to established relationships with churches on the ground."

I am honored to be part of the emerging conversation on how the church of Jesus Christ will respond with heart and hands to the challenges of our world. I have seen the passion and sense of calling volunteer faith-based people bring to the table. What an opportunity! Churches don't run from problems, they run to them. Churches are the most trusted voice in the community. Long after FEMA, Red Cross, and the National Guard are gone, the church and its thousands of enthusiastic volunteers will aid the impacted in the name of Jesus.

Philosophers, political pundits, news people, and religions of all stripes weigh in on the "why" of these disasters. Perhaps the best apologetic is, "You know, I really don't have a clue on this one. What I do know is how Jesus would respond to such loss, tragedy, suffering, and pain, because four books of the Bible tell how He did just that. We Christ-followers are trying to reach out in His way with hope, grace, help, hands, heart, money, and the message of the cross."

How about you? How do you enter a pool? Big toe dipped into the water very slowly? How about living life in a new way? By faith, attempt a cannonball—of compassion! Sure, water will go flying everywhere. Ripples will go out in every direction. Make a splash with your one and only life for God and people. Keep the "ripples" going!

Disaster

Are you allowing God to rearrange your affections, schedule, and spending habits? Are you open to having your television viewing habits adjusted? Are you willing to participate in a volunteer program, visit a shut-in or hospital room, tutor a child, serve a meal, travel across town or downtown, hold an HIV baby, go on a mission project, attend a rally, or listen to a distraught person? Will you do something kind for a widow, orphan, immigrant, poor person, prisoner, stranger, or the sick in Jesus' name? God will indeed comfort the disturbed and disturb the comfortable.

What you choose to do will RIPPLE into eternity.[1]

Chapter 17

Volunteer Revolution

One day Napoleon looked at a map of China and said, "There lies a sleeping giant. If it ever wakes up, it will shake the world." If we look at those sitting in the pews today as a sleeping giant, we could say, "If we wake up laypeople, they will shake the world." A Gallup survey showed only 10 percent of laymen are active in ministry, while 40 percent said they would like to be involved but have never been asked or don't know how.

I am a wide-eyed dreamer who believes the church of Jesus Christ can change the world. I believe the risen Jesus is the Lion of Judah who makes us more than conquerors. For twenty-nine years I prayed that at least once in my life I would get to see revival, a move of God, and an Acts 2 church in its fullness. Twenty-nine years! I just didn't know it would take a hurricane to bring it about. I have seen the church be the church and live her finest hour. I saw a nice, safe, comfortable, cozy, suburban church become a kingdom mobilization center.

It has all been a "God thing." We didn't make it up. In fact, we often didn't know what we were doing. But God! The Spirit makes streams in wastelands. Jesus brings beauty out of ashes. The Father is the Master of bringing resurrections out of death. We had our share of sorrow at night, but joy came in the morning. The big story is not the storm but what God did in and through the storm.

The thousands of volunteers from forty-two states and seven countries camped out largely in the worship center of Trinity Church. For four years, tents, RVs, trucks, trailers, vehicles, makeshift showers, and outhouses filled the property. People were everywhere, constantly. Picture a myriad of sleeping bags, untidy duffle bags, the buzz of up to three hundred volunteers weekly, and a makeshift cafeteria in a church worship center. It was not pretty, but it was beautiful to behold. Lives were transformed, and that made everything worthwhile.

It's no wonder that in time the ministry became known as "the church of the stained carpet." This was harvest time and so we chose not to shine up the tractor, plant flowers in the garden, or paint the barn. That would come later. It was time to bring in the harvest.

The weapons of this army of love were mops, buckets, bleach, chainsaws, generous hearts, hugs, listening ears, and faith, hope, and love. Tasks included cutting trees, mopping up black mold, delivering food and water, working in a free store, gutting homes, rebuilding projects, delivering medical supplies, and serving hospitals, shelters, mayors, and community leaders. Bridge builders and love extenders cared for lives, limbs, souls, and homes. Volunteers let their light shine before men in such a way that people saw their good deeds and glorified the Father who is in heaven (Matthew 5:16).

Countless people would say, "Who are you and why are you doing this?" The answer was always, "All for the love of the Lord." Good words about the church were circulating everywhere, and people thought, "I've got to check this out. This is what I've been looking for. I've never seen anything like this."

The world was visually seeing the heart and capability of the big "C" church and the little "c" churches. It was breathtakingly good. Everyone saw that it was the faith community that rose to the occasion, not the government or FEMA.

People prayed, oh how they prayed, "God, whatever it takes." Nightly sharing meetings electrified all present. Burning-bush experiences abounded. The stories were endless—it was Acts 29.

Life in many ways was complicated, but in other ways simplicity ruled because people were simply glad to be alive. Many were "dying to self" and allowing the Spirit to guide the rest. This daily surrender creates a love that bubbles to the surface, overflows, and eventually spills out toward others.

I am humbled to serve with people who love God, take risks, pay the price, sleep on floors, ride in stuffy vans, shed the old, embrace the new, understand their calling, celebrate the fruit, and do it all for God's glory. The church of Jesus Christ is being built. I feel like the turtle sitting on the fencepost. When you see this, you know the turtle didn't get there on its own! When you see what God did, you know we didn't do it on our own.

I love the story of the night Michael Jordan scored 69 points in one game. It was a blowout, and at the end of the game the coach pulled MJ and put in a little known sub who scored 2 meaningless points in the closing seconds of play. A few weeks later a reporter asked the sub, "What is the highlight of your professional career?" He said, "The night Michael Jordan and I scored 71 points together."

This is how I feel about what Jesus built at Trinity Church and TouchGlobal. Jesus is doing the work, and it is a privilege to partner with Him in His kingdom.

Volunteers

Volunteers continue to come from everywhere, and I mean everywhere!

College

During spring break, summers, Thanksgiving, and Christmas breaks, we are invaded by young adult volunteers from across the country: Harvard, Boston College, UNC, NCS, Northwestern, Georgetown, Washington State, Trinity, Moody, WBC/Capital Bible Seminary, University of Texas, Georgia, Tennessee, Virginia Tech, and so many more. They are zealous, hardworking, servant-hearted, faith-filled, choice young adults whose enthusiasm is contagious and whose compassion is unmistakable, and they almost never complain. Narcissism gives way to activism.

A new breed of college kids is emerging. One young adult from Canada spoke of finally stepping out of his typical world of computers and video games. He's changed. He's hooked. God used him.

He wants more. These modern-day Daniels, Davids, Marys, and disciples exemplify 1 Timothy 4:12: "Let no one look down on your youthfulness, but rather in speech, conduct, love, faith and purity, show yourself an example of those who believe." If we give young adults a chance, they will rock this world!

Kids and High Schoolers

A girlfriend and boyfriend decided to skip their prom and use the money to come to New Orleans over spring break to gut homes and remove caked mud that Katrina left behind. On their prom night they dressed in formal clothes they already owned, dined on salads, skipped the chauffeured limo, and saw a movie. "Going to the real prom might have been fun, but it doesn't help anyone," Patrick said. The New Orleans visit "benefited not only the people we helped, but also myself as well. It helped me grow strong in three ways: physically, mentally, and most of all, spiritually."

A young girl from Pennsylvania sent out invitations to her birthday party, but in lieu of birthday gifts she asked the guests to give a donation for New Orleans. What heart!

Adults

A seventy-year-old volunteer said, "I have never been on a missions trip my whole life." Her women's group raised money for her to come. She brought plenty of Vicodin and Ben-Gay, yet she made an outstanding contribution to our food services. You should have seen her smile.

A blind woman joined one team. Yes, blind. She went out and gutted homes with the best of them. We've had men in their eighties gutting homes as well. A dad and stepson committed to come and serve together in New Orleans. Tragically, the stepson died in a car accident the week prior to coming. The dad buried the son, and though grieving he still came to New Orleans to serve. He brought his stepson's boots and laid them before the cross located at the front of the church. Utterly inspiring!

A men's group from Chicago cancelled their annual men's retreat, forfeiting their money to serve down South. Many volunteers gave up vacations to help the devastated Gulf Coast. They often drove across the country, slept at a Motel 6, and then with one hundred others slept on our stained carpet after working in the heat all day. They are not crazy. One couple decided to celebrate their twenty-fifth wedding anniversary in New Orleans by serving the needy rather than taking a cruise. Another couple celebrated their tenth anniversary here by giving a week for others.

A woman named Dakota illustrates the compassion and zeal volunteers have to serve God. Dakota had to travel quite a distance on Christmas Day to meet the bus leaving Bethel Church in Fargo, North Dakota. As she traveled on a country road, her vehicle swerved, spun, and then flipped, leaving her semi-conscious, hanging upside-down in her seatbelt. She remained there until the police arrived. The lead policeman wanted to take her to the hospital because she was disoriented. Dakota maintained she had to catch a bus to do relief work in New Orleans. Rescue workers sensed this mission was important. Tow trucks weren't quickly available on country roads on Christmas Day, so the fire department was called to help right the flipped vehicle. Twenty firemen responded to the call and helped get Dakota on the road to catch her bus for the twenty-two-hour ride our way. As Dakota's beat-up vehicle was pulled from the ditch, the firemen promised to call her every twenty minutes as she traveled to Bethel Church to make sure she was all right. Dakota knew God called her to our mission field, and Jesus provided for her once again on Christmas Day. When our volunteers get knocked down, they get right back up. They are unstoppable.

Gene Johnson, a volunteer from Montana, returns time after time. Gene tells about fixing up a home along with a team of volunteers. For two days they labored with chainsaws and a Bobcat to clear a path. They lined the 700-foot driveway with balloons and a banner saying, "Welcome Home, Love Trinity." The homeowner's tears of despair had been turned into tears of joy. Her children said, "You gave my mother's life back to her."

Isn't the kingdom of Jesus worth celebrating? There is nothing like it.

Miracles

A pastor was trying to decide if he should bring his youth group to New Orleans or to Mexico. Would New Orleans be a real mission

Disaster

trip? Would the kids see the Holy Spirit at work? He decided to consult another group that had recently been to New Orleans.

This other team had arrived at their place of work, a home in total disrepair. The people at the door said, "Who are you?"

"We are here to help," came the joyful reply. What a difference this team made. As they built rapport that day, they learned the truth about the homeowners. Before the team members arrived, this hopeless couple had made the excruciating decision to commit suicide. The knock at the door interrupted their plan and literally hope replaced despair.

This story gets better. When the team went back to church that night to look up the records of these folks, their names didn't exist. The team realized they had gone to the wrong house ... or should we say the "right house." God sent them there as His ambassadors. Wow! Divine appointments take place every day in New Orleans.

Life Change

Hundreds of times, volunteers tell us their lives were turned upside down in New Orleans. In losing their lives, they find life. In giving, they receive. In dying, they find they are really living ... some more than they ever have in their entire lives.

- "My heart is sold out to God because of the experience."
- "I've grown more in three days than I have in the last five years. It's all because of the people at Trinity Church."
- An attorney said, "I have thought long and hard about the time we all spent together in Louisiana. With the exception of the birth of my two wonderful children and marrying my beautiful bride, it is the single greatest experience I have ever gone through....It was the most fulfilling thing I have ever done but yet it has left me with the most gaping hunger I have ever had."
- A woman who was so nervous about coming ended up saying, "It has changed my life."
- A man asked us if he one day could have a piece of the "stained carpet" to put in his trophy case as a trophy of God's grace in

Disaster

his life. He wouldn't be the last. Many wanted a piece of the stained carpet to remember where God changed their lives.

- A man named Robert E. Lee took his only vacation days and volunteered. He said, "It changed my life." He asked his wife to come and see the work for herself. She verified, "His life has been transformed." Robert has a great name to work in the South.
- One man said over and over, "I thought I had to go overseas to be a missionary. I can be one right where I live." The light bulb came on. Wow!

Evangelism

Opportunities to share the gospel exploded. One of our church members told us that so many trees had fallen on his property he hired a crew from Texas to do tree removal. They worked long days. Whenever the crew took a break, he would chat with the owner of the company. They hit it off. In fact, the church member repeatedly shared his faith in many practical ways. At the end of the three days it was time to pay up. They hadn't agreed on a price, but he knew it would be high because all paid labor was astronomical in the early days following the storm. (For instance, I had one pine tree on my house and two trees leaning against the house. I hired two guys to get the trees off the house and set them on the ground. The charge: $8,500. That's right, $8,500, for which my insurance company approved a little over two hours' work.) The owner of the Texas company said, "You don't owe me anything. You have hauled away more debris from my life than I have from your yard." They bowed their heads and the man trusted Jesus.

Another church member talked to a newcomer at church, saying, "You are in here thinking you lost everything, but you are about to gain everything." She did because she met the pearl of great price – Jesus! Another volunteer helped a man who declared himself a Jehovah's Witness. The volunteer said, "But are you saved?" The man admitted he wasn't. As the gospel of Christ was shared, God opened his eyes and the power and blood of Jesus saved him.

In time we ended up with a sea of new faces in our service. One man led individuals to the Lord on three different occasions. God opened doors. The fish were biting and conversations of eternal consequence were occurring constantly. We saw darkness get pushed back and lives get changed forever. I was on the edge of my seat wondering what God would do next. This was the thrill of a lifetime, and I had a seat on the 50-yard line. The church was being the church – caring, loving, listening, and courageously sharing Christ. The stories never stopped, and they continue to this day.

The church is being the church. Opportunities are endless. One by one people are being met and helped in the name of the Lord. God is bringing beauty out of ashes. Praise His name.

Chapter 18

Divine Appointments

"For we are His workmanship created in Christ Jesus for good works, which God prepared beforehand, that we should walk in them." – Ephesians 2:10

I'd like for you to take a visit with me back to ancient Ephesus two thousand years ago. This regional capital was a city between two worlds: Asia to the east and the Greek world to the west. It had the greatest harbor in Asia Minor and money flowed. People were opportunistic. The fabulously rich aristocrats controlled the city, but its strength was anchored in the large class of merchants and craftsmen. What stood heads and shoulders above everything else was the fact that Ephesus was the world center for worship of Artemis, or Diana as she was known by the Romans.

Artemis was the smart, ambitious, intelligent fertility goddess. Historians state that one million people would show up at the spring festival that honored her. Artemis' temple was one of the seven wonders of the ancient world, with 70,000 acres of land filled with spectacular reflecting pools and 130 pillars standing 60 feet high. Gold and jewels glistened throughout the temple. The average person did their banking at the temple bank, which was a financial powerhouse. The temple was a cultural epicenter with art shows, plays, dramas, displays of innovations, and societal gatherings.

Disaster

Heraclitus, a Greek philosopher at Ephesus, said, "The morals of the temple were worse than the morals of animals because even dogs do not mutilate each other." The temple of Artemis employed scores of prostitutes, eunuchs, priestesses, and dancers. Artemis was the center of everything. If you got a pay raise, thank Artemis. If you had a baby, it was a gift of Artemis. If you had bumper crops and good health, it was Artemis. If you had bad crops, people wondered what you did to tick off Artemis. If you didn't give thanks to Artemis, or didn't attend the dinner party at her temple, you might lose your job ... your friends ... your family ... your honored positions.

Are you getting a feel for life in Ephesus?

Christ-followers were in the minority big-time. Everything was stacked against them. Yet forty to fifty years later, Ephesus was predominantly made up of Christ-followers, and twenty to thirty years after that, John doesn't mention Artemis at all—not the temple, priests, or pagan practices. The whole thing appears to have become semi-irrelevant.

Why? How? Christ-followers discovered who they were in Christ and apprehended the truth of Ephesians 2:10, that they were God's workmanship, or "handiwork, artwork, masterpiece" (literally, it's the word *poema* from which we get our word "poem"). This word is only used twice in the Bible, here and in Romans 1:20. In Romans, we are told the physical creation is the work of a master artist, thus creation is like a great art gallery. Isn't there something in each of us that marvels at the awe-inspiring beauty of creation and celebrates the master designer? Lightning, a shooting star, or watching the fall leaves change color can take your breath away.

In Paul's letter to the Ephesian Christ-followers, we are told:

- We are God's work
- The Father's poem
- His masterpiece

It's true; you are a real piece of work! God's work! It gets better—just as the Temple of Artemis served as an art gallery for mosaics, marble, sculpture, and statues, God makes art of people. God fashions, molds, bends, and makes people as an amazing potter and artist. God doesn't make mistakes. You are no accident. You are different from a rock, a tree, and a chimpanzee. God took great care in every stroke of the brush with you, every hair, every fingerprint, and every talent given. He takes the parts that get botched up and restores and redeems.

There is a temple in Ephesus made with hands and another temple made by God and indwelt by God. You are to bring God glory through this temple. We are to be a place that touches all of life and points people to the living God. As God's masterpiece, you are here for a purpose. If you wonder why you are still here, why God didn't take you immediately to heaven when you trusted Him, Ephesians 2:8-10 gives the answer, "You are saved **by** grace, **through** faith **for** good works."

Ephesians 2:8-9 tells you *how* you were saved. Ephesians 2:10 tells you *why* you were saved. Yes, we have a God-shaped vacuum in our heart, but we also have a purpose-shaped vacuum in our heart. If you are still breathing air, He has a destiny for you. You are custom designed, one of a kind. His grace is upon you. He will give you whatever you need to get your good works done. God gave David a harp, Moses a staff, Paul a pen, Miriam a song, Gideon a fleece, Peter a nickname, Elisha a mantle, and Mary a manger. Whatever you have, God will use it—house, boat, voice, violin, computer, football ... ripple after ripple after ripple will get started.

God is raising up a whole new generation of valiant warriors to respond to the divine appointments He has prepared for them. Will you seize your destiny and serve uncompromisingly? Champions for Christ live with expectation in serving God's purposes. Don't let negative thinking, apathy, lethargy, fear, or shyness hold you back. Don't let anyone or anything outside of God define who you are. Seize the day. Shake off all excuses and compromises. Don't settle for mediocrity. You are to stand out not as a sore thumb but as a healed one for the glory of God. Inside you are gifts, talents, words, and ideas that need to be released. Love God and love people in these critical hours of world history. Move where the Holy Spirit is, hoist your sails, and enter the adventure.

I'm convinced God wants to use our lives to make a difference in the world. There is a unique plan for you and me. Psalm 138:8

says, "The Lord will fulfill his purpose for me!" We are to seize our destiny and jump into the middle of what God is doing. Awareness of these "divine appointments" can spell the difference between adventurous or lackluster faith.

- Do you realize you were born for "such a time as this" (Esther 4:14)?
- Do you own the truth that "before you were born, God had written in His book your days" (Psalm 139:16)?
- Do you embrace the fact that "good works are prearranged by God for you to accomplish" (Ephesians 2:10)? You don't have to create them or search for them. You only have to be alert and ready to act.
- Do you realize "Greater is he that is in you than he that is in the world" (1 John 5:4; 4:4)?
- Do you wake up and mutter, "Good Lord, it's morning" or do you whisper, "Good morning, Lord. This is the day You have made. I will rejoice and be glad in it" (Psalm 118:24)?
- Do you know God has a unique plan for you (Psalm 138:8)?

I've heard it said there are three groups of people in the world: the few who make things happen, the many who watch things happen, and the majority who don't know what is happening. Someone else said the world can be divided into four groups: the wishbones who wish someone would do something; the jawbones who talk a lot but do nothing; the knucklebones who knock whatever anyone else tries to do; and the backbones who get under the load, do the work, and alter the course of history.

As D.L. Moody sat on a park bench in London one day, a man by the name of Henry Varley came up to him and said, "The world has not yet seen what God will do with and in and through the man whose life is wholly consecrated to him." Moody said, "By God's grace, I'll be that man." God is always looking for a man or woman to stand in the gap.

Think of it, "The eyes of the Lord run to and fro throughout the whole earth to show Himself strong on behalf of those whose hearts are loyal to him" (2 Chronicles 16:9). God is not looking for a strong

Disaster

man or strong woman but someone whom He can be "strong on behalf of."

John Wesley, founder of Methodism said, "Give me one hundred men who love only God with all their heart and hate only sin with all their heart, and we will shake the gates of hell and bring in the kingdom of God in one generation." He also told people, "When you go out to preach, don't worry about how to gain an audience. Get on fire, and people will come to watch you burn!"

The world's strategy is to control through power, influence, money, and ingenuity. God's strategy, His Plan A, is to use the seemingly insignificant. He used a puny shepherd boy named David to slay a giant. He used former slaves to take a promised land. He used twelve unsophisticated young men to inaugurate His church.

> For consider your calling brethren, that there are not many wise according to the flesh, not many mighty, not many noble [in other wards, not the cream of the crop, the beautiful, the credentialed, the successful]. But God chose the foolish things of the world to shame the wise, and God chose the weak things of the world to shame the things which are strong and the base things of the world and the despised ... "that no man should boast before God."
>
> 1 Corinthians 1:26-29

He chose the bottom of the rung, the ones with no bragging rights. He doesn't choose perfect people but the inadequate, the weak and lowly.

God doesn't use stained-glass saints. He uses the unqualified to do the impossible. If you don't believe me, think of the unqualified people God used. If you feel foolish, weak, or ordinary, welcome to the club. The things you think disqualify you actually qualify you. And if you think God couldn't use you after what you've done, think again.

- ➢ Noah – drunkenness and lewdness
- ➢ Abraham – lying, adultery
- ➢ Isaac – lying

- Jacob – extortion, manipulation, deep insecurities, passivity in fathering
- Moses – murder, anger in striking a rock
- Aaron – rationalization, led an orgy around a golden calf
- Rahab – prostitution
- Gideon – low self-esteem and at first little confidence in God
- Samson – lust
- Ruth – an accused Moabite
- David – lady's man, murder, adultery, hands so bloody he couldn't build the temple
- Solomon – polygamist extraordinaire
- Jonah – runaway prophet, hatred of the Ninevites
- Paul – former Christian killer, pride
- Peter – impulsive, braggart, big-mouth
- John – arrogance, anger ("son of thunder")
- Matthew – tax collector, thievery
- Simon the Zealot – terrorism, fiery temperament
- Bartholomew – prejudice, superiority

As Hudson Taylor said, "All God's giants are weak people ... God uses ordinary people with shortcomings and weaknesses who are willing to trust God." I know it sounds upside down, but that's the way it works. If you were to select twelve guys to turn the world upside down, would you have picked the same twelve Jesus picked? Imagine if Jesus submitted the resumes of His twelve to a modern-day HR department. The results might read like the following.

To: Jesus, Son of Joseph. Woodcrafter's Shop. Nazareth
From: Jordan Management Consultants. Jerusalem.
Subject: Staff Aptitude Test.

Thank you for submitting the resumes of the twelve men you're considering for management positions in your new organization. All of them have taken our battery of tests, the results of which we've run through sophisticated computer analyses. We've also arranged personal interviews for each candidate with our psychologist and vocational-aptitude consultant.

It is our staff's unanimous opinion that most of the nominees are lacking in qualifications for the type of enterprise you are undertaking. We recommend that you continue your search for persons of experience and managerial ability and proven capability.

We find that Simon Peter is emotionally unstable and given to fits of temper. He seems far too impulsive to be put in a position of oversight. Andrew has absolutely no qualities of leadership. The brothers James and John place personal interest above company loyalty. And they seem to be impatient with others. Due to this impatience and ambition, they could one day become disgruntled employees.

Thomas demonstrates a questioning attitude that could tend to undermine morale. We feel it is our duty to tell you that Matthew has been blacklisted by the Greater Jerusalem Better Business Bureau.

In closing, one of the candidates shows great potential. He is a man of ability, resourcefulness, and ambition. We recommend Judas Iscariot as your comptroller and right-hand man. All the other profiles are self-explanatory.

Sincerely yours,
Jordan Management Consultants, Jerusalem[1]

It's Energizing

There's a constant buzz that comes with living inside the will of God. It's the helper's high. It's joy in serving Jesus. It's energizing even if you get tired. It's adventure living at its best.

In John 4, Jesus took His initial team on a little cross-cultural training trip to Samaria. At Jacob's well, the boys encounter a Samaritan woman. One good look at her and they think, "Her, a divine appointment? You have to be kidding." Why mess with the mission field on a mission trip, right? Besides, their stomachs are growling and it's lunchtime. The disciples go into town while Jesus has a spiritual feast with this lowly, empty lady whose soul longs for living water. Eventually the disciples return totally oblivious to the movement of God that is afoot, a harvest being picked.

In the meantime, the disciples say, "'Rabbi, eat.' But He said to them, 'I have food to eat that you do not know about.' The disciples therefore were saying to one another, 'No one brought Him anything to eat, did he?'" (John 4:31-34) Can't you hear Jesus sighing right here? I'm guessing it's Peter doing the talking. They don't get it. Jesus said to them, "My food is to do the will of Him who sent Me and to accomplish His work" (John 4:31-34).

Jesus was making a profound statement that went right over the disciples' heads, and maybe yours and mine also. You could substitute the word "energy" for food. The right food gives energy. The right food is entering into the will of God. Jesus just had a steak dinner and His disciples had a skinny hotdog (you get the point).

What is your food? What makes you feel most alive? What gives you the highest buzz? Jesus says there is nothing like entering the redemptive drama, living the spiritual adventure through obeying God. It is the ride of a lifetime. It's pure energy.

It's Adventurous

One day, Jesus decided to take His apprentices on a fieldtrip to Caesarea Philippi (Matthew 16:13). It's easy to skip over this geography. When a good Jew heard the words "Caesarea Philippi," all lights would begin to blink on the dashboard. You didn't go there if you were a good Jewish boy or girl. Caesarea Philippi was the world headquarters for the worship of the Greek god Pan. Pan was half goat and half god, a nasty creature to be sure. People from all over the world traveled to this destination. There was a cliff with a giant crack from which Pan-followers believed the spirits of hell would come and go from the earth. The crack was known as the "Gates of Hell." A temple to Pan existed at the base of the cliff, and pagan rituals in the courtyard consisted of unspeakable acts with goats.

Imagine Jesus taking these good Jewish boys, some teenagers, to the ledge of this cliff, twenty-six miles from Galilee. Trust me, their families never took a summer camping trip to Caesarea Philippi. Imagine the disciples thinking, "If our parents find out, we're busted..."

Jesus gives a little pop quiz. "Who do people say that I am? ... Who do you say that I am?" Jesus' response to Peter's declaration that He was the Messiah: "Upon this rock I will build my church and the Gates of Hell shall not overpower it." In other words, upon this Rock (Christ) I will build communities of faith, and the gates of hell (like the one right over there at Pan Headquarters) won't stop Me. The church of Jesus won't be stopped by goat movements, the powers of darkness, or anything else. The church is advancing here – not hell.

This is not a call for the church to be a fortress defending weak saints from wolf packs. Nor are we to be independent Holy Huddles building goofy subcultures. Rather, the picture here is of people trapped in confusion, fear, and sin and Christ-followers going after them. It's a call to go in love. It's believing that the gates of hell are not a threat to us. We have been held hostage at the "gate" point for too long. It's high time we push off the intimidation and get into the game. This is a call to play offense and get outside the walls of the building. It demands remembering that life is too short and hell is too hot to play church. It's a call to adventure.

Jesus' disciples never forgot this day, and neither will you when you choose to step out. If Jesus could take His disciples to the most pagan, secular, sexually avant-garde, spiritually broken city in the world, wouldn't He call us to places where sin gets excused, kids are forgotten, people are confused, the Bible is unknown, and God's love isn't embraced? This is the gates of hell. It's where Jesus says, "Follow Me."

Do you want to come? Are you willing? Are you willing to be made willing? This is where the adventure is. Are you willing to join the adventure and be part of something bigger than yourself?

Perhaps the greatest gift we can give to some Christ-followers today is this sense of adventure. Far too much of what we do as Christians is about do's and don'ts, duty and how-to's—but where is the adventure? Living on the edge is met with raised eyebrows. One time Mark Buchanan was speaking at a camp:

> I held up two video cases for a group of about seventy teenagers to see. One was the case for the first Indiana Jones movie, where the archaeologist-adventurer goes flinging across continents, brawling with a host of rivals and enemies, swimming

oceans and scaling stone walls, in a race to find and take the ark of the covenant. The cover had a picture of Indiana's sweat-soaked face, a cut wet with blood across one cheek. Around him were pictures of a Nazi villain, a hooded cobra, a ship under siege.

The other video cover showed a sewing machine with a swatch of cloth clamped beneath its chrome foot. The swatch was rough-hewn on one side, neatly stitched on the other. It was a training video for using the machine.

I asked the young people, "When you look around at churches today, which of these videos would you say best captures the essence of the Christian life?"

Every single one of them said the sewing machine training video.[2]

May adventure be restored ... for Jesus' sake ... for the kingdom's sake ... for our soul's sake.

Do You Get it?

Periodically, when speaking to a group, I'll try to gauge whether they personally own the truths in this book with a diagnostic question.

"How many of you are in full-time service for Jesus Christ?" I ask.

People look at me and the wheels start to turn mentally. The pastor and missionary types in the room immediately put up their hands, then a few committed laypeople. Many look confused about whether to raise their hands. Then I clarify: "I didn't say how many of you are in full-time vocational Christian ministry, but how many of you are full-time for Jesus Christ?"

People smile. The light comes on. Many more put their hands in the air.

I want to blow up the myth that only a few pastor types are full-time for Jesus Christ. The day you trusted Christ, you got a full-time ministry contract for Jesus. You are "a plain clothes agent in the Jesus Revolution – the only revolution that will ultimately be successful."[3] Royal blood flows through your veins, and you have an inheritance that makes Bill Gates' money look like petty cash. You are a kingdom player, pulsating with the life of the Spirit. Fasten your seatbelts and live.

I love it when I see a church bulletin that reads:

Ministers: The Entire Congregation
Staff: (a few names are listed)

I've got a secret longing for each of you reading this book. I would love to have you stand to your feet in front of a gathering of your family and friends and say to you, "It is my privilege to ordain you to the ministry." After a prayer, all would celebrate your calling and full-time status. You are gifted, connected to the Vine, Jesus Christ, and His grace flows through you. Divine appointments await!

Could it be that we are in the midst of a second reformation? The first Reformation involved getting the Scriptures into the hands of the laity. The second reformation is getting the ministry into the hands of the laity. If necessary, may this chapter be your burning bush, a defining moment to full-time service for Christ. This could change everything. Don't let your life slip by without seeing God show Himself mighty on your behalf.

Do You Have 'Eternity Thinking'?

Draw a line with an arrow in each direction.

The line represents eternity. There is no beginning or end. Within eternity is your life here on earth, represented by the small dot in the center. Looking at the line you would have to conclude that your life is indeed very short. Eternity is *very* long.

We need to live life in light of the line and not in light of the dot. We need to live in light of eternity.

Epilogue

God Doesn't Play Dice

God has a way of strategically positioning us to be in the right place at the right time. Call it providence. Call it divine appointments. Call it sovereignty. This is a God-thing, and this perspective changes the way life is lived. Acts 17:26 says, "From one man He made every nation of men, that they should inhabit the whole earth: and he determined the times set for them and the exact places where they should live." Count on it, our chronology and geography are ordained by God.

Now it's certainly possible that being in the right place at the right time may feel like the wrong place at the wrong time. When we get pushed out of our comfort zone or go through hard times, it can seem like that. Yet often God uses hard times or closed doors to transition us from one place to another or cause us to consider other options.

I have pondered the sovereign hand of God in bringing me to New Orleans for such a time as this. For most of the first forty-one years of my life, I lived in the Washington, D.C., area. All of our family and friends resided there, and our plan was to stay local. But after I finished my doctoral program at Dallas Seminary my plan fell apart. A big door closed. My only option was to enter the adventure and wait on God. As Albert Einstein said, "God doesn't play dice." Oswald Chambers, author of the famous *My Utmost for His Highest*, coined the phrase "Let God engineer." There is no guesswork with God. His timing is perfect.

I'll never forget the call that came unexpectedly from New Orleans: "We have your resume. Can you send us a packet of information?" My reply, "Who are you and how did you get my name?" The answer was an outdated resume that Dallas Seminary put into the hands of the Trinity Church pastoral search committee. I said I would send some information, but I wondered, "Who are these guys?" When I told Donna, her first words were classic: "Louisiana? Who would ever want to live in Louisiana?"

I think now about all I would have missed if I had stayed put in Maryland. So many good things can be traced back to that one small step, that one giant leap in following God's leadership twelve years ago. I can't imagine not being a part of the strategic spiritual mobilization that God has in New Orleans as an epicenter of hope for people here, near, and far away. A big boulder was thrown into our pond called New Orleans that has created a volunteer revolution of compassion that is rippling across the world.

As I write the final words of *DISASTER*: *Betting the Farm on God*, our wild, adventurous God has wanted to see once again if I really believe what I have written. God has stirred my nest once more. My new assignment is to lead a new ministry called GRACE ADVENTURES. This Christ-centered, grace-motivated, kingdom-focused ministry is dedicated to transforming our world for Christ, one leader at a time. No longer will I pastor one church but will pastor at large in the community. George McCloud said, "The cross must be raised again at the center of the marketplace as well as on the steeple of the church. I'm claiming that Jesus was not crucified in a cathedral between two candles, but on a cross between two thieves on the town garbage heap at a crossroads so cosmopolitan they had to write his title in three languages: Hebrew, Latin & Greek. The kind of place that cynics talked smut and thieves cussed and soldiers gambled because that is where he died and that is what he died about and that is where churchmen ought to be and what churches ought to be about."[1]

I thank God for the comfort and adventure that flows from His sovereignty. I thank God He brought me to New Orleans, Louisiana.

What about you? Are you sensing God pushing you out of a nice, comfortable nest? Are you ready to spread your wings and fly? You were made to fly even above the storms. Will you dare to take a risk? Will you catch the wind of the Spirit and soar? Go ahead and bet the farm on God. A *grace adventure* awaits you!

Appendix

Externally Focused Churches

I'm thankful today that more and more churches are asking, "How do we move the church out of the church?" "How do we get out of the four walls," and "How do we reach our full redemptive potential?"

Many churches want to be externally focused and "missional." Here are the principles we are learning:

1. It starts in the heart of leaders
2. Teach the biblical foundation
3. Understand the culture
4. Pray for compassionate hearts and eyes
5. Align mission, vision, values, staffing, resources
6. Examine the needs of the community
7. Utilize a blessing strategy
8. Train in evangelism
9. Build strategic partnerships
10. Action orientation

It Starts in the Heart of Leaders

In order to get an outwardly focused church you need outwardly focused people, and to get outwardly focused people you need outwardly focused leaders. The speed of the leader is the speed of the team. When God wants to do something significant, He always raises up a man, a woman, a team, or a couple. Always.

Someone with fire in their bones is seized by a call. Someone draws a box around himself and says, "The revival starts with me." Often God uses hardship to break them, make them, call them, and compel them to zealously reach the community.

Teach the Biblical Foundation

Leaders must not only model an outward focus but also teach, preach, and train until they are blue in the face. Vision leaks. People need to get God's heart for the world and its theological underpinnings. The following Scripture passages will help you teach an outward focus:

- Matthew 28:19-20
- Acts 2:42-47
- 1 Peter 2:11, 12; 3:15
- Luke 10:30-37
- Micah 6:8
- Matthew 5:13-16
- Ephesians 2:10
- Luke 15
- Jonah 4
- 1 John 3:17-18
- Matthew 25:35-46
- 1 Peter 4:10
- Matthew 16:18

Did you know that four hundred passages in the Bible demonstrate God's heart for...

- Poor
- Sick
- Orphans
- Widows
- Incarcerated
- Aliens

- Homeless
- Immigrants
- Disabled
- Hungry

Jesus lived an outward focus, His teaching emphasized this focus, He trained His disciples in this ministry, and the disciples lived and continued Jesus' pattern. Externally focused churches emphasize both good deeds and good news to become an outwardly focused church.

Over the years the people of God proclaimed the gospel as well as helped overcome slavery and child labor issues, started orphanages and hospitals, and enhanced foster care. John Stott suggests there was a commitment to both good deeds and good news before the twentieth century.

In the twentieth century, evangelicals largely disconnected from the good deeds side and focused almost exclusively on saving souls, serving the church, and defending the faith. Stott thinks the evangelical church changed and lost some of its rich heritage of charity, community, concern, and sacrificial works of service.[1]

Today, many churches are realizing there doesn't have to be the tyranny of an either/or approach—good news or goods deeds—but rather the genius of both/and:

Both/And	
Demonstration	Proclamation
Proof	Truth
Good Deeds	Good News
Bridge Builders	Hope Sharers
Serve the Least	Save the Lost
Great Commandment	Great Commission
Incarnation	Evangelization
Common Grace	Amazing Grace

In New Orleans, we have seen over and over that good deeds lead to good rapport, which leads to good words, which lead to the good news of the gospel.

Understand the Culture

Long ago, the sons of Issachar understood their culture and knew what to do (1 Chronicles 12:32). So today we must understand our culture. We live in an age of suspicion and cynicism. When a call comes at dinnertime and the caller mispronounces your name and says, "I'm so glad to talk to you ... I want to introduce you to a product that will change your life," we think it's probably not an act of pure altruism. When we get mail from an unfamiliar organization that says "check enclosed," we think "this will cost me something, somehow, somewhere." After a while, we think everyone is selling, hyping, or spinning.

This has spilled over to thoughts of the church as well. The church is more marginalized and less influential. In one survey people were asked, "What is the first thing you think of when you think of Christians?" The number one answer: "They hate gays." Oh, for the day when the first thing people think of is "love," "humility," "great artists," "justice," or "servants." The church is often long on "mad" and short on "mercy."

I'm convinced many are open to hearing about God, but there's a question they have to get past first: "Are you one of the narrow-minded, bigoted, hate-filled, intolerant types of Christians I've heard about?"

What they really want to know is whether we promote hate or love. I'm also convinced if we are not in the compassion game to some extent, it's hard to be in the evangelism game at all because many will not even give us a hearing in today's culture.

A new day is arising when the church will be outwardly focused yet working quietly in the shadows, humbly, counter-culturally, and almost subversively doing radical acts of service in the name of Jesus, wanting nothing in return. These expressions of compassion don't grab the headlines, but they turn heads and lead to changed lives. This radical goodness is often irresistible in getting people's attention. We have found the weapons of the kingdom are often brooms, rakes, visits, listening ears, open hands, and generous hearts.

We have found over and over in New Orleans that if you go out in Jesus' name and serve people wanting nothing in return, they will at first be skeptical, but in time they will ask, "Who are you?" and "Why are you doing this for free?" The answer is always, "Only because God loves you and so do we."

What an approach. No agenda but God's. No angle but love. Doors in time fly wide open for the gospel of Jesus Christ when you don't care about people's zip code, race, address, denomination, or what they can do for you in return. We have seen more saved through the good deeds/good news approach than any canned approach.

Pray for Compassionate Hearts and Eyes

What would happen if we had a paradigm shift in how we see people? In his book *The Seven Habits of Highly Effective People*, author Steven Covey tells about a memorable experience:

> I remember a mini-paradigm shift I experienced one Sunday morning on a subway in New York. People were sitting quietly—some reading newspapers, some lost in thought, some resting with their eyes closed. It was a calm, peaceful scene.
>
> Then suddenly, a man and his children entered the subway car. The children were so loud and rambunctious that instantly the whole climate changed.
>
> The man sat down next to me and closed his eyes, apparently oblivious to the situation. The children were yelling back and forth, throwing things, even grabbing people's papers. It was very disturbing. And yet, the man sitting next to me did nothing.
>
> It was difficult not to feel irritated. I could not believe that he could be so insensitive as to let his children run wild like that and do nothing about it, taking no responsibility at all. It was easy to see that everyone else on the subway felt irritated, too. So finally, with what I felt was unusual patience and restraint, I turned to him and said, "Sir, your children are really disturbing a lot of people, I wonder if you couldn't control them a little more?"

The man lifted his gaze as if to come to a consciousness of the situation for the first time and said softly, "Oh, you're right. I guess I should do something about it. We just came from the hospital where their mother died about an hour ago. I don't know what to think, and I guess they don't know how to handle it either."

Can you imagine what I felt at that moment? My paradigm shifted. Suddenly I saw things differently, and because I saw things differently, I thought differently, I felt differently, I behaved differently. My irritation vanished. I didn't have to worry about controlling my attitude or my behavior; my heart was filled with the man's pain. Feelings of sympathy and compassion flowed freely. "Your wife just died? Oh, I'm so sorry! Can you tell me about it? What can I do to help?" Everything changed in an instant.[2]

Just as Covey was transformed by a paradigm shift, so can we. What if we started looking at people through the eyes of God? What if we realized every person we set eyes upon matters to God, everyone is one humble prayer away from being a brother or sister in Christ? What if we looked through the redemptive lens for what could be? It might change us and our churches. Yet it is so easy to get busy and miss people. Not so with Jesus. Matthew says, "Seeing the people, He felt compassion for them" (Matthew 9:36).

One of the experiments I do in churches when I teach on this subject is to show a one-minute video of two teams passing a basketball back and forth. I ask the group to count how many times the ball gets passed. What is not expected is that at the 35-second point a gorilla enters the picture and stands among the basketball players, pounds his chest for 9 seconds, and then exits. I ask the group, "How many times was the basketball passed?" Then I ask, "How many saw the gorilla on the screen?" Amazingly, over 50 percent of the observers don't see the gorilla at all because they are so focused on counting the passes.[3] Psychologists call this "unintentional blindness." May we become a people who don't get so distracted we miss out on compassion. May we see, really see, those around us. May we see with the eyes of God. This paradigm will redefine the way

Disaster

we love. Our mission is not to beat people up, judge, or condemn but to show mercy, encourage people to take a sip of living water, and cheer them on as they cross the line of faith.

There is power in an experience. When people move out of their comfort zone and meet a real person with a real need, it transforms. People come alive and get the ministry buzz. They experience the "helper's high." It is something that reading a book or hearing a sermon can't accomplish. God is using you in an endeavor much bigger than yourself. You taste and see that it is good.

An inner-city kid came up to me and asked, "If I were to get shot two hundred times but God wanted me to live, would I live?" I was immediately grieved that this question had to be asked, but I realized this is what kids in Central City, New Orleans, think about constantly. Whereas other kids are thinking about college, sports, friends, vacation, and riding their bikes, many inner-city kids think about when they will catch a bullet and die. I'll never forget it. I had so much compassion for this youngster and took the time to talk to him about the God who would watch over him on this side and the next. The truth is almost everyone who has a compassionate heart looks back to some experience that was life-changing.

The stories are endless of how compassion experiences lit a fuse in people.

> A church I visited in January recently had a few families from a Bible study pass out flyers for a neighborhood barbecue; 175 people showed up. As people talked, many people were griping about one neighbor who never mowed the lawn. The paint was peeling, and the screens were out. This house was bringing down the value of everyone's home. The conversation headed south until they found out who lived there – a single mom with kids whose husband was serving in Iraq. Ouch! Church people and many neighbors scheduled another party. What if they were the hands and feet of Jesus to that woman? The next Saturday they showed up to mow the lawn, paint the house, and repair the screen.
>
> I have to confess I really didn't want to go on this trip. I only went because my husband, Bob, wanted me to go. I had no

expectations about the trip, no plans of reaching out to anyone or being moved by what I saw, but what I experienced changed my life.

I was overwhelmed by the devastation and how widespread it was. I was shocked by the FEMA trailer stories that so many people wanted to share with us. But I was truly blessed on Super Friday.

I am not a compassionate person; I keep to myself and try not to get involved with other people's problems. What I experienced on Super Friday changed that. I saw a three-year-old girl helping to haul out her family's personal belongings to the curb. I met Jarrod, a young black man with dreadlocks down to his waist, and I confess that if I had run into him anywhere else, I probably would have crossed the street to avoid him. He was working by himself, gutting his home on the street we were cleaning. I went right up to him and we talked. He didn't know he could get help from your organization so I gave him some phone numbers. I called over a couple more team members and we gave Jarrod a Bible and prayed with Him. He was so grateful. Every time I think of him I weep. I seem to be doing a lot of that lately! I believe God is working in me to change my heart and my attitude.

I applaud you for your work down in New Orleans. I wrote an article for my school paper about my experience with your church and the cleanup down there. New Orleans changed my view on the world and how I see people. I met a young man whose mother was suffering from drug addiction. He changed my life even though I only talked to him for a little while and we did not talk about his mother's drug addiction. When we were "destroying" his house, I found a letter stapled to the wall, it read, "Dear God, please save my mom from drugs." It was signed by the young man, his sister, and his cousin. It broke my heart. I wept with some volunteers outside the house and then we prayed over the letter for the young man and his family. I have a picture of the young man, and I pray for him and his sister whenever I see it and think about it. New Orleans is a place of renewal. It is not wiped out because of all the sin. I still have that letter. I found it in my hope chest because that woke me up that there are people out there with more problems than my own. Someday I hope that this story will be told. A story of hope and secrets found in the aftermath of Hurricane Katrina. And someday I hope that that boy will return to God through all his pain and anger. The last words I told the boy were, "Don't give up on God. He is listening to you." He gave me a weird look and then he left. At least he knows someone cares and is praying for him. I wish that I could meet him again and give him a glimpse of hope. Thank you for your actions and work for the Lord. They have been a blessing. Thank you for letting us volunteer and stay at your church. I thank you from the bottom of my heart. New Orleans has changed a big part of my heart.

Align Mission, Vision, Values, Staffing, Resources

It is important to make an outreach focus operational rather than just sentimental. This takes intentionality. Once the outreach focus is envisioned, leadership can then bring wisdom into how to create systems to turn vision into reality. Existing ministries can be evaluated to reach their outreach potentials. Staff can be leveraged to unleash training, systems, and time for evangelism and compassion ministry. Budgets can be evaluated to reflect new priorities.

Some churches work toward making 25 percent of the budget for outreach. Some churches build outreach components into every small group two times a year. Some churches have an annual all-church outreach event. In so doing, the church becomes not just the keeper of the aquarium, but also the fishers of men.

Examine the Needs of the Community

Year after year we have told New Orleans volunteers to go home and look for "little Katrinas." There are hurricanes in every life and community. Mother Teresa brought a little heaven to a hellhole. She would tell people, "Find your own Calcutta." Henry Blackaby encourages people to see where God is working and jump in there. Every church can exegete their community to see where the needs are.

At Trinity Church we had people or teams reaching out in the following identifiable ways:

Free Store	Urban Impact
Life Coaches	Katrina Relief
Crisis Pregnancy Center	Voter Registration
Food Bank	Desire Street
Campus Life	Gift Cards
Dance	Jail Ministry
Christian Business Men's Committee	Business Forums
	Grief Care
Christian Coalition	Divorce Recovery
Northlake Christian School	Support (12-Step)
Alliance Defense Fund	Crown
Habitat for Humanity	Mother's Day Out
Free Dental Clinic	MOPS

Here are some examples of how churches have found open doors by exegeting their communities:

> One church determined the greatest need in their community was overwhelming consumer debt in families. Some people were being charged up to 40 percent interest on their on credit card debt. The church responded with a no-interest loan to people in the community if they would commit to work down their debt and be held accountable by meeting weekly with a mentor to learn biblical financial principles. The loans were funded by people in the church who, at the time, were only making 1-2 percent on their own money; $2.6 million was available to be loaned out. The payback rate to the church has been 97.5 percent. Many people who would never have gotten out of debt are experiencing financial freedom. People are finding Christ through this kindness.

> Christian businessmen working out of Hong Kong are starting manufacturing plans in mainland China in rural areas based on practicing the great commandments (love God, love people) and the Great Commission. Poor people

are paid a fair wage, given doctor and dentist care, and the women receive surprise manicures and pedicures at work. They observe, "The gospel shouts when it comes through love." The leaders report between 40-60 percent of the factory workers have come to know Jesus as Savior.

- A church in Florida was burdened to reach out to prostitutes living in their community. They sponsored a "Queen for a Day" banquet. The pastors and elders rented tuxes and served the women from the community and the church. There were free pedicures and manicures for the guests. One of the women said, "I knew your church was here, but I didn't know this church cared for prostitutes!"
- Another church took a large team to paint, landscape, and do a makeover of some rooms at their local public school. One teacher was amazed and said, "We thought Christians hated public schools." Walls, misconceptions, and stereotypes were blown up and a relationship began.
- One church came to realize their community included many elderly residents. Many of those seniors couldn't climb ladders to check the batteries in their smoke detectors. The church partnered with Wal-Mart (who provided free batteries) and went door-to-door serving the elderly for free in the name of the Lord. They also partnered with the fire department, which sent their fire trucks around the community with sirens to create a buzz. Firefighters joined the church people in this effort. Many conversations took place about Jesus.
- One church went out one-thousand-strong to a challenged, dirty area of their city with buckets, trash bags, shovels, and brooms to pick up broken glass, litter, and cigarette butts, etc. By the end of the day, the community was overjoyed. Over and over people asked, some with tears of joy, "Why are you people cleaning up trash?" The answer each time was, "If Jesus was in our city, He wouldn't just be preaching in a church, He'd be out sharing His love in practical ways. So we are out cleaning up trash in the same spirit."
- A youth pastor just returned from Africa and showed the congregation slides of children's feet in oversized shoes. These

people discovered that kids couldn't go to school without shoes so the parents gave their kids their shoes and they had to work barefoot. After sharing the missions report the pastor gave the people the opportunity to come forward and donate shoes. Some asked if they could write a check instead. The answer, "No, today you have to give shoes." 95 percent of the people gave the shoes. All through the week the people of that church got to say to friends, "You wouldn't believe what I did this Sunday!" They were then able to have spiritual conversations about Jesus Christ.

Utilize a Blessing Strategy

What if we thought more in terms of a blessing strategy rather than an evangelism strategy? Remember, God called Abraham to "blessing" as a way of life in the Abrahamic covenant. God would bless (the word is used five times in Genesis 12:1-3) Abraham. Abraham would bless others, including those outside of his tribe. Even those he didn't know! A cycle would start and the whole world would be blessed. God, in the midst of a world that can be hellish at times, *blesses* so that those blessed can create a revolution one person at a time. When the Blessing Strategy is caught, others get exposed and it spreads like a virus. It can create a pandemic.

The truth: **You are not designed to be a receptacle but a pipeline.** You are like the UPS guy who is entrusted with a parcel he must pass along to the right person. God says, "You are my UPS guys. You are my pipeline to extend blessings in a sometimes hellish world." This is a strategy of intentional, Spirit-led acts of kindness and blessing in the name of Jesus. It works.

- I was with a guy who regularly prays for people. He finds that people don't turn down prayer. He was recently at a restaurant and asked the waitress if there was anything she needed prayer for. She said, "Pray for my sick mom and one other thing." He prayed before he ate. Twenty minutes later she excitedly came to his table and said, "God did it. What did you pray?" He said, "I asked God to bless your life because He loves to bless." She said, "My boyfriend walked in after our big fight this morning

and gave me twelve roses. That was the other thing I needed prayer for." He then talked about Jesus. Our job is not to convict or convert but to bless. The Holy Spirit does the inside work.
- A pastor named Steve Sojourn has a church that deploys a "blessing strategy." He was on the radio in his community when a businessman called in saying, "There I was downtown running to my car, fully expecting a parking ticket. Instead of a ticket there was a card that read, 'Your parking meter looked hungry, so we fed it!'" He went on, "I stood there stunned. My first thought was, I don't deserve this. I should have gotten a parking ticket, but instead I got love." After a pregnant pause on live radio Steve said, "That's exactly the point, sir. You probably did deserve a ticket, but we extended a bit of grace to you in the form of a dime in your meter and a card explaining what we did. In exactly the same way, Jesus Christ has extended His love and grace to each of us, even though not a single one of us deserves it."

Blessing and kindness knock down barriers that prevent people from seeing God clearly. Many times when people experience a kindness expression, they are puzzled at first and then it sinks in and they are amazed. Sometimes people's mouths drops open or they get teary-eyed or just laugh with delight. We always ask our Katrina volunteers to value people over tasks. It has paid off. The weapons of our warfare are not waged with raw force but simple yet powerful kindness and love.

Isn't this the exact "blessing" method Jesus taught? For example:

- Love your enemies (Matthew 5:33).
- Whoever slaps you on your right cheek, turn the other to him also (Matthew 5:39).
- If someone wants ... your tunic, let him have your cloak also (Matthew 5:40).
- If someone forces you to go one mile, go with him two miles (Matthew 5:41).

It's easy to think we are to withhold the blessing until someone deserves it or only bless the right people. Jesus calls us to **bless everything that moves**, intentionally.

What if you went out this week and blessed three people, and made sure at least one didn't deserve it. Give it a whirl and see what happens.

Train in Evangelism

It is easy to be good at good deeds and not so good at the good news. It is easy to be good at friendship but not so good at friendship evangelism. Yet it's easy to just be into "niceness." Good deeds are not a substitute for the good news. In fact, many people left to their own will come to the wrong conclusions as to who you are or why you are serving them. We see examples of this in Scripture. In Acts 2 at Pentecost, God supernaturally allowed His disciples to speak in different native languages. The crowds were amazed and "bewildered" at this work of God. Their conclusion: "the disciples had too much wine." Fortunately, Peter stepped up and told them they were not drunk as they supposed. It's not happy hour. It's only nine in the morning. He proceeded to preach the sermon of his life, and three thousand were saved.

In Acts 3, God used Peter and John, and a disabled man walked. The man jumped to his feet and caught the attention of everyone. The crowds couldn't figure it out and concluded the power was from Peter and John, not God. Peter made sure he proclaimed the "Jesus" behind the story. Both deed and word were needed.

In Acts 14, Paul and Barnabas met a lame man, and God, through Paul, healed him. What a miracle. Did the people of Lystra interpret the event properly? No, they mistook Paul and Barnabas for Zeus and Hermes and wanted to offer sacrifices to them. Good deeds create goodwill, but also sometimes the wrong perceptions. Paul had to share the good news to set the record straight.

The goal is not just to let people think Christ-followers are nice people, but to share the hope that is within us (1 Peter 3:15) and to introduce others to Jesus Christ. Faith comes by hearing and hearing by the Word of God. It isn't enough to simply allow our life to speak. We are to speak of Jesus.

Build Strategic Partnerships

Hurricane Katrina knocked down huge walls, barriers, and petty differences that existed between churches and between churches and community organizations. In one treacherous day, we all realized how interconnected we were and how much common ground we possess. Incredible relationships have been formed with pastors, police chiefs, firefighters, mayors, civic groups, and community organizations – Red Cross, Salvation Army, schools, shelters, urban/suburban friendships. It took a hurricane to get us to work together, but that isn't required for you.

The good news in becoming more outreach oriented is you don't have to reinvent the wheel but can take advantage of strategic partnerships. This may require expanding your boundaries beyond what you have done in the past. I'm not talking about compromising convictions here but stretching where partnerships are possible. In our case we will work with an organization that is morally positive, spiritually at least neutral, and cares about what we care about. This is people of good faith working with people of goodwill. We want to care for our community with others and make a difference for Christ.

Look for good matches. Look for where God leads. Test the waters. Step out. You'll be amazed.

Action Orientation

In the early days only a remnant of people remained in the community, yet God arranged for a kingdom ambassador to land literally on my doorstep. His name was Pete. He was the national director for Food for the Hungry in the aftermath of the tsunami in Indonesia. He had seen the gospel move in a predominantly Muslim nation through the principles of good deeds and compassion. A work of Christ was going on among the people even though this would never be reported in the media. Devastated people met Christians who cared and helped.

Pete was in New Orleans just after Katrina hit, without a place to stay, and God brought him to me. What provision! In picking his brain, the first principle I received was to be proactive and have a bias for action. There is a solution for everything. Get in the game.

Play offensively, not defensively. Don't worry about making turnovers. Be known for what you are for rather than what you are against. Step out in faith.

What counsel. We followed it and the rest is history. You can have an "action orientation" as well. Jesus said after telling the story of the Good Samaritan, "Go and do likewise" (Luke 10:35-37).

I'm learning a little of what Keith Johnstone said: "There are people who prefer to say, 'Yes,' and there are people who prefer to say, 'No.' Those who say 'Yes' are rewarded by the adventures they have, and those who say 'No' are rewarded by the safety they attain."

ABOUT THE AUTHOR

Dr. Michael Sprague is the president of Grace Adventures, a Bible-based, Christ-centered, grace-motivated, kingdom-building ministry in the greater New Orleans region. Michael served as Senior Pastor at Trinity Church in Covington, Louisiana, for eleven years and fifteen years at Forcey Memorial Church in Silver Spring, Maryland. He helped launch the TouchGlobal Crisis Response Ministry for the Evangelical Free Churches of America that is now multiplying churches and compassion ministry around the world after natural disasters. Michael received his Doctor of Ministry degree from Dallas Theological Seminary. Michael and his wife, Donna, have been married for twenty-nine years and have one son, Jonathan. He blogs at www.graceadventures.info.

Thank you for reading the book! Every reader has a different experience. I would delight in discovering what you found helpful or thought-provoking. Maybe you have questions...or disagree with something I've said. That's okay too! We are all pilgrims on a journey and need to learn from one another.

You can also learn more about GRACE ADVENTURES, a Bible-based, Jesus-focused, grace-based, kingdom-centered ministry that reaches out to political, business and spiritual leaders. Michael is available for preaching, retreats, and conferences. Here's how to contact him:

Grace Adventures
Michael Sprague
701 Rue Marseille
Mandeville, LA 70471
Telephone: 985-502-4265
MDSprague00@bellsouth.net
www.graceadventures.info

The recovery of New Orleans and the Gulf Coast is still a work in progress. Individuals and teams come on a weekly basis to rebuild homes and lives for the glory of God. Go to www.efca.org or www.urbanimpact.org for more information.

See you in New Orleans. It is bound to be a life-changing experience.

NOTES

Introduction

1 Amanda Ripley, *The Unthinkable: who survives when disaster strikes and why* (New York: Random House, Inc.), xvi.

Chapter 1: Your Faith

1 John Ortberg, *When the Game is Over, It All Goes Back in the Box* (Grand Rapids: Zondervan, 2007), 238-240.

Chapter 2: Surrender—God's Plan is Better

1 John Ortberg, *The Life You've Always Wanted: Spiritual Disciplines for Ordinary People* (Grand Rapids: Zondervan, 2002), 214.

2 Phil Vischer, *Me, Myself and Bob: A True Story about God, Dreams, and Talking Vegetables* (Nashville: Nelson, 2006), 245.

3 Ibid., 196.

4 Ibid., 231.

5 Ibid., 232.

6 Ibid., 235.

7 Ibid., 237.

8 Ibid., 251.

9   Ibid., 239.

10 G.K. Chesterton, *Orthodoxy* (Sioux Falls, SD: NuVision, 2007), 18.

11 Oswald Chambers, *My Utmost for His Highest* (Toronto: Dodd, Mead & Company, Inc., 1935), 120.

12 "The Road of Life," author unknown.

Chapter 5: Your Calling

1   Jim Pace and Richard Warren, *Should We Fire God?: Finding Hope in God When We Don't Understand* (New York: FaithWords, 2010), 83.

2   Ibid., 53.

Chapter 6: Our Culture

1   David Kinnaman and Gabe Lyons, *UnChristian: What a New Generation Really Thinks about Christianity . . . and Why it Matters* (Grand Rapids: Baker, 2007), 48.

2   Robert and Cindy Sterling, *The Choice*, copyright 1992 Word Music, 38, as quoted in Dean Merrill, *Sinners in the Hands of an Angry Church* (Grand Rapids: Zondervan, 1997), 30.

3   C.S. Lewis, *God in the Dock* (London: Curtis Brown, 1970), 199.

4   Phillip Jenkins documents the exponential growth of Christendom and the recent rapid expansion into Africa, Asia, and Latin America. He predicts that if current trends continue, by the year 2050 only one-fifth of the world's Christians will be non-Hispanic Caucasian. Phillip Jenkins, *The Next Christendom. The Coming of Global Christianity* (New York: Oxford University Press, Inc., 2002).

5   Dean Merrill, *Sinners in the Hands of an Angry Church* (Grand Rapids: Zondervan, 1997), 59.

6   Ibid., 60.

7   Ibid.

8   Reggie McNeal, "It's A.D.30 All Over Again," Reformed Church in America's One Thing Conference, February 2009.

9   Merrill, 60.

Chapter 7: Where Is God When Things Go Wrong

1   Anne Lamont, *Bird by Hand: Some Instructions on Writing and Life* (New York: Doubleday, 1994), 22.

2   C.S. Lewis, *The Problem of Pain* (New York: Macmillan, 1943), 160.

Chapter 8: God of the Resupply

1   Rodney Stark, *The Rise of Christianity* (San Francisco: HarperCollins, 1997), 160.

Chapter 9: Our Jesus

1   Gene Weingarten, "Pearls before Breakfast," *Washington Post*, April 8, 2007. http://www.washingtonpost.com/wp-dyn/content/article/2007/04/04/AR2007040401721.html

2   J.I. Packer, *Knowing God* (Downers Grove, Illinois: InterVarsity Press, 1973), 21.

3   John Ortberg. "Making Ordinary Days Extraordinary." Menlo Park Presbyterian Church. Menlo Park, CA. Feb. 22-23, 2008.

4   Leonard Sweet and Frank Viola, *Jesus Manifesto* (Nashville: Thomas Nelson, 2010), 100.

5   Brennan Manning, *The Importance of Being Foolish: How to Think Like Jesus* (Harper Collins Publishers: New York, 2005), 173.

Chapter 10: Surviving Bouts with Doubts

1   Jesus was quoting the prophetic passage about the coming Messiah (Isaiah 61:1) knowing John would recognize it and put two and two together (prophecy and Jesus' works) thus authenticating Messiah Jesus.

2   Frederick Dale Bruner, *The Churchbook: Matthew 13-28, Matthew: A Commentary* (Grand Rapids: Eerdmans, 2005), 456.

3   Frederick Buechner, *Wishful Thinking* (New York: HarperCollins, 1973), 20.

4   Rufus Jones, *The Radiant Life*, quoted in Gary E. Parker, *The Gift of Doubt: From Crisis to Authentic Faith* (San Francisco: Harper & Row, 1990), 71.

5   Francis Bacon, *The Advancement of Learning* (1605), book I, v, 8.

Chapter 11: Sustainability—Surviving for the Long Haul

1   Richard Swenson, *The Overload Syndrome* (Colorado Springs: NavPress, 1998), 123-124.

2   This illustration is adapted from a story told by Mindy Caliguire, "Soul Health Mind," *Leadership Journal*, Summer 2004: 41.

3   Gordon MacDonald, *The Life God Blesses* (Nashville: Thomas Nelson Publishers, 1997), 124-125.

4   Ibid., 125-126.

5   Henry Cloud, "Wise People, Foolish People and Evil People," Willow Creek Community Church (Barrington, Illinois), week 32, 2009.

6   Dallas Willard, *Spirit of the Disciplines* (New York: HarperCollins, 1988), 81.

7   Leith Anderson, *When God Says No* (Minneapolis: Bethany House Publishers, 1996), 56.

8   Ann Wells, "What Special Someday are we Saving for?" *Los Angeles Times*, April 1985.

Chapter 12: When Sheep Act Like Wolves

1   Blaine Allen, *Before You Quit—When Ministry Is Not What You Thought* (Grand Rapids: Kregel Publications, 2001), 23-24.

2   Larry Magnuson and Mike Schafer, Sonscape Retreats Newsletter, Dec. 3, 2010, 1.

3   Focus on the Family and Barna Research.

4   Dr. James Dobson, "The Titanic. The Church. What They Have in Common," *Focus on the Family*, August 1998, www2.focusonthefamily.com/docstudy/newsletters/A000000803.cfm

5   Hillary Wicai, "Ill-Behaving Members Lead to Clergy Burnout," *Baptist Standard*, April 23, 2001, www.baptiststandard.com/2001/4_23/pages/burnout.html.

6   Don Cousins, *Experiencing LeaderShift* (Colorado Springs: David C. Cook, 2008), 55.

7   In the foreword to Stephen Mansfield's book, *Rechurch* (Carol Steam, IL: Tyndale House Publishers, 2010), ix – xi, George Barna tells his chilling stories of what it was like to experience his own personal pain in successive churches.

8   Ibid., xii.

9   Sheldon Van Auken, *A Severe Mercy* (San Francisco: Harper & Row, 1977), 85.

Chapter 13: Spiritual Warfare

1   R.C. Sproul, *Essential Truths of the Christian Faith* (Wheaton: Tyndale House Publishers, Inc., 1992), 85.

2   John Trent and Gary Smalley, *The Gift of Honor* (Nashville: Thomas Nelson, 1987), 9-10.

3   Mark Buchanan, "Fight the Good Fight," *Leadership Journal*, Fall 2004: 52-53.

Chapter 14: Be Dangerous

1   David Platt, *Radical* (Colorado Springs: Multnomah Books, 2010), 164-165.

2   Steve Farrar, *Study Tall* (Sisters, Oregon: Multnomah Books, 1994), 86-87.

3   Erwin McManus, "Seizing Your Divine Moment," *Preaching Today*, no. 252.

4   Platt, 175-176.

5   John Foxe, *Foxe's Book of Martyrs*.

6   *Apologeticus*, 50, 13.

7   Josephus, *Wars of the Jews*, 2.8.1.

Chapter 15: Do Good Deeds

1   Rick Rusaw, "Living a Life on Loans," Externally Focused Church Conference, LifeBridge Christian Church (Longmont, CO), 2007.

2   Eric Swanson, "Evangelism and Externally Focused Church – 201," Externally Focused Church Conference, LifeBridge Christian Church (Longmont, CO), 2007.

3   Philip Jenkins, *The Next Christendom: The Coming of Global Christianity* (New York: Oxford University Press, 2002), 71.

4   Rob Moll, "Mission Incredible," *Christianity Today*, March 2006, 28.

5   David A. Livermore, *Serving with Eyes Wide Open: Doing Short-term Missions with Cultural Intelligence* (Grand Rapids: Baker Books, 2006), 33.

6   Thom S. Rainer, "7 Sins of Dying Churches," *Outreach Magazine*, Jan.-Feb. 2006, 16.

7   Rodney Stark, *Discovering God: The Origins of the Great Religions and the Evolution of Belief* (New York: HarperCollins, 2007), 319.

8   John Ortberg, "Healers Anonymous," Menlo Park Presbyterian Church (Menlo Park, CA), Feb. 21, 2010.

9   Timothy K. Jones, "Dying for Jesus," *Christianity Today*, March 19, 1990, 12.

Chapter 16: Ripples

1   Sonja Schneider, *EFCN Life*, October 2009.

Chapter 18: Divine Appointments

1   Unknown. This story has been around for years.

2   Mark Buchanan, *Your God is Too Safe* (Sisters, Oregon: Multnomah Publishers, Inc., 2001), 60.

3   Larry Poland, *Rise to Conquer* (Chappaqua, New York: Christian Herald Books, 1979), 47.

Epilogue: God Doesn't Play Dice

1   David McCasland, *Oswald Chambers: Abandoned to God: The Life Story of the Author of "My Utmost for His Highest"* (Grand Rapids: Discovery, 1993), 190.

Appendix: Externally Focused Churches

1   John Stott, *Human Rights and Human Wrongs: Major Issues for a New Century* (Grand Rapids: Baker, 1999), 21-22.

2   Steven Covey, *The Seven Habits of Highly Effective People* (New York: Simon & Schuster, 2004), 30-31.

3   This account is from "None So Blind" by Michael Shermer. *Scientific American*, February 9, 2004, www.sciam.com.

CPSIA information can be obtained at www.ICGtesting.com
Printed in the USA
242456LV00001B/7/P